Luminos is the Open Access monograph publishing program
from UC Press. Luminos provides a framework for preserving and
reinvigorating monograph publishing for the future and increases
the reach and visibility of important scholarly work. Titles published
in the UC Press Luminos model are published with the same high
standards for selection, peer review, production, and marketing as
those in our traditional program. www.luminosoa.org

Silicon Elsewhere

Silicon Elsewhere

Nairobi, Global China, and the Promise of Techno-Capital

———

Andrea Pollio

UNIVERSITY OF CALIFORNIA PRESS

University of California Press
Oakland, California

Suggested citation: Pollio, A. *Silicon Elsewhere: Nairobi, Global China, and the Promise of Techno-Capital.* Oakland: University of California Press, 2026. DOI: https://doi.org/10.1525/luminos.262

Library of Congress Cataloging-in-Publication Data

Names: Pollio, Andrea, author
Title: Silicon elsewhere : Nairobi, global China, and the promise of
    techno-capital / Andrea Pollio.
Description: Oakland, California : University of California Press, [2026] |
    Includes bibliographical references and index.
Identifiers: LCCN 2025027368 (print) | LCCN 2025027369 (ebook) |
    ISBN 9780520425842 hardback | ISBN 9780520413085 paperback |
    ISBN 9780520413092 ebook
Subjects: LCSH: Technological innovations—Kenya—Nairobi—21st century |
    Information technology—Kenya—Nairobi—21st century | Investments,
    Chinese—Kenya—Nairobi—21st century | Globalization—China
Classification: LCC HC865.Z9 T47 2026 (print) | LCC HC865.Z9 (ebook) |
    DDC 338.2/60967625—dc23/eng/20250915

LC record available at https://lccn.loc.gov/2025027368
LC ebook record available at https://lccn.loc.gov/2025027369

GPSR Authorized Representative: Easy Access System Europe,
Mustamäe tee 50, 10621 Tallinn, Estonia, gpsr.requests@easproject.com

34 33 32 31 30 29 28 27 26 25
10 9 8 7 6 5 4 3 2 1

CONTENTS

How does a city in Africa become a capital of technological innovation? How did Nairobi, Kenya's capital city and home to the Silicon Savannah digital ecosystem, become the experimental testbed of China's high-tech presence in the African continent? What would it mean to write about Chinese technology from Nairobi, against the backdrop of rising geopolitical anxieties over the US-China digital rivalry? Are there different trajectories of techno-capital beyond the Silicon Valley imagination that dominates the world of technology? These questions animate the pages of *Silicon Elsewhere*.

Over the years that it took me to finalize this book, on a topic as controversial as China in Africa, friends and colleagues would often ask how I ended up researching something as daunting and complex. In response, I had a few stories that I would use interchangeably. One of these stories begins in a pub in Sydney, Australia, where I lived during my doctoral studies. It must have been the beginning of summer 2017, when I was busy writing the last chapter of my dissertation. During the previous three years, I had been researching the interface between Silicon Valley's entrepreneurial cultures and the world of antipoverty in Cape Town, a city that portrayed itself as yet another start-up capital—Africa's Silicon Cape.

Somebody had forwarded me an email from a younger student interested in digital innovation. He was considering the idea of enrolling in a graduate program, and, three years into my doctorate, I was the right person to talk to for advice. When we caught up, on a warm and wet Sydney evening, I told him about my work, about how wonderful and intense my field research in Cape Town had been, and how fascinating it was to think about the technopolitics of digital entrepreneurship in urban Africa. He listened quietly, his foam-ringed beer glass almost empty, and then asked, "But what about China?"

I was puzzled. I replied, "What about it?" Until then, China had never been within the horizon of questions that I had come to expect and fear as a doctoral student. In response, my interlocutor explained that with the Digital Silk Road and other infrastructural investments in Africa, he thought I would have something to say about the Chinese digital presence in the continent. Was it a neocolonial strategy? Had China inaugurated a new era of technological development? What were African start-ups doing to attract Chinese capital? Were the Chinese setting up hidden backdoors in their equipment to spy on African governments?

I sheepishly responded that I had nothing to say about China. But suddenly that question—What about China?—seemed to be everywhere. It was around then that large Chinese technology companies like Alibaba and Tencent began appearing in Western media more and more frequently, often shrouded by a mix of cybersecurity concerns and sinophobic tropes. Only a few weeks after that first conversation, for example, the African Union scandal broke out. An investigative piece in the African edition of the French newspaper *Le Monde* alleged that computers in the African Union's headquarters in Addis Ababa were connecting every night to servers in Shanghai and that the futuristic building—funded, designed, and developed by the Chinese—was bugged. Whether the allegations were true or false, the more sinister, post-Snowden face of digital technology now belonged to China too.

With all this in mind, I started thinking about the China question. Eventually, early in 2019, I moved back to Italy, my home country, because of an unexpected short-term job offer. By then, China's twenty-first-century maritime Silk Road had reached European shores, with a windfall of controversial small and big bilateral agreements. I thus realized that it would be strategic to craft a research project about the new Silk Roads in Africa and apply for funding from the European Union (EU) at a time when emotional responses to China's geoeconomic power reverberated loudly in the European collective imagination. With a mix of luck and privilege, timeliness and chance, in 2020 I was awarded a Marie Skłodowska-Curie fellowship from the European Commission, which funded three of the five years of research for this book.

This is my full disclosure. I started working on *Silicon Elsewhere* funded by a large geospatial institution—the European Union—to study another large geospatial phenomenon of our time—digital global China in Africa. And although I do not know to what extent my success in getting funding from the EU was aided by the choice of a fitting topic at a fitting moment, the reason I start from this autobiographical story is because books like this begin from a single data point—the conditions of possibility of research—in which the interaction of geopolitical and personal parables is inextricable.

But the conditions of possibility of research extend much beyond the money that funds it and beyond the geopolitics of research grants. Over the past decade, I have had the inexplicable fortune of being supported, helped, guided, and befriended by a cohort of people to whom I owe an immense debt of gratitude. As trite as this statement sounds, books are always the product of collective work and of shared conviviality.

Liza R. Cirolia has been a friend, a generous mentor, and a thinking partner in more ways than words can express. Without Liza, this project would never have seen the light of day. From morning coffees to late-night queer parties, via our daily WhatsApps, she has been my sounding board for everything life, relationships, work, and cringy memes. Ilia Antenucci has been my sister in crime since the day we met, a decade ago. Zhengli Huang, whose networks in Nairobi are unrivaled, has been an indispensable companion in our respective research. Jack O. Odeo, insightful and brilliant, has taught me about the lives of technology in the Silicon Savannah more than any book or paper could. Sue Parnell has been a deus ex machina throughout my career, magically appearing with the right piece of advice at the moments when I needed it the most. Liam Magee has done the same, always cultivating material and intellectual care.

My research journey started long before this book project. In Torino, during my early steps in academia, Francesca Governa and Marco Santangelo instilled the belief that I could pursue a life of passionate work. Sharing an office with Francesca today completes a full circle that reminds me every day of how lucky I was to receive her mentoring in 2012 and how fortunate I am to still be learning from her. Meeting Michele Lancione on a winter morning in 2013 was a life-changing chance. As a returnee, a sea turtle now, I am grateful for the camaraderie of Silvia Aru, Mara Ferreri, Chiara Iacovone, Carlo Salone, Alberto Valz Gris, and the scholars at the Department of Urban and Regional Studies (DIST) of the Polytechnic of Turin. Behind the scenes, Stefania Guarini and everyone in the administration has provided me with invaluable support for navigating the idiosyncrasies of Italian bureaucracy.

At the African Centre for Cities (ACC) of the University of Cape Town, my second academic home, I could not have found a more unsparing platform, even at the peak of COVID-19, when this generosity was mediated by multiple screens. My relationship with ACC began during my stay at the EGS in 2015, when Mercy Brown-Luthango taught me some of the tricks of thoughtful research. It was then that I met Pippin Anderson, Sharon Adams, Suraya Scheba, Jeronimo Delgado Caicedo, and other EGS people who keep inspiring me and checking on me via Instagram. Since joining ACC in 2020, I have benefited from the friendships and intellectual guidance of Edgar Pieterse, director, and Andy Tucker, deputy director, along with heeten bhagat, Alicia Fortuin, Gareth Haysom, Laura Nkula-Wenz, Nokukhanya Mncwabe, Nobukhosi Ngwenya, Ali Pulker, Anna Selmeczi, Rike Sitas, Warren Smit, Tammy Wilks, and everyone else. Whether at a reading group or in a café, in a meeting room or on a Zoom call, I have always felt stimulated—by caffeine, by South African wines, but especially by ACC's impactful research. I am particularly grateful for Andy taking a chance on me and signing a commitment letter in fall 2019 but never stopping at the bureaucratic side of things; for Laura's and Anna's unwavering kindness and for leading the way in an exciting, cosmopolitan urban studies pedagogy from Cape Town; for the chats with Rike and Ali, whose humor always makes me crack up; and for Alicia, waiting for more e-scooter adventures. Although she only recently rejoined ACC, the support and encouragement I have received from Nancy Odendaal goes back to a meeting in her Centlivres office ten years ago. At ACC I also had the fortune of collaborating on a couple of research projects that have in part seeped into the pages of this book. I am particularly grateful for the Platform Politics and Silicon Savannahs (PP&SS) team (funded by a Volvo Research and Education Foundation, Mobility and Accessibility in African Cities program)—Alexis Gatoni Sebarenzi, in addition to Alicia, Jack, Liza, and Rike—and for every WhatsApp message in our shared archive of friendship and digital platform research. Throughout my time there, ACC's administration team—Maryam, Ameerah, Shakira, Marlene, and Ithra—made sure that the complications of multiple research accounts ran smoothly. Alma Viviers somehow made everything beautiful with her touch. Ultimately, ACC could not have been more welcoming. My hope is to one day honor this debt.

My third academic home is UTA-Do. Wangui Kimari is an inspiration for how to do things with research. In UTA-Do's ever-growing network, I cherish the friendships of Mwangi Mwaura, Jethron Akallah, Amollo Ambole, Prince Guma, Smith Ouma, MK Mbugua, Miriam Maina, Junnan Mu, Medhanit Ayele, Elisabeth Bollrich, Mariam Genes, and Albert Nyiti. At each UTA-Do workshop, I have had the chance to learn from both the guest scholars and the participants who joined the collective laboratory that Wangui, Liza, and Prince got off the ground in 2022. Being UTA-Do's KYM is the best side gig I could ask for.

During my academic detour in Sydney, I had the good luck to meet a number of people who inspired me and continue to do so, including my supervisors, Donald McNeill and Sarah Barns. I am sure that throughout the pages of this book Donald and Sarah will recognize some of the seeds that they thoughtfully planted. At the Institute of Culture and Society (ICS), Western Sydney University, I also learned a lot from Ien Ang, Brett Neilson, Liam Magee, Juan Salazar, Gay Hawkins, Greg Noble, Megan Watkins, and Shanti Robertson and enjoyed the days at Kathryn Gibson's house with the Community Economies Research Network. I am especially grateful for my doctoral colleagues Tsvetelina Hristova, Giulia dal Maso, Jack Parkin, Giovanna Luciano, Cecelia Cmielewski (and Nigel, of course!). At ICS, I also met my blood brother, Jasbeer Mustafah Mamalipurath, who makes my life fuller even at a distance.

I presented sections of this book on various occasions, and I am indebted to the feedback I received every time. I want to acknowledge the following:

· the Parables of AI in/from the Global South workshop, organized by Data & Society in the boreal fall of 2021 (Marie-Therese Png, Seyram Avle, Alessio Koliulis, Hannah Claus, Tom Cowan, Ranjit Singh, Rigoberto Laura Guzmán); some of the opening lines of this book have appeared in the anthology curated by Ranjit, Rigo, and Patrick Davison;
· the various events of the global infrastructure–led urbanization network, especially Simone Vegliò, Jon Silver, Elia Apostolopoulou, Alan Wiig, Astrid Safina, Leonardo Ramondetti, Evelina Gambino, Yannis Kallianos, Seth Schindler, Biruk Terrefe, Francesca, Alberto, and Giulia;
· the Mapping Asia China Connections in a Changing World 2024 workshop at the University of Pretoria's Centre for Asian Studies in Africa, especially the organizer, Alf Gunvald Nilsen, and the tips I received from C. K. Lee, Maria Repnikova, and Tommy Tse.
· the Geopolitics of Digital Africa 2023 conference at the Institut Français des Relations Internationales (IFRI), especially Sina Schlimmer;
· the various engagements with Ian Klaus at the Carnegie Endowment for International Peace;
· the panel on African statecraft at the intersection of urbanization and financialization at the European Conference on African Studies 2023, chaired and organized by Sylvia Croese and Matt Lane;
· the Beyond Splintering Urbanism workshop in Autun, 2023, especially the organizers (Alan Wiig, Colin McFarlane, Andy Karvonen and Jon Rutherford) and those who offered their thoughts on my work there (Steve Graham and Sophie Schramm);
· the first China-Africa conference of the Associazione Italiana Studi Africa-Cina (the Italian chapter of the Chinese in Africa/Africans in China Research Network), especially the brilliant cofounders, Antonella Ceccagno, Costanza Franceschini, Elisa Gambino, and Mariasole Pepa; and
· the Incompleteness and Conviviality 2024 disobedience workshop organized by Divine Fuh and HUMA, where I typed the conclusion of this book.

Four additional cohorts of colleagues deserve a special mention: my friends and comrades in the Flow/Overflow/Shortage research collective (Chris Mizes, Demetra Kourri, Moritz Kasper, Sophia Abbas, and Suyash Barve); the editors at *Platform and Society* (Niels Van Doorn, Rafael Grohmann, Cheryll Soryano, and Julie Y. Chen); the doctoral students (Razaz Basheir, Archie Muzenda, Emanuele Sciuva, Malte Stein) who have allowed me to learn from them as they pursue their journey and their passion; and the Smartness as Wealth team, Armin Beverungen, Marc Steinberg (who is an inexhaustible source of good recommendations), Orit

Halpern, Anindita Nag, Randi Heinrichs, and everyone else. I cannot wait to see what this collaboration has in store for us.

This book is better thanks to the thoughtful readers who pushed me to write and think better. My hat tips to Tsvetelina Hristova, Liam Magee, James Christopher Mizes, Liza Rose Cirolia, Devra Waldman, Mwangi Mwaura, Nancy Odendaal, Alicia Fortuin, Ryan Burns, Morgan Mouton (who helped me with the paper version of chapter 2) and the editors at the University of California Press, Michelle Lipinski and Jyoti Arvey, who carefully read each chapter of my manuscript. While mistakes remain mine only, having a small army of readers was invaluable, including the three reviewers who generously commented on the manuscript.

Written pages are also a function of fleeting oral conversations: with Sharad Chari on a wintery yet sunny morning; with Julien Migozzi over red wine and WhatsApp; with Amir Anwar and Michel Wahome during a rainy workshop; with Dennis Muthama on many occasions; and with Ali Bhagat during a summer of new friendships.

And finally, I am indebted to those who make home home, in different geographies. In Italy, my parents, Marika and Tony, Alessandro, Laura, Matteo, Valeria, Yulya, Merve, Cristian, Fiore, MT, Francesco, Elena, Nica, Giovanna, and Carolina. In Kenya, Allan, Jillian, Chloe, Jerotich, Yasmine, Abdi, Kenny, Lindi, Cesco, Keren, and Alexandria Williams, who provided assistance for the early stage of research. Majalla and Bemnet are my Nairobi family, the love throuple that never was but is. In South Africa, Scott, Rashiq, Rifquah, Lufefe, Anisa, Johan, Marnus, Libbie and Martjin, David, and Basani. Adriaan Bester and Lauren Hermanus, who always shine. In Sydney, Luigi di Martino, Heather Ford, Chris, Federico. And across many oceans, Sean.

James Scott hilariously wrote that after finishing his dissertation he felt "a little stupider" than when he started.[1] I don't know if after completing the manuscript of this book I feel stupider, but I definitely feel a deeper sense of impostor syndrome. For all the hours spent reading, interviewing experts, and researching digital entrepreneurship in Nairobi, the subjects of this book remain moving targets. China, Kenya, technology, digital platforms . . . All of them change so quickly, so radically, I have had to lean into the impossibility of completeness, as Francis Nyamnjoh teaches us.[2] I hope that *Silicon Elsewhere* offers a snapshot of a recent present that, albeit incomplete, speaks to the meanings, the limitations, and the possibilities of technology elsewhere and otherwise.

Sections of chapter 2 were published in a different form in Pollio, "Of Bloatware and Spreadsheets"; and the section "Platforming the Last Mile, with Chinese Characteristics," was adapted from Pollio et al., "Algorithmic Suturing."

The project behind *Silicon Elsewhere* received funding from the European Union's Horizon 2020 research and innovation program under the Marie Sklodowska-Curie grant agreement no. 886772. The open access publication was kindly supported by the Smartness as Wealth project funded by VolkswagenStiftung (Perspectives on Wealth).

ABBREVIATIONS, CHINESE PINYIN TERMS, AND KISWAHILI AND SHENG TERMS

ABBREVIATIONS

AISI	African Information Society Initiative
API	application programming interface
BPO	business process outsourcing
BRT	bus rapid transit
B2B	business-to-business
CBK	Central Bank of Kenya
CGTN	China Global Television Network
CIPS	Cross-Border Interbank Payment System
CLT	central location test
CMA	Capital Market Authority
C2M	consumer-to-manufacturer
DSR	Digital Silk Road
ERS	Economic Recovery Strategy
FMCG	fast-moving consumer good
GCCN	Government Common Core Network
ICT	information and communication technology
ICT4D	information and communication technology for development
IMEI	International Mobile Equipment Identity
IMF	International Monetary Fund
IPO	initial public offering
ISO	International Standards Organization
ISP	internet service provider
IoT	Internet of Things

IT	information technology
ITU	International Telecommunication Union
KICTANet	Kenya ICT Action Network
KIF	Kenya ICT Federation
KoTDA	Konza Technopolis Development Authority
KT	Konza Technopolis
KYC	Know Your Customer
MAS	Monetary Authority of Singapore
MEI	Mass Entrepreneurship and Innovation program
MVP	minimum viable product
NESC	National Economic and Social Council
NIC	new infrastructure construction
NOFBI	National Optic Fibre Network Backhaul Initiative
NTSA	National Transport and Safety Authority
PACT	Partnership for Africa–China Technology
PEP	politically exposed person
PPP	public-private partnership
SAL	structural adjustment loan
SDO	Standard Developing Organization
SGR	standard gauge railway
SOE	state-owned enterprises
SWIFT	Society for Worldwide Interbank Financial Telecommunication
TEAMS	The East African Marine System
3GPP	3rd Generation Partnership Project
UNCTAD	United Nations Conference on Trade and Development
USSD	Unstructured Supplementary Service Data protocol
VC	venture capital
WSIS	World Summit of the Information Society
WTO	World Trade Organization

CHINESE PINYIN TERMS

863 jihua	863计划	Programme 863
baijiu	白酒	traditional fermented liquor (lit., white liquor)
chi ku	吃苦	persevering (lit., eating bitterness)
feiqian	飞钱	flying money
geren waihui	个人外汇	personal foreign exchange
guanxi	关系	personal and business network or obligation (lit., close system)

ju sha cheng ta	聚沙成塔	piling sand makes a tower
Hongmeng	鸿蒙	HarmonyOS (Huawei's operating system)
Hulianwang jia	互联网+	Internet Plus
gaige kaifang	改革开放	reform and opening-up
ping'an chengshi	平安城市	safe city (program)
renminbi	人民币	Chinese official currency (yuan)
renlei mingyun gongtongti	人类命运共同体	community with a shared human destiny
sange daibiao	三个代表	Three Represents
shanzhai	山寨	copycat innovation (lit., mountain fortress)
shengtai wenming	生态文明	ecological civilization
shishi	石狮	stone lion
zaofan youli	造反有理	rebellion has a motive
Zhong Fei hezuo luntan	中非合作论坛	Forum on China–Africa Cooperation
Zhongguo zhizao erlingerwu	中国制造2025	Made in China 2025
zouchuqu zhanlue	走出去战略	go-global strategy

KISWAHILI AND SHENG TERMS

Asante, Rais	Thank you, President
boda boda	motorcycle taxi
chinku	(Chinese) knock-off
dawa	nonalcoholic warm drink made with honey, ginger, and lime (lit., medicine)
imbo	imported (or of bad quality)
jua kali	informal economy (lit., strong sun)
kabambe (phone)	feature phone
kadogo	a little
kuwa nawe, kua nawe	being and growing with you
KYM	handyperson, factotum
madaraka	self-rule (independence)
matatu	privately owned minibuses used as share taxis (prob. from Kikuyu)
Mchina, Wachina	Chinese
mitungi	jerry cans
UTA-Do	What are you going to do about it?
wananchi	ordinary people

Introduction

The Silicon Savannah's Beijing Connection

Nairobians have different stories about their first encounter with China. One begins in Kilimani, a hilly, middle-class suburb west of the city's central business district. Once a leafy residential area reserved for British settlers during colonial times,[1] Kilimani started to change again in the 1990s, with the opening of large malls and the relocation of private corporations into newly built office towers. Another wave of transformation followed in the 2010s, with the proliferation of high-end apartment blocks replacing the guarded, tree-shaded estates that had survived in the postcolonial city. Still today, Kilimani is a never-ending construction site. For every brand-new unit that opens its doors to fresh generations of Kenyan tenants and international Airbnb guests, a new crane is erected somewhere around the corner. But the story I want to recount is less about real estate, although that is part of it, and more about the place of Nairobi in a changing world. Let me begin there.

For many in Nairobi, the first contact with China's global economic expansion took place in the quadrant of Kilimani that serves as its retail hub, around Ring Road and Ngong Road, the highway that links the city to the green gorges of the Great Rift Valley. In 1992, this is where Yaya was inaugurated—the first large American-style shopping center in the area. With its exclusive shops, marble floors, and unfinished hotel tower, Yaya soon became a landmark of Kilimani and of Nairobi as a whole. But by the mid-2000s, a small number of alternative shopping destinations had appeared around it. These were Chinese malls, selling everything from synthetic wigs to cheap electronics, clothing, and groceries. They catered to locals as well as to an increasing mobile population of Chinese workers who had relocated to Nairobi to work for state-owned companies. Those were the years of Kenya's "Look East" shift. Several infrastructure projects—port berths, dams, highways, fiber-optic networks, and geothermal power plants—funded by agencies of Beijing's state council were being built at a rapid pace by the overseas units of China's impressive construction and engineering firms. China had quickly become Kenya's main economic partner and largest holder of bilateral foreign debt.

In Kilimani, the "Look East" transition was palpable. Some of the Chinese malls doubled as guest houses. Eventually, a proper Chinese hotel opened just a few hundred meters from Yaya, its gate guarded by two spectacular *shishi*, the stone lions that protect the material and spiritual wealth of those inside. At some point, even the Chinese embassy's economic office operated on the same road. The red-painted compound of the diplomatic mission wasn't far away either. Everywhere in Kilimani, Asian hotpots and grills cropped up. Construction companies like China WuYi, the overseas arm of the Fujian Construction Engineering Group Company, established their headquarters in the area. Chinese media companies followed suit: in the mid-2000s, Xinhua News's regional offices moved from Paris to Nairobi, China Global Television Network (CGTN) found a home just a couple of blocks away from Yaya, and *China Daily* set up its East African base in an extravagantly decorated business center on Ngong Road. All around, investors from China began staking their bets on many of the high-rise buildings that were crowding the previously flat skyline of the city's western suburbs. Had Kilimani become Nairobi's idiosyncratic Chinatown?

"You could see the sea change," I was told by a Kenyan journalist. "Cities are strange this way. Change starts very small, barely visible, a Chinese mall on a corner, . . . and then the whole country enters a new era." Like elsewhere in urban Africa, these Chinese spatial markers had signaled the arrival of Chinese capital, as well as deeper geopolitical rearrangements in an increasingly sinocentric continent.[2] But for Kenya, the first decade of the new millennium had not just kindled a yuan-fueled infrastructural friendship with China. It had also inaugurated a period of fast technological change. In 2007, for example, an aid-backed experiment, mobile money, radically transformed the financial landscape of a country where until then the majority of its people did not have access to legacy banking systems.[3] Leveraging the "quick codes" that cell phone users typed in to check their airtime balance,[4] a whole new way to transact money was introduced by Safaricom, the former parastatal network operator that had been in part sold to Vodafone. M-Pesa, which literally means "mobile money" in Kiswahili, borrowed the extant practice of using scratchcards to remit money at a distance and incorporated it into a much larger telecommunication system.[5] Kenyans became able to send virtual currency from one SIM card to another but also to cash in and out using money kiosks attended by human tellers.[6] A plethora of payment experiments ensued, targeting all facets of life in Nairobi.[7]

Still, M-Pesa was just the tip of the iceberg of an exhilarating technological acceleration that placed Kenya at the forefront of Africa's foray into the digital economy. In the aftermath of the 2007 election violence, which I address in chapter 1, a made-in-Nairobi crowdsourced platform—Ushahidi—offered a new standard for crisis mapping that was later adopted across the world.[8] An emergent yet incredibly vocal Twittersphere prompted journalists and pundits to ask whether Kenya had leapfrogged from one-party state to digital democracy.[9] The introduction of several international undersea cables along the coast of Mombasa, Kenya's main port city, promised at once to increase the country's integration into the global internet industry and decrease the cost of access to connectivity for a brewing ecosystem of offshored services.[10] An exceptionally proactive Information and Communication Technology (ICT) Ministry, under the leadership of Professor Bitange Ndemo, made digital technology a key agenda of the nation, enshrining it as one of the flagship strategies of its long-term developmental plan, *Kenya Vision 2030*. In 2010, from a nondescript office building not far from Kilimani's Chinatown, a US entrepreneur started iHub, Africa's best-known incubator of digital start-ups. It is here that, years later, Facebook's founder, Mark Zuckerberg, would make a surprise visit "to learn about mobile money" and publicize his controversial Internet.org campaign to bring free internet to the poor of the world.[11]

By the time of Zuckerberg's trip, in 2016, Nairobi had consistently featured in the tech media as one of the up-and-coming innovation capitals of the world and garnered the nickname of Africa's "Silicon Savannah."[12] With cash to burn and ideas to test, entrepreneurs from the African diaspora, together with a "creative class" of adventure seekers from other parts of the world, had started flocking to the city.[13] More and more incubators, start-up accelerators, venture-building programs, makerspaces, coworking facilities, and hip cafeterias were ready to welcome them. Nairobi brimmed with promissory hopes: digital technologies, and the zealous start-ups crafting them, pledged to fix the ills plaguing the African continent.[14] Broken democracies, ingrained poverty, infrastructural divides—all sorts of pilots blossomed, predicated on the possibility of using technology to do good while doing well financially. Other entrepreneurs and investors simply wanted to unleash the untapped profits of marginal economies that could be digitally upgraded or algorithmically augmented.[15] In less than a decade, Nairobi's Silicon Savannah had become one of the most exciting frontiers of global techno-capital. As recently as 2023, Kenya was crowned the leading destination of venture capital (VC)— high-risk equity investments—for the entire African continent.[16]

Back on Ngong Road, meanwhile, Nairobi's busy Chinatown remains a visual reminder of China's economic presence in Kenya. Incidentally, or perhaps not, it was the same strip of offices and malls that Nairobians recognized as the original location of the Silicon Savannah, the place from which the fledgling idea of an African hub of technological innovation took off, some fifteen years ago. So what have these two stories got to do with each other? Aside from the spatial proximity and the temporal overlap, how is the emergence of the Silicon Savannah entwined with Kenya's Look East transition and with China's technological rise? These are the questions at the heart of this book.

At first sight, China's economic ties with Kenya are not limited to construction firms and sovereign loans earmarked for the development of ports, railways, and highways. China's *digital champions*—companies like Huawei, ZTE, and China Mobile—have been active in East Africa for more than two decades, delivering all sorts of infrastructure projects: undersea cables, fiber-optic backbones, mobile telephony networks, data centers, and so forth. Chinese manufacturers of affordable hardware, including smartphones, have come to dominate the electronic sales market in Africa at large. Scores of tech entrepreneurs, software developers, and elusive investors have followed in the footsteps of these state-driven initiatives and become integral to Nairobi's tech scene. In this sense, the ascendancy of the Silicon Savannah is inextricably tethered to the bombastic appearance of China as a global techno-power, capable of rivaling the United States in its digital hegemony.

But this is only part of the answer. At a deeper level, the Silicon Savannah's "Beijing connection," as one of my interlocutors called it, has been a terrain of promises that is forging new meanings and trajectories of techno-capital.[17] Ironically, while Nairobi's tech scene unequivocally borrows its moniker from Silicon Valley, the putative birthplace of everything digital, it would be impossible to understand the Silicon Savannah's place in the economy of technology without tracing the circulations that intersect the integration of China's digital industry in Africa. In other words, and this is the main argument of this book, the Silicon Savannah is the experimental site of a technological transition that, in spite of the Silicon Valley's dominance in the global imagination of the digital economy, begins at the encounter of an African city with Chinese ideas, experts, entrepreneurs, start-ups, investors, platforms, business models, and electronic equipment. This is a story of ingenuity and adaptation that, against the backdrop of rising geopolitical anxieties about a "second cold war"—the escalation of a US-China rivalry increasingly fought over and through technology—offers an alternative view of this worldly turbulence.[18]

At the very least, it is the vantage point of this book that is different. How, I ask, has a city like Nairobi—booming, fragmented, chaotic yet cosmopolitan, inventive and fast-changing—become the experimental site of the encounter between the tech-infused developmental aspirations of an African state and China's digital ambitions? Or better, can Nairobi be the foil against which to read the technological shifts of digital capitalism in the context of mutating geopolitical alignments? In asking these questions, *Silicon Elsewhere* focuses on an African city—and its *Beijing connections*—to capture a snapshot of technological change that does not begin either with Silicon Valley or with China's digital power alone. Much like historians have used other African cities such as Algiers, Dar Es Salaam, and Durban to write about internationalism in the revolutionary contact zones of the Cold War, *Silicon Elsewhere* is an ethnography of contact zones, of the asymmetrical interfaces between the many impulses of contemporary techno-capital writ large: foreign powers, big tech companies, inevitably, but also local state authorities with their long-term planning goals of transforming Kenya into Africa's digital engine, and scores of emergent start-ups and investors who are reimagining Nairobi's urban economies within and beyond the structural legacies of colonialism, in a *reoriented* technological world.[19]

My hope with this book is to show that the Silicon Savannah is not a periphery of techno-capital, yearning to catch up with a technological present that Silicon Valley has already left behind, or a passive landing pad for China's geopolitical ambitions. What may seem marginal contact zones are in fact the sites of some of the most advanced forms of speculation and experimentation in technological change, not just the frontiers of innovation *from elsewhere*, but, as the historian of technology Clapperton Mavhunga suggests, *an elsewhere* itself of technicity and reinvention, a geography from which new techno-economic forms originate and emanate.[20] Or so they might.

DIGITAL GLOBAL CHINA IN AFRICA

The temporal conjunction at which the Silicon Savannah and digital China found one another, at the dawn of the new millennium, trailed the course of a longer history of Sino-African relations. A tradition of bilateral friendships had already begun in Chairman Mao's era (1949–67), when China and newly independent African nations bonded over their revolutionary slant. Leaders like Kenya's Odinga, Zanzibar's Babu, and Congo's Lumumba had even appeared on a series of Chinese postage stamps that, under the banner of *zaofan youli*—"rebellion is justified"—celebrated the Republic's solidarity with the anti-imperial plight of oppressed peoples around the world. While China under its first leader is often imagined, at least in the West, as internationally isolated, the country continued to forge alliances in Africa. These alliances included military and strategic support for liberation movements but also more technical and developmental assistance. Small turnkey infrastructure projects, friendship farms (agro-technical pilots), and industrial partnerships for manufacturing upgrading began in earnest in the 1960s.[21] By the early 1970s, the People's Republic had unseated the rival Republic of China (Taiwan) at the United Nations Security Council, thanks to a large number of African diplomats voting in favor of the replacement, and China was funding and building its largest overseas infrastructure project to date: Tazara, or the Great Uhuru Railway.[22] An 1,800-kilometer-long rail link connecting landlocked Zambia to the coast of Tanzania, Tazara foreshadowed a coming future of infrastructure-tied aid, technological circulations, and Sino-African geoeconomic ties.

Under Deng Xiaoping, China's second leader (1978–89), relationships with African countries mostly stayed positive but fell into the background of other more pressing concerns. Those were the years of gradual but radical economic reforms, the *gaige kaifang* that opened China to foreign businesses, and Deng's pledge to realize the "four modernizations"—in agriculture, industry, defense, and science and technology—outlined by his predecessor, Zhou. To rejuvenate China, technical advancement was necessary; it required help from the outside and a nationwide program at all levels of government. As China's socialism entered its "socialism with Chinese characteristics" phase and ushered in a period of unprecedented economic takeoff, "Africa was seen as largely irrelevant to the increasingly commercial nature of the PRC's external relations," the scholar Ian Taylor observed.[23] In other words, while the global reintegration of China accelerated, Sino-African trade and aid relationships stagnated.[24]

Things began to shift at the end of the decade. A major reevaluation of China's foreign policy on Africa followed the Tiananmen events of 1989, when a violent crackdown on protesters, described by the Chinese government as counterrevolutionary rioters, precipitated a highly mediatized global backlash. Isolated again, the People's Republic rekindled some of the Third Worldist promises of mutual help. Clambering to win over its former African allies and pointing out the West's double standards and unending meddling in the continent's political affairs, Beijing began recementing Sino-African partnerships.[25] This new diplomatic offensive was about aid, but it was also, increasingly, about economic affairs. By the end of the 1990s, the annual growth of China's trade to Africa was running at double figures. At the heart of this rapprochement was Beijing's pledge to never intervene, either directly or with economic conditionalities, in the internal politics of sovereign nations.[26] More importantly, perhaps, China had now banked a few decades of experience with receiving foreign aid and investments and could use that experience for its own engagement with African nations.[27]

If the Tiananmen incidents marked an uptick in China's engagement with Africa, this acceleration was also a function of the go-global policy—*zouchuqu zhanlue*—a strategy that Jiang Zemin, the third leader of the People's Republic, inaugurated toward the end of the twentieth century. Recognizing a slowdown in the domestic market, Beijing's state council started a number of initiatives to encourage domestic enterprises, particularly state-owned firms at the beginning, to find foreign markets. Through its increasingly liquid policy banks, China could, for example, tie project loans for African infrastructure to domestic construction firms while at the same time creating the demand for Chinese-made machinery and building material. Put differently, decades of soft diplomacy and small projects (with few exceptions in scale, like Tazara) could be called on for a new, much more grandiose Sino-African fellowship made of preferential buyers' loans, joint industrial ventures, export credits, and sovereign loans.[28]

The circumstances could not be more ripe. At a time when Western aid and development banks prioritized other kinds of interventions,[29] often demanding the scaling back of state expenditure, China's promise of noninterference and of investing in (or lending money for) desperately backlogged infrastructural and industrial systems was incredibly timely. African states needed vital infrastructure and the money and expertise to build it. Through its policy banks and engineering contractors, Beijing offered both. By the late 2000s, China had overtaken the United States as Africa's largest trading partner: under the aegis of the Forum on China–Africa Cooperation, the *Zhong Fei hezuo luntan* launched in October 2000 (and an ancillary variety of smaller bilateral agreements), a windfall of projects had set a renaissance of infrastructure-led development in motion.[30] Eventually, in 2013, China's current leader, Xi Jinping, reframed his country's promises of increased global integration within the Belt and Road Initiative (BRI). Also known as the One Belt One Road or the New Silk Road, the BRI rebranded existing partnerships and poured money into infrastructure projects that, while increasing connectivity across Asia, Europe, and Africa through a network of land and sea routes, would also generate profit opportunities for China's outgoing companies and capital, and shift the center of gravity of the world's economy.[31] Connectivity, Xi announced in 2017, was the foundation of a new era of development. And albeit fuzzy, Africa's New Silk Road has instigated even deeper infrastructural and financial ties with China, all of them predicated on the mantra of South–South cooperation.[32] Yet, as the political scientist Lin Chun has observed, Beijing's hefty presence on the world stage today is less about anti-imperial internationalism, despite Xi and Hu's *renlei mingyun gongtongti* (community of a shared future) philosophy, and more about the global integration of its economic fortunes.[33]

In this context, accounts of China in Africa teem with hopes and anxieties. More than anything else, these sentiments have been symbolized precisely by large-scale infrastructure systems, from railway corridors to undersea cables and 5G towers, which have been the currency of both popular and academic debates about China's going-out capital reaching the shores of the African continent. Optimistic narratives point to the fact that Chinese loans and state-owned contractors, after the "lost" decades of structural adjustment–enforced austerity, have helped fill the gaps of incomplete, undermaintained, or even absent infrastructural networks.[34] Ports, highways, light rails, and fiber-optic networks funded by agencies of the state council in Beijing, and delivered by China's overseas companies, have pledged at once to improve Africa's connectivity and its integration into a world economy shifting toward the East, and to offer a more equal set of geopolitical relations than older forms of Western support for infrastructure development.[35]

Conversely, critics have drawn attention to the numerous pitfalls and contradictions of these infrastructural promises. As we have briefly seen, China's engagement with African countries in the 2000s responded to an explicit policy framework designed to find new markets for large (state) corporations whose profits had faltered in the context of a saturated domestic economy.[36] Therefore, some have argued, China's capital-export regime is not far off older developmental programs in which aid money was tied to the commercial interests of Western companies and states.[37] Even though the notion of "debt-trap diplomacy" has been carefully debunked, it is undeniable that new forms of dependence, extraction, and accumulation mark the strides of Chinese capital in the continent.[38] Much has thus been written about the environmental costs, the asymmetrical labor regimes, the restructuring of landownership, and the unequal patrimonial relations that are beholden to Chinese-built infrastructure corridors.[39] And although less attention was initially paid to ICT networks, louder and louder alarms have been raised against the authoritarian model of digital sovereignty and tech-enabled surveillance that the Chinese state purportedly exports through its giant ICT companies like ZTE and China Mobile.[40] At times, China's high-tech presence in the African continent has been even described as a form of "digital neocolonialism," a subtle form of dispossession based on data and not on tangible resources.[41] I return to this issue in a few pages.

Kenya, as readers will have already surmised, is no exception. In Nairobi, aside from Kilimani's Chinatown, it is impossible to ignore how the physical landscape of the city has been forever altered by the "marriage of convenience" between the Chinese construction sector and domestic ambitions of growth and development.[42] The standard gauge railway (SGR) built by the China Road and Bridge Corporation (CRBC) that connects the city to Lake Naivasha, for example, drifts over the gazelles, ostriches, and zebras of Nairobi National Park.[43] In 2019, then–President Uhuru Kenyatta, who had made infrastructure a signature issue of his tenure, called it "the Golden Belt of the BRI" in East Africa.[44] Along the peripheries of the city, new road bypasses link and sometimes cut through suburbs that, according to colonial planning, were never meant to be well connected.[45] The new city-to-airport expressway now casts its brutalist shadow over the leafy Uhuru Park that the Nobel Prize–winner Wangarĩ Maathai famously saved from bulldozers in the late 1980s. And throughout the city, the horizon is marked by a swelling number of tall skyscrapers erected at a rapid pace by the same Chinese companies that have built these city-modernizing infrastructures and are now hedging their bets on Nairobi's real estate boom.

Yet the conspicuous presence of these overseas construction contractors is only one of the corporate forms of China in Nairobi. Perhaps less visibly, Chinese digital champions have been active in Kenya for a long time. Network equipment providers like Huawei and ZTE, for example, have been fundamental partners of the Kenyan government in delivering the widespread internet access on which Nairobi's regional advantage as a technology capital rests. Anecdotally, one of the first ever Chinese concessional loans made to Kenya was earmarked for a digital connectivity project in a rural county. And the latest loan (to date) from the Export-Import Bank of the Republic of China (Chexim) to the Kenyan treasury has allowed Huawei to deliver the national data center and the smart-city grid in Konza, a new satellite town poised to become the country's digital hub. Sometimes these projects fly the flag of the Digital Silk Road (DSR), the high-tech sub-brand of the broader BRI.[46] Yet large state companies and large contractors, I argue in this book, are but the tip of the iceberg of much more variegated circulations of techno-capital between the Silicon Savannah and its Chinese counterparts.

How to make sense of these circulations? *Silicon Elsewhere* stands on the shoulders of a body of studies that has been labeled as "Global China" and inspired by Ching Kwan Lee's landmark book, *The Spectre of Global China*. In her research on Chinese mining and construction companies operating in Zambia, Lee made the point that China's going-out capital is a palimpsest of different actors, rationalities, and relations. There is more than the Chinese state in Global China: myriad entrepreneurs, private companies, investors, experts, and elite networks shape China's overseas footprint.[47] At times, these networks use the BRI and other going-out strategies as bridgeheads; at times, they precede them; at times, they are completely disconnected from policy goals. In other words, only by recognizing different varieties of capital can one trace the different logics of accumulation and their ensuing regimes of labor, management, and so on. The idea of Global China also foregrounds the need to not lump everything Chinese, in Africa or anywhere, under a master narrative of geopolitical domination (or an attempt thereof). This is of particular importance in the study of the Chinese presence in the African continent, where overemphasizing China's strategic goals infantilizes African states and peoples as unwitting pawns.

The same is true not just of construction and mining companies, Lee's object of study, but also of the digital economy, my concern in this book. Building on the research agenda inaugurated by *The Specter of Global China*, the following pages focus not solely on Chinese tech companies but also on the many homegrown start-ups and initiatives that seek to build economic bridges or attract investments from the Asian giant. In doing so, my hope is to explore a specific destination of *digital Global China*,[48] following the trail of more and more works dedicated to China's place in global technology markets seemingly dominated by ideas and players emanating from Silicon Valley.[49] Then again, as Ivan Franceschini and Nicholas Loubere have noted, "only by understanding global capitalism can one understand China" and "only by understanding China can one understand global capitalism," in Africa and elsewhere.[50] My proposition in this book is less ambitious. If there are different varieties of capital in Global China's presence in Africa, I ask, can the same be said of varieties of techno-capital and of digital technologies at large and, therefore, of their logics and modes of existence? And what does Nairobi, a Silicon Elsewhere, tell us about these questions?

SILICON ELSEWHERES: BEYOND THE PERIPHERY AND THE FRONTIER

"Silicon Savannah," explains the famed tech entrepreneur Jimmy Gitonga in *Digital Kenya*, is an oddly ill-fitting name for a made-in-Nairobi innovation ecosystem. "We need to recognize this," he writes, "because nowhere in Africa is silicon itself being used to innovate through production," and "though 'savannah' is used to depict an African landscape, it is not an African word. It comes from a Native

American community for the grassland prairies they inhabited."[51] Worse still, the implied reference to the US Silicon Valley, a geography of techno-capital with its own unique history, seems to suggest that Nairobi's tech scene is a derivative affair. Meanwhile, as both Michel Wahome and Alev Coban argue in their respective books on the Silicon Savannah, the latter is animated by mimicries of Californian entrepreneurialism as much as by aspirations to trace alternative futures for homegrown digital technologies.[52] While often contradictory, these futures are predicated on the possibility of digital technologies that respond to local needs and somehow cut ties with what Erin McElroy describes as "Silicon Valley imperialism": a mobile frontier of digital domination that finds new terrains of profit and exploitation by making the post-colonial and post-socialist world in its image.[53] Add digital Global China to the savannah landscape, as I do in this book, and the picture becomes even more muddled and ambiguous.

My point of departure is that to understand the Silicon Savannah as an optimistic project of technological emancipation one does need to look at Silicon Valley but also engage China's digital presence in the African continent and Kenya's own trajectory and relations with China. It is germane to this effort to follow Lee's suggestion to look at different varieties of capital (e.g., across state and private actors) to foreground the diverse logics that distinguish Global China, both within and without. But here's the rub: if tracing different varieties of capital challenges the assumption that there are universal logics in capitalist enterprises, does tracing different varieties of techno-capital also map the cosmopolitan specificity of digital technologies themselves?[54] To be more specific, we could ask whether digital platforms that are created elsewhere are the same as those that originated in Silicon Valley. We could reflect on whether different practical concerns, or different state-market relations, different cultural norms, different geopolitical alliances, and so on, ultimately coalesce into one single version of digital technology, or into a terrain of technological difference, where universality and specificity coexist.[55] My broader point is that the *techno-* part of techno-capital cannot be left unaddressed.

This is a complex proposition with which scholars of science and technology have long grappled.[56] I am particularly inspired by the philosopher Yuk Hui's thesis that there is no single, anthropologically universal technology; rather multiple ontologies, epistemologies, and moral cosmologies of technics exist and have always existed in the world. He writes that while "there is a general misconception that all technics are equal, that all skills and artificial products coming from all cultures can be reduced to one thing called technology," technicity exists across very different moral and cosmological registers.[57] These horizons, Hui suggests, could be called "cosmotechnics" and deployed to challenge a "universal history describing one technology with various stages of development." Instead we could chart technological change through the colliding orbits of techno-diversity. Not incidentally, it is through the example of Chinese technological thought that Hui unearths a lineage of cosmotechnical imagination that both diverges and converges with the European episteme.[58] And yet techno-diversity does not imply falling into the trap of cultural relativism or, worse, orientalism. The crucial question, after all, is not what is Chinese about Chinese technology, or what are African technologies, but what is technology beyond the universalizing categories of Western technics.

Such a philosophical undertaking is beyond the scope of this book.[59] Still, the notion of technological diversity, as a domain of the varieties of techno-capital that I address in these pages, remains useful. It remains useful in a practical and, I would say, geographic manner. As the words of the entrepreneur Jimmy Gitonga remind us, the Silicon Savannah is seemingly oriented to a geography of techno-capital that has its North in the Bay Area of California. But this may well be fiction. Writing more broadly about knowledge production, the historian Dilip Menon makes this case using the Chinese compass as a device for rethinking the assumption of our orientations.

> One could have used the metaphor of the compass oriented toward the North to characterize intellectual production in the former colonized world. However, this image itself is a normalized one, reflecting amnesia. The Chinese, as we know, created their compasses to point to the true South which was their cardinal direction: geographical as much as ethical (in the sense in which we use the phrase moral compass). The orientation to the "South" was not only about physical direction but about metaphysical balance. The users of early Chinese compasses were as much concerned with orientation as an ethical and metaphysical imperative—in line with the compass's primary geomantic purpose—as they were about finding physical directions in the physical universe.[60]

While the metaphysical and cosmological dimensions of techno-diversity are too complex to address here, the ethical and the pragmatic horizons shaping the encounters of digital Global China with the Silicon Savannah are key concerns. In this effort, *Silicon Elsewhere* is as much about technology as it is about Nairobi as a city, a *capital* of innovation in a conjuncture of global turbulence. When we read technologies, explains Eden Medina, we are reading history.[61] Yet we are also reading, no less importantly, their geographies.

By centering Nairobi's tech scene, using it as a vantage point for technological change that seems predetermined by geopolitical rivalries and global hegemonies, my goal is to capture a sliver of techno-capital through a geographic reorientation *from* one of the world's Silicon Elsewheres.[62] This approach follows in the footsteps of the many scholars who have sought to chart both genealogical and ethnographic accounts of technology from its peripheries,[63] or at least from what may seem its peripheries but are in fact experimental terrains of technological otherwise. In doing so, *Silicon Elsewhere* also responds to Mavhunga's invitation to consider Africa not as a mere frontier of innovation *from* elsewhere but as a geography of technology in its own right.[64] Digital Global China in Nairobi, in other words, is an empirical excuse for a double displacement of perspective. Away from Silicon Valley and away from China, Nairobi is a Silicon Elsewhere that, like many others, forces us to rethink the universal trajectories of digital development. Multiple geographies of innovation, as we will see, are constantly and effectively mustered in this project.

This framing is slightly different from seeing Nairobi as a digital periphery or as a frontier of techno-capital, even though these are equally important and critical intellectual endeavors. Anita Chan's notion of the "networked periphery," for example, sheds light on the violence and dispossessions through which digital capital leverages the discursive and material reality of marginal places.[65] "Cultural ambivalence and technological complexity," she writes, "much as they happen in the centres[,] . . . weave connections at the periphery of digital economies."[66] But peripheries, she goes on to explain, are hardly ever passive or uninventive.[67] As digital technology is inevitably translated in languages that reinscribe its meanings, so too is the periphery itself, as "it becomes at once a site, a node, and an outcome of information flows."[68]

Conversely, the notion of the "frontier" speaks to Erin McElroy's theorization of "Silicon Valley imperialism" as an exportable formula, an entrepreneurial promise of technological profit that erases the racial and supremacist nature of expropriation and destruction produced along the way of its expansion. This imperialism, McElroy writes, is "a global condition in which Silicon Valley's existence is necessitated by its unending growth and in which it penetrates and devours people's intimate lives, local epistemologies, and personal data while also consuming global and even outer space imaginaries in novel ways."[69] In making and remaking frontiers, "Silicon Valley conjures fantasies of liberal assimilation despite the material and imaginative violence it yields."[70] It is digital technology at large, as the media scholars Nick Couldry and Ulises Mejias note, that rests on a frontierist project by which data colonizes all aspects of life that have hitherto escaped the possibility of being monetized.[71]

In a context like Nairobi, frontiers take on even more substantive meaning. On the one hand, African "frontier markets" are an emic category through which popular media and organizations like the International Monetary Fund (IMF) depict the whole continent, as the next, or last, perimeter to be crossed for global economic players.[72] Meanwhile, both Global China and global techno-capital in the African continent have been scrutinized under the rubric of coloniality. Accordingly, while China uses its capital-export regime to forge new frontiers, creating new forms of dependence via sovereign debt and unequal trade relations, digital technology cannibalizes formal and informal economies alike.[73] Combining both concerns, warnings about "Chinese digital neo-colonialism in Africa" abound,[74] even though, as Yuchen Chen and her colleagues have observed, these readings sometimes lump disparate things and practices together in the same black box.[75] But the bigger point remains valid, as the "siliconization" of the world follows the traces of previous colonial relations and is ridden with new forms of enclosure and predatory inclusion that mirror the past.[76] Extractive digital economies rely

FIGURE 1. A small edge data center built by a Chinese start-up to provide last-mile connectivity in Nairobi's peripheries. Photo by author.

on labor made cheap and disposable by the enduring inequalities that have their origins in the imperial project of Africa's economic subjugation.[77]

Both the idea of the digital periphery and the idea of the digital frontier, in these critically informed perspectives, refute Silicon Valley as "the zero point of spatiotemporal and technological analysis."[78] My complementary project with this book, as it should be clear by now, is to adopt yet another point of observation. What if we start with Nairobi as a capital of technological change and not a peripheral frontier? The Silicon Savannah may well be constituted by powerful ideas that travel there from the Bay Area of Northern California and by colonial remains, but it may be the case that Nairobi is also the experimental site where, if we look at digital Global China instead, one can trace the techno-diversity of global techno-capital. This is not just a shift in the conceptual grammar that I use, albeit an important one. It is also a way to avoid reducing Silicon Elsewheres to locations of mere *tinkering*, as Mavhunga argues, of artifacts that originated some other place.[79] Phrased in another way, borrowing from Sabelo Ndlovu-Gatsheni's provocation, *Silicon Elsewhere*'s broad objective is to provincialize Silicon Valley while deprovincializing the Silicon Savannah.[80] To do so, I trace the Silicon Savannah's Beijing connection as a project that is at the center, not at the margins, of global anxieties over the rise of China and its purported neocolonial tendencies, marked by ingenuity and manipulation, failure and adaptation. In the conclusion of the book, I return to the openings that "multiple elsewheres," as Jenny Robinson puts it, create for thinking not just about the diversity of techno-capital, and challenging totalizing narrations that attribute to it an intrinsic nature, but also about the otherwise of technology.[81]

AN ETHNOGRAPHY OF TECHNO-OPTIMISM

The technological acceleration that Nairobi has become known for, at least since the launch of mobile money in the late 2000s, was not over by the time I started the research for this book, in 2020. At the outset of the COVID-19 pandemic, while middle-class Nairobians sheltered in place and poorer Kenyans working in the *jua kali* (informal economy) were forced into even more precarious conditions, a new wave of made-in-Nairobi digital platforms flooded existing urban economies.[82] From last-mile logistics to warehouse management, from humanitarian platforms to crowd-work portals, from pay-go kits to crypto-wallets, a range of new digital applications appeared on the market, seeking to produce value through the algorithmic optimization of economies that seemed in need of a digital fix. Attesting to the hype, investors too began rushing to Nairobi.

Despite this, 2020 and 2021, when I first landed in Nairobi for my field research, were not easy years to study digital Global China in Kenya. Global pandemic aside, with its fears, curfews, lockdowns, and travel bans, many Chinese entrepreneurs and investors had since left the country. Things would gradually change, but starting this work in a time of crisis felt incredibly daunting. Not only was I an outsider, both to Nairobi and to the Silicon Savannah's Beijing connection; I was unsure that there was a there there after all. Perhaps the Beijing connection had wilted away, and my prior desk research—my endless googling of Chinese start-ups in Nairobi—had turned futile. Soon, however, I realized that the crisis was just a placeholder to describe a momentary reshuffle. The Beijing connection was still alive. More importantly, the pandemic was just one of the structural ruptures of life in Nairobi. The city was and is beset by all kinds of infrastructural, social, economic, and environmental predicaments. And these issues, with or without the COVID-19 virus, were being made into technical problems that could be solved through the augmentation of digital technologies. This was the hope of the Silicon Savannah at large: techno-capital would fix the ills of an African city while producing profits, jobs, innovation, development, democracy, and financial independence.[83] The pandemic had not dimmed these aspirations. If anything, it had pushed technological experimentation even further. And the Chinese start-ups, managers, coders, data scientists, analysts, and investors who remained were not only imbricated in this speculative enterprise. They were at the forefront of pilot programs and test beds that sought to arbitrage China's technological rise by making it into an actionable program for the Silicon Savannah. There was a there there, and this was a technological promise.

But how does one study such a vague and fleeting object? From the very beginning, my ambition was to enter the field through the networks of expertise that primed the encounter between digital China and the Silicon Savannah. I spoke with renegade tech entrepreneurs who left the hardened corporate environment of China's state companies to build their own Africa-centric start-ups, innovative investors who were betting on the possibility that Kenya would follow the same technological path as China a decade before, local software engineers and bureaucrats who sought to mobilize Chinese capital to overcome the structural dependencies of Kenya's economy, and many other skillful experimenters, adventurers, and state planners. The approach of this book could thus be broadly described as an ethnography of expertise. This was only one side of the equation of techno-capital in the Silicon Savannah.[84] Yet having experts as ethnographic muses allowed me to capture the tireless work required to construct the Beijing connection,[85] as well as bypass the problem of studying techno-capital through concepts that seem to have an a priori coherence but do not. Start-ups, corporations, platforms, tech ecosystems, and VC investments, through the eyes of the experts punctuating the stories of this book, do not feature as accomplished facts, or linear discourses, but as fraught, incomplete, personal, and collective projects to be cultivated. There were obviously other ethnographic objects that belonged to the realm of expertise: policy documents, technical standards, tech news, and others. These too appear in this book.

Tying everything together shifted my ethnographic effort from experts and expertise to a somehow deeper constitutive frame of action, namely, technological optimism. This was the moral horizon of a collective desire to use technology for both social improvement and personal gain. As we will see, techno-optimism is deeply entwined with Silicon Valley narratives but also with the possibility of eschewing the rules and the models of siliconization by multiplying the concerns and references of digital *things*.[86] This kind of optimism is one of the engines of techno-capital in the Silicon Savannah. In chapter 6, at the close of this book, I detail how researching techno-optimism was equally a practical and an epistemic affair. Without giving too much away now, the final chapter reflects on four aspects of this ethnographic venture.

First, technological optimism was vehicled by a lingo, the language of disruption, that tied my biography to those of the interlocutors who generously shared their stories with me. Language proficiency, or lack thereof, modulated my privileged access to the Beijing connection. Second, technological optimism was networked in a way that blurred the lines between researcher and informant, work and leisure, observation and participation, trust and wariness. Third, technological optimism was never in a single place or performed in specific choreographed events but distributed and ephemeral. In this way, it required rethinking some of the qualities traditionally associated with the thickness and depth of ethnographic work. Fourth, techno-optimism primed my research project itself. *Silicon Elsewhere*, as one of my contacts claimed, was (still is?) a "start-up." And, as such, this book too belonged to the many, diverse experiments of the Silicon Savannah's Beijing connection. Ultimately, this forced me to rethink the possibility of straddling critical proximity and critical distance, the complicit nature of research in expertise, and the debits of scholarly privilege that are easily buried under grand arguments and big theories of capitalism.

OUTLINE OF THE BOOK AND ITS ARGUMENTS

Each chapter of *Silicon Elsewhere* offers a unique vantage point, tracing different aspects of the interface between Global China and the Silicon Savannah: from large-scale developmental projects to affordable smartphones, from the platform pilots that aim to optimize Nairobi's informal economies to the trials of new cross-border payment standards that seek to build new China-Africa financial corridors, and the fervor of Chinese investors who place their bets on all these experiments.

Chapter 1 begins by charting two parallel story lines. On the one hand, I briefly summarize the ascent of China's digital industry and its sudden integration into the most competitive and advanced forms of transnational techno-capital, constantly seeking new frontier markets. On the other hand, I follow Kenya's developmental program that placed ICTs and digital entrepreneurialism at the center of the country's ambitions of economic statecraft in its new democratic era (after 2002). In other words, the chapter asks how Nairobi became Africa's "Silicon Savannah" and consequently a destination of digital Global China. My argument is that the encounter between Nairobi's innovation scene and digital Global China was, at least in part, engineered by state-driven ambitions and programs. To illustrate this point, chapter 1 brings together existing work on the boom of China's hardware manufacturing and digital industries in the post-reform era, in particular in the early 2000s, and my own archival work on Kenya's state policies that foregrounded ICTs as a national agenda. Through parliamentary records, policy documents, and reports, I trace the moment at which a number of strategic and serendipitous moves of the Kenyan state made the country prime for the arrival of both China's "digital champions" and, later on, swarms of smaller entrepreneurial experiments. In recounting these two overlapping stories, of Kenya's technological ambitions and China's going-out digital capital, the chapter sets the scene for the remainder of the book. Anchoring the discussion, the main case study of the chapter follows the development of Konza Technopolis, a satellite "smart city" on the outskirts of Nairobi, which embodies the aspirations and the contradictions of Kenya's ICT developmentalism.

Chapter 2 narrates the recent history of affordable Chinese phones in Nairobi. Cheap handsets manufactured in China are the material commodities that enable an increasingly competitive datafication of urban life, especially at its informal edges. Low-cost phones are known as "chinku," a vernacular that denotes their suboptimal quality but also their ubiquity and affordability. In fact, and in spite of their bad reputation, chinku phones are one of the data materialities on which new avenues of digital accumulation are premised and promised. Chinku phones are the enablers of new datafied economies, from crypto-wallets to distributed logistic platforms, that seek to transform and incorporate so-called frontier markets—informal economies that have thus far escaped the circuits of digital capital. Combining an oral history of affordable Chinese cell phones with an ethnography of the experts that enable and manage the value chains of this commodity, the chapter portrays Nairobi as a city of experiments and recoils amid increasing competition for markets and standards.[87] In doing so, it challenges some of the assumptions about the notions of frontier and frontier markets that are commonplace in both critical and popular accounts of techno-capital in Africa. To make this point, the chapter is centered on the case of Transsion, the Shenzhen-based phone maker that currently dominates mobile sales in Kenya and beyond.

Chapter 3 delves into a particular set of techno-capital experiments in Nairobi—experiments that seek to incorporate existing urban economies, many of which only exist informally, into digital platforms. These pilots combine behavioral trials and incredibly sophisticated practices of data capture, seeking to make economic activities legible to digital platforms even when they are fragmented, haphazard, and precarious. Obviously, this is not just a story of Chinese companies and entrepreneurs. In fact, business models based on the platformization of informal economies abound across the Silicon Savannah. From last-mile logistics to e-mobility, from pay-go solar kits to restocking apps for small businesses, from e-commerce to crowd-work, American, Arab, Chinese, European, and Indian entrepreneurs compete for markets and for access to capital in Nairobi. But as I explain in the chapter, digital Global China remains an important reference point for these new platform economies. On the most superficial level, as the previous chapter shows, affordable hardware often comes from China, and therefore it is Chinese start-ups that have a unique advantage in negotiating imports and deals. Most importantly, however, many platform experiments happening in Nairobi seek to arbitrage business models and marketing strategies that originated in China more than a decade ago and made the fortunes of companies like Meituan, Pinduoduo, and Alibaba. In other words, for many start-ups, the rise of digital China offers the Silicon Savannah an alternative pathway to that of Silicon Valley, especially insofar as China's digital boom started with and from making hardware and software for the masses, the "information have-less" of digital capitalism.[88] Taken to Nairobi, this trajectory offers a model for the algorithmic suturing of urban infrastructure that are optimistically recast as terrains of digital optimization at the lower-income margins of the city.

Chapter 4 addresses one of the most fraught and fastest-changing geopolitical terrains of our time: the making of technical standards. Once dominated by Western companies in forums like the International Standards Organization (ISO) and the International Telecommunication Union (ITU), the making of international standards is now a more plural arena of tussles and negotiations. This is the result of China's unequivocal ambition to shift from being a standard follower to being a standard-bearer, especially in critical sectors like digital industries. Against this backdrop, often overdetermined by geopolitical disquiet, Nairobi's Silicon Savannah presents us with an alternative perspective. Far from grand geopolitical moves, standards existed in the worlds of my interlocutors across many different registers. Standards were seen as a negative, inefficient status quo and as an aspiration, that of setting new rules, starting from Nairobi. So standards manifested as protocols to be challenged but also as opportunities to create new uniformities. Through the testimony of my interlocutors, chapter 4 charts the making of new standards in the domain of China-Africa cross-border transactions enabled by new financial technologies (fintech). Although tentative and exploratory, these experiments contained and articulated a clear geopolitical program. But it wasn't a grand narrative—the Chinese century, the tech cold war, or the like. Rather, it was a minor, pragmatic kind of geopolitical project, which I describe as "microgeopolitical" for its modest, run-of-the-mill approach to cross-border payment inefficiencies that were linked to intractable and much bigger global misalignments and downloaded, literally and figuratively, into something as small as a digital application running on a cheap smartphone.

Chapter 5 turns to the capital of techno-capital itself, asking how Chinese digital entrepreneurs and investors make the Silicon Savannah worth investing in in the first place. Behind the bullish, at times superficially irrational optimism that

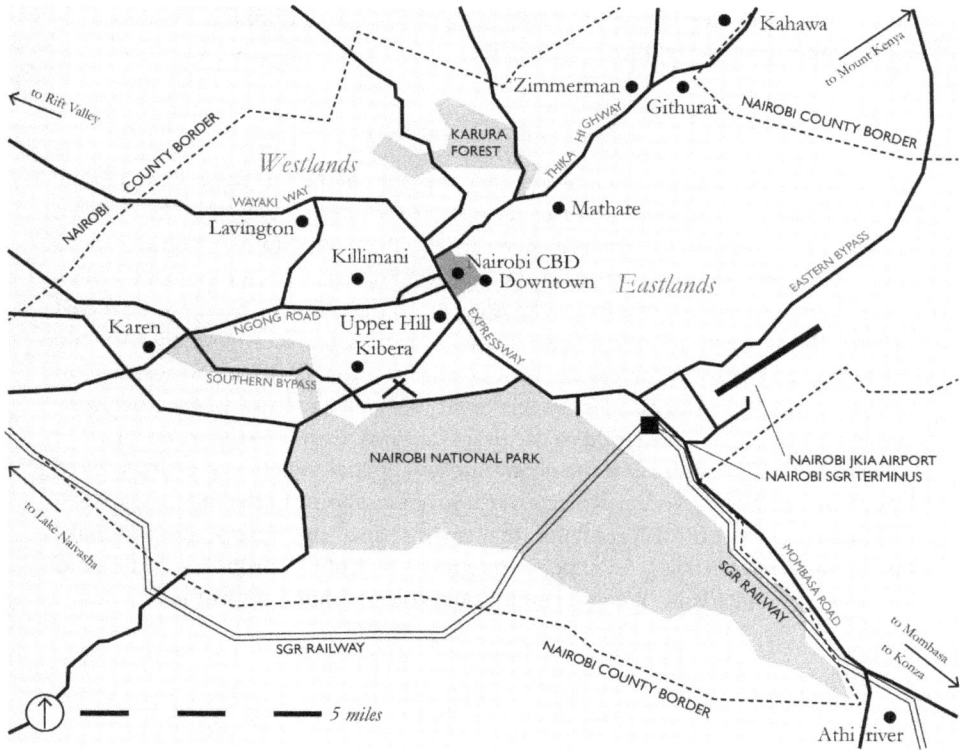

MAP 1. Nairobi, showing locations mentioned in the book. Drawn by the author.

animates start-up life, cultivating the possibility of injecting cash and hopes in uncharted innovation requires laborious cycles of derisking and deleveraging. In the chapter, I showcase how the venture capital investments that happen at the interface of Global China and the Silicon Savannah are contingent on two different, overlapping forms of labor: the making of entrepreneurial solidarities,[89] offline and online networks of mutual hopefulness through which transnational techno-capital finds a home in Nairobi; and the careful derisking of venture capital investments that are failure-prone and punctuated by losses. These different practices serve the purpose of making uncertain presents legible as the starting point of future gains, but chapter 5 argues that they are also techno-speculative acts that perform the investability of Nairobi's Silicon Savannah as a project of technological change.

Chapter 6, as mentioned, retraces the thread of technological optimism that somehow weaves together each chapter, focusing on the methodological implication of my ethnographic encounter with the Silicon Savannah's Beijing connection. And finally, in the coda of the book, I return to Hui's question of technological

diversity, with a reflection on the stakes and possibilities of thinking about technological otherwises from Silicon Elsewheres.

A NOTE ON NAIROBI

Just as this book frames a thin, momentary snapshot of digital Global China in the
Silicon Savannah, it also captures a very narrow topology of Nairobi. The city that
appears in the following pages is a very partial reflection of an African metropolis
that is far more complicated, contradictory, and fractured than the image I offer.
Most Nairobians do not live in and have access to the places of privilege traversed
by my ethnographic research. Tree-shaded coworking spaces, rooftop bars, hip
cafeterias, and upscale conference venues echo a colonial, decadent portrayal of
Nairobi as the "green city under the sun" that is skewed and incomplete. Therefore,
and where possible, I have tried to use notes to point readers to the works of other
scholars who have addressed the economic and spatial violence of a city scarred
by colonial and postcolonial projects. If these issues appear in the following pages,
they appear as technical "problems" that my interlocutors were seeking to make
into terrains of technological experimentation and profit. Nairobi is a "ridiculous
hurricane of capitalism," Wangui Kimari once told me, but not just that.

1

Silicon States of Development

A VERY JACK MA EVENING

July 2017. On a partly cloudy Nairobi afternoon, students, academics, journalists, and government officials had gathered in the auditorium of the new twenty-two-story tower of the University of Nairobi. Designed by Kenyan architects and contracted to one of the Chinese state-owned companies that dominated the construction market in Kenya, the toothpaste-colored building had only recently altered the brutalist, low-rise skyline of the university's central campus. The reason for the forum was a public lecture by Jack Ma, founder of the Alibaba e-commerce empire and, at the time, one of China's wealthiest entrepreneurs.

It was his first-ever trip to Africa—a trip on which he was accompanied by an entourage of other Chinese investors and entrepreneurs and by unprecedented media coverage on both Chinese and Kenyan news outlets. Prior to the gathering, Ma had met with local start-ups at iHub, one of Africa's most talked about tech incubators, had rubbed shoulders with business leaders of the powerful Kenyan Private Sector Alliance, and entertained private talks with government officials. As a final act, Ma would be saluting Nairobi with a lecture titled, "Empowered African Young Entrepreneurs and Small Businesses—A Game Changer," an event cohosted by the United Nations Conference on Trade and Development (UNCTAD), to which Ma was a special adviser.

Energetic and witty, Jack Ma knew how to hold the stage. It wasn't his first talk of that kind. With Alibaba raising more than US$20 billion in what was the biggest-ever IPO in 2014, Ma's picaresque tale of success had traveled the world. In the wake of the company going public, his crisp, mandarin-collar shirts and blue suits had become just as famous as Alibaba's foundation story. Perhaps this

21

was one of the peculiarities of Jack Ma's presence at the University of Nairobi. Before his disappearance from public life, he was one of very few Chinese tech entrepreneurs whose charismatic personae were well known outside of China, Africa included. More subtly, however, Ma's trip, his entourage of millionaires, the media frenzy, and the shared feeling that the tour would inaugurate a new season of China–Africa business partnerships, were all reminders of another tradition of Chinese visits to Africa.

With annual cadence since 1991, Chinese foreign ministry leaders have toured Africa to discuss both business and aid opportunities. Between 2009 and 2018, eighty-two visits by China's political leaders took place in forty different African countries.[1] Even before then, albeit more sporadically, as Deborah Brautigam discusses in *The Dragon's Gift*, African tours had been a cornerstone of Sino-African partnerships—with the first diplomatic and aid missions dating to Mao's era, when upper-echelon Communist leaders started a long tradition of strategic multilateralism in the continent.[2] In more recent times, it was during a South African trip in 2015—at the second summit of the Forum on China–Africa Cooperation—that Xi Jinping inaugurated a new season of "win-win cooperation and common development" based on five principles and ten action points.[3]

It was in light of this history that Jack Ma's mercurial speech in Nairobi was also oddly unique. Not only was Ma a private entrepreneur whose fraught relationship with the Chinese government would later culminate in his disappearance from the public eye, but his address was an overt critique of state intervention in business. At times, his speech was hilariously dramatic: "I'm not a politician, I am a business-people [*sic*]. As businesspeople, we are result driven. We're efficiency driven. We're fair driven. We are result driven because you have to get results. Otherwise you only talk, no results, you die."[4] At other times, his pragmatic business philosophy echoed China's stated noninterventionist foreign policy on Africa (spelled out, for example, in Xi's five pillars): "Businesspeople can never force people to do business with me. It's about a fair trade, so, I would say, let's move up. Africa will be the next driving force, or driving energy of the world, after today's Asia. And this is what I truly believe. And [as] I come here, I don't want to sell anything to you guys. I want to help you sell your great stuff to the world, using [the] internet." Aside from evoking the figure of "Africa rising," a common trope that recursively appears and wanes in portrayals of the continent's economic outlook,[5] Jack Ma's words were both prophetic and misleading. If they did foreshadow a coming wave of diverse, technology-related experiments and partnerships between China and Kenya and an optimistic faith in the emancipatory gifts of digital entrepreneurship, as this book shows, they also underplayed the role of both states in the making of fertile terrain for cross-national techno-capital. Or at least the promise thereof.

The argument that I want to outline in this chapter is that the rise of the Silicon Savannah, and the fact that it became an experimental ground for digital

SILICON STATES OF DEVELOPMENT   23

Global China in Africa, should be read, at least in part, as the trajectories of two states seeking to reinvent themselves so as to be at the forefront of the new technology economies of the twenty-first century. It is true that Jack Ma's controversial belief that business-driven technological innovation would accelerate development against an army of inefficient politicians, slow bureaucrats, and corrupt state officials was a powerful one. Those who are familiar with the history of development will no doubt recognize a particular flavor of neoliberalism in this worldview—one that became dominant in the 1980s with the World Bank's and IMF's structural adjustment programs and with the Washington Consensus. Kenya's own trajectory had been indelibly marked by this doctrine, which had charged the local bureaucratic apparatus with putative neopatrimonial tendencies and forced at least two decades of austerity and privatizations during the complicated years of President Daniel Arap Moi's oppressive rule (1978–2002).[6] Even before the shock therapy of so-called structural adjustment loans (SALs) in the 1980s, the second-ever IMF loan to Kenya, in 1978, had already imposed a wage-restraint conditionality for public servants.[7] According to development analysts of the time, an overblown state budget and diffused corruption had caused Kenya to lag behind, and important parastatals tasked with the delivery of vital infrastructure had been mired by inefficiencies. These deep, often ill-advised, anti-state sentiments, as Thandika Mkandawire and Charles Soludo have explained, were then baked into the reform programs forced onto most African states between the late 1970s and the late 1990s.[8] With very little results. And even though Moi's government did push back against some of the SAL prescriptions,[9] little could be done about the prevailing notion that the falling productivity of sub-Saharan economies like Kenya's should be interpreted as failures of the "African state"—more or less what the World Bank's famous Berg Report had made crystal clear in 1981.[10]

But 2017 Kenya, despite Jack Ma's misgivings about bureaucratic inefficiency, was not the ailing Kenya of the 1980s or the 1990s. Kenya in 2017 was Africa's upcoming bulwark of digital innovation, its Silicon Savannah. Contradictions aside, Kenya was a rapidly growing economy, one increasingly imbricated in the most advanced forms of digital capital that existed in the continent. "Some of the most innovative ideas in the world [could] come from places like Kenya," Melinda Gates would observe a year later, on a trip during which she launched a platform for poverty reduction through technology.[11] From mobile money to crisis mapping software, from widespread internet access to political spats on Twitter, Kenya was leading the way in the internet era.[12] And none of that could have happened at the hands of savvy businesspeople alone. During the "golden" decade of Mwai Kibaki's presidency (2002–13) and under the helm of an overarching development strategy, *Vision 2030*, the Kenyan state had pledged to be and indeed acted as an investor in the much-yearned-for transition from a traditionally agricultural to an advanced economy, centered on knowledge and innovation.[13] Kenya had become an "investor state" beyond the digital economy, leading and facilitating several infrastructural visions of progress and development.[14] Behind the scores of entrepreneurs and techies who heralded and championed the Silicon Savannah as the next capital of technology, the patient, optimistic, at times incongruous work of state bureaucrats and ambitious politicians had, quite literally, laid the discursive and physical foundations of the story of this book. And if Jack Ma's words about the role of the state in Kenya's buoyant foray into the digital economy were misguided, they were even more so about the inextricable, not less contradictory, alliance of the state and the private technology sector that had ushered in China's digital boom. Ironically, as Hong Sheng explains, even Alibaba's success with e-commerce had been, perhaps counterintuitively, entwined with several programs of the Chinese investor state.[15]

What to make of these stories of entrepreneurial statecraft—specifically, of the Kenyan state and the Chinese state intervening and creating the conditions for transnational digital economies to thrive? While these stories are not identical, as the macroeconomic policy issues that Kenya was trying to address were often not the same as those that China prioritized, they reveal how, across the world, states are not quiet bystanders of thriving or failing innovation economies.[16] National and local governments in different geographies and from different sides of the political spectrum have long rushed to digital economic policy for all kinds of reasons, from securing critical industrial capacity to rescuing postindustrial cities from stagnant decline and even addressing matters of nation building.[17] Nonetheless, the entrepreneurial paths of Kenya and China are hardly just variations of what political economists have described as the resurgence of "state capitalism"—a brawnier presence of the state in the economy through public enterprises, wealth funds, and other kinds of government-controlled corporate entities and financial mechanisms.[18] As Isabella Weber reminds us, China is a good example of how the involvement of the state in the making of capital has a complex intellectual history, merging developmental ambitions and the desire to fend off imperial subjugation.[19] And even a small snapshot of the year 2000 in Kenya, as we will see, reveals a complex landscape of state rationalities that defies easy categorizations.

In charting the parallel and then entwined story lines of the Silicon Savannah's blooming and China's digital expansion in Africa, this chapter follows Kenya's developmental programs that placed ICTs and digital entrepreneurialism at the center of the country's ambitions of economic statecraft in its new democratic era (after 2002) and that eventually primed Nairobi for the arrival first of China's "digital champions" and later on a swarm of much smaller corporate entities, start-ups, and zealous investors. Placing such enterprising experiments against this backdrop gives us a genealogy of techno-capital in the Silicon Savannah that is not solely oriented to a single North, that of Silicon Valley, but traces some of the many strategic and sometimes serendipitous path alignments that shaped its promises.

THE "GOLDEN" DECADE (2002–2012)

"Everywhere I went, I heard the same words," wrote the Kenyan novelist and editor Byanivanga Wainaina in a 2007 *Vanity Fair* piece, recalling the months that preceded the 2002 election. "Roads. A new constitution. Taps. Water. Electricity. Education. The usual tribal chauvinism and crude political sycophancy vanished. Nations are mythical creatures, gaseous, and sometimes poisonous. But they start to solidify when diverse people have moments when aspirations coincide."[20]

Wainaina's reflections captured the perhaps cruel optimism that led up to Mwai Kibaki's presidency and the overwrought hope for structural reforms that infused his first tenure. Some long-awaited democratic changes did take place in those years. "Multiple and unpoliced spaces of popular expression, including expanded airwaves, a vibrant Internet and the runaway success of mobile telephony, turned the Kibaki presidency into a teeming marketplace of debate on each and every political and non-political issue," would write Joyce Nyairo in her book marking fifty years after Kenya's independence (1963–2013).[21] Kibaki's cabinet had also stood by the promise to shift the course of the Kenyan economy. After two decades of performances perceived as sluggish, the country was roaring at more than 5 percent GDP growth. "The Nairobi Stock Exchange," Wainaina pointed out, was "on fire. Since 2002 the index ha[d] risen 787 percent in dollar terms, making it one of the world's best-performing markets."[22] The national budget for primary education had risen by 5 percent on overall state expenditure. Important infrastructure projects had begun to hit the ground. Foreign investments, both from international players and from the Kenyan diaspora, were finally pouring into Nairobi's real estate. Most importantly, Kenya had aspirationally embraced the possibilities of a nascent economic sector—all things related to ICTs—and heeded the call of ICT4D (ICT for development) proponents, who had for some time advocated digitalization as a means to unleash industrial growth, foster inclusion, and fix social pains.[23] Moreover, in a country scarred by the corrupt and opaque if not outright violent policing of dissent in the Moi era, information technologies also embodied the possibility of new spaces of democratic participation and debate.[24]

It wasn't long after Wainaina's optimistic piece in *Vanity Fair* that history would dampen the hopefulness that had sustained Kenya's early steps into its multiparty, postcolonial democratic era. Signals were already there. Corruption scandals had not disappeared, even at the top of the government establishment.[25] Neither had the unsavory practice of intimidating journalists. While elites were accumulating wealth, inequality in an already unequal country had continued to rise. Clashes over who-belonged-where had reemerged from the ashes of a long saga of ethnicity being weaponized as a divide-and-rule colonial technique. Ultimately, as the historian Daniel Branch explains, all political parties in power, even in those years that brimmed with the desire to chart a different trajectory for the country, had relinquished any kind of redistributive agenda.²⁶ This wasn't new. Kenya had for decades been an anticommunist rampart in a region swept by more radical movements. The very engineers of independent Kenya, the likes of Jomo Kenyatta (its first president) and Tom Mboya (its first economic planning minister), had believed that the preservation of private property and economic development had to be prioritized over redistribution. This is a simplification of political figures whose thought cannot be reduced to that of laissez-faire crusaders. For instance, Tom Mboya and Mwai Kibaki, then permanent secretary at the Treasury, had even coauthored a paper, *African Socialism and Its Application to Planning in Kenya* (adopted by the parliament in 1965), in which they had championed a nonaligned, state-planned, yet free-market economy, where principles of social justice and the expansion of welfare were pegged to the imperative of economic growth.²⁷ By the time Kibaki was president, however, these discussions about the features of African socialism seemed very distant. Eventually, the lack of structural reforms geared to economic justice, never dormant matters of land distribution in the Rift Valley and elsewhere, combined with the failure to modify the constitution and proven ballot frauds, led to the 2007 postelection violence. The cheerful Kenya of Wainaina's portrayal, just a few months old, turned into a realm of dark brutality.²⁸

Only a power-sharing agreement between Kibaki and Raila Odinga, his former rival turned ally turned rival again, tentatively put an end to the violence, a few months after the 2007 elections. It also inaugurated another period of intense economic development policy, which began in earnest with the approval of *Kenya Vision 2030* in June 2008. *Kenya Vision 2030* was an ambitious, all-encompassing national development plan that, at the time of this writing, still frames the country's aspirations. It was followed by the much-anticipated constitutional reform, which initiated a halfhearted devolution project.²⁹ Kibaki's new "grand coalition" was eager to leave behind the trauma of violence, to which cabinet members themselves, according to a later inquiry of the International Criminal Court, had allegedly contributed. In turn, Kibaki's ministers embraced a developmentalist agenda that was not just ideologically committed but also pragmatic.³⁰ As the West and China were tracing two completely different responses to the shock of the great financial crisis, one of state retrenchment and austerity and one that would lead to the state capital–fueled Belt and Road Initiative,³¹ Kenya could finally rely on a wider gamut of possible alliances. Beyond the usual suspects, such as the World Bank and other development banks, China, Japan, and South Korea emerged as possible partners of *Vision 2030*. With export credits to going-out companies and new forms of project financing usually devoid of the strict conditionalities of the World Bank's "good governance" mantra, a whole new set of infrastructural geopolitics seemed attainable. Later on, journalists would call it Kibaki's "Look East policy" shift, accenting Kenya's increasingly deep economic and diplomatic ties with China.[32] It is in this context of developmental thrusts and new international alliances that the seed of a Silicon Savannah was planted. But let's start from the beginning.

During Kibaki's first term (2002–7), the complex task of accelerating economic growth and reducing poverty was entrusted to Peter Nyong'o, then minister of planning and national development. A graduate of Makerere University in Kampala, just like Kibaki, Nyong'o had been one of the key political figures behind the rainbow coalition that had defeated Moi. He was thus seen as a mediator who could get the different souls of the motley alliance behind a single policy plan. Known for his thoughtfulness, Nyong'o did so in two ways. First, he stressed the gravity of nationwide reforms. After all, Kenya's economic numbers were not rosy: over the previous decade, per capita income at purchasing-power parity had plummeted, and more than 55 percent of the country was living in poverty. In sub-Saharan Africa, Kenya had the lowest connectivity per capita rate in terms of basic infrastructure like electricity and internet access.[33] This sense of urgency was communicated by the very name of the set of policies concocted by the ministry: the *Economic Recovery Strategy for Wealth and Employment Creation*.[34] Second, Nyong'o strategically marshaled a broad range of experts in the preparation of the document, drafting a new generation of optimistic technocrats, often with vast international experience, into a wide consultation process. Unsurprisingly, the strategy was not only embraced by the political alliance; it soon obtained the green light of the IMF- and World Bank–backed donor consultative group and was enshrined in a four-year investment program—Investment Program for the Economic Recovery Strategy (IP-ERS)—that prioritized state spending for certain components of the plan.[35]

It is with the implementation of the Economic Recovery Strategy that Kenya launched itself into the digital era as a matter of policy. Only a few years earlier, Nyong'o would recall, public officials were barred from using email.[36] Adopting some of the aspects of the African Information Society Initiative (AISI), a blueprint endorsed by the African Union in 1996, the ERS shifted course entirely, even suggesting that ICT industries could decrease the country's reliance on agriculture.[37] To do so, the strategy outlined, Kenya needed cross-cutting reforms (such as the implementation of e-governance and digital literacy initiatives across different sectors) as well as outright supply-side investments in connectivity infrastructure: a full-blown industrial policy.[38] The ERS also pledged to develop a dedicated ICT master plan, another component of the AISI framework.[39] In its last few years of power, Moi's government had already succumbed to international pressure to liberalize telecommunications.[40] The 1998 Communications Act had created the conditions for Kibaki's cabinet to operate in a context of relative ease,[41] and, if not swimmingly, a national ICT policy draft was out for stakeholder comments by late 2004, the same year in which a further liberalization of the licensing structure had taken place in the telecommunications sector.

Under Permanent Secretary James Rege, a Kenyan engineer who had led the successful entrance of Vodafone in Tanzania, an impassioned coalition of private sector representatives, civil society groups, academics, and government technocrats emerged. Two examples from this period are telling of the fervor with which debates over ICT policies took center stage, at least in the realm of experts. On the one hand, the powerful Kenya Private Sector Alliance birthed a two-hundred-member lobby group, the Kenya ICT Federation (KIF), which included both large IT businesses and representatives from informal cyber cafés. KIF not only participated in and organized various consultations, but vocally advocated the developmental intervention of the Kenyan government in support of this nascent industry.[42] Only a marriage of convenience, experts argued, a careful balancing act between regulation and facilitation, would truly unleash the potential of ICTs to foster economic growth and reduce poverty. The question of universal access was particularly relevant: a committed developmental state, it was recognized, was needed for the uneconomical project of providing infrastructure to the poorest sections of the country.[43] Meanwhile, these goals had also brought together a much larger network of interested parties in the Kenya ICT Action Network (KICTANet), an email-enabled debate space that formed as a multistakeholder advocacy group leading up to Kenya's participation at the 2005 World Summit of the Information Society (WSIS).[44] Combining debates about the geopolitics of internet governance, which had been unsuccessfully tabled at the previous WSIS, and domestic concerns over how the government should act with respect to ICTs, KICTANet and its mailing list would become an important player in many of the policy changes that ensued.[45] Still today, the network is one of the loudest civil society voices in the country's ICT governance sphere.

While these discussions flourished, another team of experts was busy assessing the outcomes of the ERS and envisioning a longer-term plan. This was Kenya's National Economic and Social Council (NESC). As part of the ERS, NESC was chaired by the president and included key cabinet ministers, business leaders, and carefully chosen international consultants. NESC's task was not only to evaluate the outcomes of the implementation of ERS—which had been admittedly designed, according to Peter Nyong'o, to "get the quick wins"[46]—but also to muster political consensus for longer-term development objectives. NESC had to be both visionary and pragmatic.

Inspiration to achieve these goals came from a visit of NESC officials and staff to Malaysia, where long-term economic statecraft, under the *Wawasan 2020* plan, had radically transformed the country in the space of a generation.[47] For Kenyan officials, while the East Asian experience could not be simply cut and copied, it could still provide clues, since Malaysia too had been a multiethnic British colony.[48] Even more than *Wawasan 2020*, NESC planners insisted, Kenya needed a holistic plan in which social, economic, and democratic goals coexisted. This view was crystallized in a paper that was approved in January 2006, after a cabinet reshuffling that had ousted all ministers who had campaigned against the constitutional referendum of November 2005, including the architect of the concept note, Professor Nyong'o.

Finally, in June 2009, a year after its approval, *Kenya Vision 2030* was launched, together with the first medium-term plan for its implementation. It was the first important government move of the power-sharing coalition that had been negotiated in the aftermath of the postelection violence of 2007–8. By then, a new NESC had been formed, this time with all its four international experts coming from East Asian countries—Japan, Malaysia, Singapore, and South Korea. As Elsje Fourie writes, the emulation of an Asian developmental paradigm "echoe[d] the early years of post-colonial Kenya, when technologically optimistic planners such as Tom Mboya sought to guide the country along the path of modernization, deploying tools such as technocratic rule, rapid economic growth, and social engineering."[49] Significantly, *Vision 2030* listed diverse projects as part of its three pillars of social, economic, and political development, including the formulation of a new constitution and the mandate to carry on a devolution of power to subnational entities. Alongside this, the most important feature of the plan was an ambitious push toward infrastructure-led growth. Recognizing the actual budget limitations of the state coffers to achieve such an overarching scheme of modernization, the strategy also argued that both private and bilateral finance had to be mobilized, whenever necessary.

If the ERS plan had made timid references to ICTs, *Vision 2030* did not shy away from positing that technology and innovation were the very foundations of the kind of socioeconomic change envisioned by the strategy. But the architects of *Vision 2030* did not conceive ICT just in instrumental terms. ICT-enabled economies needed to be a focus of industrial policy. This was a speculative gamble. For instance, of the six macroeconomic areas that the plan identified as strategic for the state to actively invest in, four were already the largest GDP contributors to the country's economy at the time, namely, agriculture, tourism, manufacturing, and retail, but two—IT-enabled business process offshoring and financial services—only minimally contributed to Kenya's GDP.[50] In other words, they required a full-fledged industrial policy, the likes of which the country had never seen. This industrial policy materialized in very specific initiatives, like the plan for a new city on the outskirts of Nairobi, as I discuss later, but also in more mundane and less lofty policies of import substitution, lifting of certain custom duties, subsidies, streamlined approvals of experimental protocols like mobile money, and the delivery of basic digital infrastructure across the nation.[51] The latter, in particular, was one of the major ICT supply-side interventions of the early years of *Vision 2030*, including the commissioning of a Government Common Core Network (GCCN), a national data center, and fiber-optic links connecting each of the county capitals to the internet backbone, referred to as the National Optic Fibre Network Backhaul Initiative (NOFBI). Since then, and despite change in governments and political alliances, *Vision 2030* has hatched several specific ICT-centered strategies, from the 2013 *Towards a Digital Kenya* to the more recent *Digital Economy Blueprint* of 2019 and the *National Digital Master Plan* of 2021.[52]

Together with these strategic and speculative long-term visions, Kibaki's second mandate, like his first one, was marked by the fast-moving "political entrepreneurialism" and quick wins of individual leaders.[53] No one perhaps was more active than the permanent secretary of the ICT Ministry, Bitange Ndemo. With no political experience but a career as a World Bank consultant and an academic at the University of Nairobi, Ndemo was still remembered at the time of my field research as the true mastermind of Kenya's digital transitions (even though, by then, he was posted in Belgium as ambassador to the European Union). He had been appointed after the first cabinet reshuffle in 2005 and then confirmed after the election. During his time in office as the head of the civil servants in the ministry, Ndemo oversaw important shifts in the ICT industry, including the market liberalization of the communication sector initiated but never fully acted on until then. He steered the country's first open data policies. He also seized important opportunities that would later turn out to be crucial in Kenya's digital transition. For instance, he put his weight behind the approval of M-Pesa in 2007, at a time when the Central Bank's acting governor had carefully declined to greenlight a proposal crafted by Safaricom, the country's recently privatized mobile telecommunications company. With M-Pesa, Safaricom was shouldering an innovative mode to transact money through the USSD protocol—the quick-code system used by mobile providers to recharge airtime. Those were the years of Safaricom's listing on the Nairobi Stock Exchange and of a series of events that, as Emma Park writes, consecrated a new kind of "corporate" belonging for Kenyan citizens.[54] Ultimately, Ndemo's push for an alliance between ICT and financial regulators established Kenya as a leader in mobile money innovation, and M-Pesa became an inextricable part of the country's formal and informal economies.[55] In fact, a big push for the quick adoption of M-Pesa as an alternative to cash, when only 5 percent of Kenyans had access to financial services,[56] was precisely the election instability of 2008 and the ensuing need to safely remit money—to "send money home," as Safaricom's slogan put it—across urban and rural divides.[57]

Another good example of tactical moves that would accelerate the country's digital transition was the landing of internet cables. Until June 2009, Kenya and the rest of East Africa remained one of the few regions in the world without hardwired internet access. Connectivity was provided by costly and increasingly uneconomical satellite links. By the end of July, however, two of four planned internet cables had gone live along the coast of Mombasa, Kenya's second city and main port. Ndemo, himself a prolific writer, would recall the story of one of these cables, the East African Marine System (TEAMS), a few years later, as an exemplar of his unwavering political entrepreneurialism.

When I joined the Ministry of Information and Communications, there was an initiative to provide high-speed connectivity and lower the cost of accessing the Internet by linking East Africa to the rest of the world through a fiber optic cable. . . . For six years, the 22-country project had remained at the planning stage. . . . Ultimately, after numerous discussions, it became clear that forging ahead with the project successfully was going to require a unilateral approach. Our Ministry decided to abandon the regional initiative in favour of a Kenyan-led project. . . . We faced a policy challenge. In 2008, Kenya did not have a policy to govern public–private partnerships. Yet, such a policy was necessary to convince stakeholders that Kenya would lead the project. To save time, we proceeded to get Etisalat Telecommunications Corporation in the United Arab Emirates as a junior partner (15%). Once we had secured this initial deal, we came back and mobilized local operators to invest in the remaining 85% of the project. To calm investors, I created a board consisting of all of those who had expressed interest in being part of the process—largely local telecommunication companies. And with that TEAMS was born.[58]

As a government outfit, TEAMS pioneered one of many experiments of infrastructure project financing that bloomed in the years to come. By the time Bitange Ndemo left office, on the occasion of the new presidential elections of 2012, Kenya was no longer a disconnected nation. In fact, data showed that internet penetration was now higher than in most other parts of Africa and that the contribution of ICTs to the GDP was steadily increasing. Obviously, tales of individual leadership, like that of Ndemo, only capture a sliver of the story. But they nonetheless foreground the contradictions and hopefulness of post-Moi Kenya, a country in which technological advancements and the propulsion of techno-capital became matters of both emancipation and belonging in the rebuilding of a nation scarred by its recent past. If it is true, as Wainaina wrote, that nations are "gaseous" creatures that come alive when collective aspirations suddenly coincide, then the "golden" decade of Kibaki was precisely this, at least for the political and bureaucratic machine of the country. In truth, many had been left behind by these techno-political promises of inclusion through infrastructure and entrepreneurialism. By the time I finished my fieldwork, I realized that a general sense of ambivalence toward Kenya's embrace of techno-capital was common among friends and colleagues. Some were rightly critical of how little social justice had mattered in the rebuilding of the country through information technologies. Some would defend the techno-liberal hopes that had nurtured the statecraft experiments of the 2000s, yet shake their heads in resignation at how that project had eventually unfolded.

Still, among bureaucrats and state planners, the technological optimism of Kibaki's era had not withered away. The next government, spearheaded by Jomo Kenyatta's son Uhuru, did not turn its back on the infrastructural thrust initiated by Kibaki's cabinet (of which he had briefly been a member). Ultimately, Kenyatta pressed the alliance with China even further, stressing the importance of foreign capital to realize the ambitious projects of *Vision 2030*, including those that encapsulated the transition to an ICT-driven economy. But before turning to one such project, it is worth taking a step back and looking at China's own trajectory with digital technology, one that culminated more or less at the moment when the Silicon Savannah was ready to welcome China's outgoing techno-capital.

DIGITAL CHINA: GOING OUT TO KENYA

From WeChat to TikTok through indestructible Lenovo laptops, nimble Xiaomi phones, and AI-powered Hikvision cameras to lithe DJI drones and many other pieces of software and hardware equipment, few would not concede that China is a world-leading nation in almost all facets of the digital economy, only a close second to the United States. Even areas of technological production in which the gap between the two states has long seemed unbridgeable, like the manufacturing of cutting-edge microchips, are gradually becoming terrains of competition. During the writing of this book, for example, Huawei caught several pundits by surprise with Kirin 9000S, a phone chip that experts assessed to be only a year behind Qualcomm's top-notch, comparable products, despite (or perhaps because of?) the US sanctions that had crippled China's best-known "digital champion."

However, the recognition of China as a superpower of innovation is rather new. In the West, the orientalist view of a technologically sleepy giant has only recently faded away.[59] In contrast, a conundrum was shared among historians of technology and sinologists who wondered how it was possible that a millenarian empire had produced so little techno-science. Most famously, this was "Needham's grand question." Joseph Needham (1900–1995), a British scientist and historian of China, had asked, "Why did modern science, . . . with all its implications for advanced technology, take its meteoric rise only in the West at the time of Galileo?"[60] This was especially puzzling because, Needham had written, "between the first century B.C. and the fifteenth century A.D., Chinese civilization was much more efficient than occidental in applying human natural knowledge to practical human needs."[61] Even in more recent times, the technological achievements of early twenty-first-century China have often been portrayed as copycat emulations rather than genuine ingenuity, as discussed in more detail in chapters 2 and 4.[62]

Needham's question has since received two kinds of responses. A more conceptual rejoinder has pointed to the Eurocentric nature of the question itself. Even though Needham's work did much to shed light on important Chinese technological developments, the economic historian Andre Gunder Frank would later observe, its implicit assumption entailed a rather linear conception of progress and of the relationship between science and innovation.[63] For the philosopher Yuk Hui, it is a limited view of technicity, one primed by fundamentally Western-centric notions of "technics," that places the West as the sole originator of technology.[64] A second kind of response to Needham's grand question has been grounded in empirical studies of technological advancement in China.[65] Accordingly, Beijing's digital primacy should be read against a long trajectory of experimentation with decolonization, industrial policy, military programs, market reforms, nationalism, and socialist rationalities. This complex history reveals not just how inaccurate the idea of a sluggish nation suddenly awakening is but also how different techno-scientific ambitions have long been at the center of Chinese statecraft, at least since Mao's era. Needless to say, as Franceschini and Loubere explain, this perspective doesn't make Chinese state-driven techno-capital exceptional per se.[66] Rather, it recognizes China as one of the motors in the globalization of technology, a motor without which we would only grasp a partial, Euro-American picture of the digital economy. Notwithstanding this, China's rapid rise as a technology giant deserves some attention—certainly more than what can be done in the short space of a paragraph—because it is on the back of this growth that digital China's overseas expansion eventually reached the shores of Kenya.

A good point of historical departure is perhaps *863 jihua*, Programme 863, approved by Deng Xiaoping in 1986. During Mao's time, China had experienced a number of important scientific achievements, including the development of laser technology, thermonuclear fusion, satellites, and semiconductors, but top scientists believed that innovation had been stifled by the bureaucratic apparatus and too little had been done to truly address the country's gap with Western nations. In 1986, four of these well-known scientists expressed this concern in a letter to Deng, outlining a plan for how the state could better support basic research and its industrial application. With the backing of then–Prime Minister Zhao Ziyang, who had been influenced by the Silicon Valley evangelist Alvin Toffler (we will reencounter him later),[67] the plan was enshrined in policy a year later, as Programme 863. The scheme, implemented over the next thirty years, was meant to nurture the development of indigenous innovations in a wide range of fields, decreasing China's costly reliance on foreign high-tech products. In fact, the program dovetailed with Deng's reforms, which had selected key industries, including ICT, to experiment with foreign investments and partnerships. Imports of electronic telephone switches and fiber-optic cables, for example, were among the first to be liberalized, in those same years. The rationale of this move was to take a necessary "intermediary step" toward "self-reliance and catch-up."[68] Meanwhile, at least at the beginning, Programme 863 produced a radical departure for decision making in national R&D, centralizing power into an organ led by expert scientists and not party cadres.[69] And though this shift was later reversed, the plan provided both financial and techno-political opportunities: while funding ushered in important milestones like the commissioning of the Tianhe supercomputer, the overall framework—that is, fast technological catch-up with more advanced nations—offered a shell for the flexible integration of foreign and domestic companies in the making of cutting-edge technology in the years to come. Ultimately, Programme 863 established the centrality of IT-related industrial policy, in all its shades, to the boosting of domestic technology markets first and then to their global expansion.

The 1990s turned out to be an important decade for this industrial shift.[70] While China had become known as the factory of the world, the contradictions of this industrial boom had soon become clear to Beijing's economic planners. Export-oriented manufacturing, often catering to low-tech, low-cost commodities and concentrated in few areas of the country, was not sustainable in the long term. In response, Jiang Zemin, China's third leader, accelerated a number of initiatives designed to further industrial upgrading, decrease reliance on foreign patents, diversify manufacturing verticals, address regional disparities, and attract human capital back from the West. The formation of dedicated Ministries of Science and Technology and of Information Industry in 1998 signaled that these fields of state-craft needed dedicated attention, especially as the country had by then joined the internet and a new generation of IT value-added services was emerging.[71] However, ICT manufacturing in the 1990s remained couched in an export-processing mode of industrialization, driven by a developmental state that was at once trying to rebalance regional disparities (by encouraging relocation of assembly factories in less industrialized western China) and further integrating into global trade.[72] Notwithstanding these contradictions, Jiang's leadership crystallized the importance of technological advancement as the very bedrock of the relationship between the Chinese Communist Party and the people of China. With the theory of the *san ge daibiao*, the Three Represents, ratified at the 2002 congress, Jiang (himself an engineer) established that the party had to act for the "most advanced" productive forces of the country.[73]

In tandem with these inward-looking reforms, by the late 1990s certain industries were seen as ripe not just for global integration but also for global competition, which again needed a supporting investor state. It was the famous *zouchuqu zhanlue* policy of 2000 and 2001: the going out (or going global) of designated national champions, enterprises that could be backed to compete on international markets. Going global was a response to internal crises of accumulation whereby certain domestic markets had already reached a stage of stagnation or overcapacity or where competition with foreign companies was harsh.[74] This was especially the case for network equipment manufacturers like Huawei, whose going-global story is rather exemplary.[75] Founded in the late 1980s in the special economic zone of Shenzhen, Huawei had initially imported network switches from Hong Kong while seeking to reverse-engineer them to start domestic production. Its founder, Ren Zhengfei, as he himself would later write, was motivated by the same ambitions of catch-up and self-reliance that had come to prime China's techno-nationalist outlook.[76] Eventually, with a unique employee-owned corporate structure, Huawei had found success in the deployment of communication equipment to parts of the country, especially rural areas and lower-tier cities, left out by the foreign vendors' joint ventures that dominated more lucrative urban markets. Replicating

Mao-inspired strategies of targeting marginal areas first ("encircling the cities from the countryside"), Huawei had perfected the capacity to build network kits that were comparable in quality but much cheaper than their foreign-patented alternatives. When the going-out policy was announced, Huawei had the option of relying on state-provided, low-cost capital to accelerate its foreign expansion. As the same competitors that had crowded out China's top market, the likes of Nokia, Alcatel, Lucent, Fujitsu, and Ericssson, already dominated sales in high-revenue countries, Ren opted for revising the "encircling cities from the countryside" and instead encircled "developed markets from emerging markets."[77]

In practice, Huawei aligned its own strategy of market expansion with the geopolitical moves of China seeking partnerships outside the West, especially in the Global South and in former socialist countries. Even before the official going-out policy, Huawei had made its first appearances in Russia, the Middle East, Southeast Asia, and eventually Africa. In 1998, an intrepid group of Huawei salespeople and technicians had set up business in Kenya.[78] Some of my contacts remembered them fondly. According to urban legend, they had lived together in a cheap hotel and kept busy around the clock, seven days a week—almost a caricature of the Chinese expatriate laborer in their "eating bitterness," *chi ku*, work ethic.[79] Their room doubled as an office. After a few years, they had managed to get the first contract with the ICT Ministry to build internet infrastructure in rural regions of the country. In 2002, this was one of the first loan agreements between China and Kenya, and it established a long alliance between Huawei and Beijing's State Council on one side and Kenya's ICT Ministry and Treasury and local telecoms on the other.

Huawei's arrival in Kenya could not have been more timely. The early 2000s were the years of Kibaki's ERS, and ICTs were gradually becoming a state priority. In the meantime, structural adjustment reforms had liberalized the telecommunication sector across most parts of the African continent, while at the same time they had curbed the capacity of African governments to invest public funds in the delivery of this infrastructure. In addition, private Western operators had shown little interest in deploying ICT infrastructure in areas like Kenya, which implied costly upfront investments and low, long-term returns.[80] As a result, Kibaki's cabinets embraced China's promise of development finance with fewer strings attached, even if that meant that funding would be vehicled through Chinese companies. In the telco space, Huawei ended up being in competition with (or in the same value chains of) state-owned enterprises like ZTE, China Mobile, and others that had also, by then, started business in Kenya. Anecdotally, while Huawei won its first bid with the ICT Ministry, its rival ZTE had grabbed one with the government-owned Telkom in the same years. One of my contacts, a young salesman working for ZTE, elaborated that it had been the "managed competition" between these different Chinese network equipment providers that had accelerated Kenya's connectivity leap.[81] He told me, as an example, that Huawei and ZTE

5G base stations cost more or less the same but a third of the Nokia option. No wonder that these two companies had become by far the largest ICT vendors in Kenya, and in Africa at large, he observed.

Huawei had also diversified its footprint. From network equipment, the Shenzhen company had branched into data centers and cloud services, mobile phones and software applications. When with some colleagues I met with Huawei executives in Nairobi, in the summer of 2024, the latter showed us a mind map of the different components of their business in Kenya. In the grand boardroom of the company's headquarters, the slide recited, "Kenniya Huawei 20 nian, women zuole shenme?"—Twenty years of Huawei Kenya, what have we done? It then listed the variously integrated facets of the company's market in the country, including personal connectivity, fiber-to-home infrastructure, cloud services to both private and public entities, smart healthcare, smart mobility, financial backends, and the controversial "safe city" tool kit (*pingan chengshi*)—an AI-powered surveillance platform that has had critics concerned with Beijing exporting digital authoritarianism overseas.[82] Under the Kiswahili tagline *kuwa nawe, kua nawe*— being and growing with you—Huawei had partnered with all the shades of Kenya's governance and corporate landscape. They had provided part of the NOFBI, digitized medical care in rural counties, and built cloud-powered IT services for financial institutions like ABSA, NCBA, and DTB, all important banks in the country. Most importantly, perhaps, Huawei had assembled the infrastructure underpinning the transition of M-Pesa from low-tech USSD-based transactions to a much more sophisticated digital stack. The migration of user data from IBM servers in Germany to purpose-built facilities in Kenya was the stuff of legend among experts in the field. Overnight, or so the story went, Huawei had patented several components of the sophisticated techno-financial architecture that Safaricom needed to scale its M-Pesa operations. Fuliza, for example, the popular service that allows customers to continuously overdraw to make payments (with a very small charge if refunds are rapid) had been engineered by a Huawei team.

Some three years before visiting their Nairobi headquarters, I had asked another Huawei executive how it was possible that M-Pesa, a source of such nationalistic pride for several Kenyans, ran on a Chinese stack without raising questions of digital and financial sovereignty.[83] He had smirked and answered that not only was M-Pesa ultimately "Kenyan," as it operated within the strict boundaries set by local regulators, but Huawei had managed to be regarded as a principled partner by politicians and state bureaucrats. Rarely involved in controversies, or even in rumors like the African Union–gate in Ethiopia,[84] the Shenzhen company had aligned itself with the goals of *Vision 2030*—goals that provided market opportunities for Huawei and stories of infrastructural success for state officials. Examples abounded, from the already mentioned NOFBI to the migration of all National Transport and Safety Authority (NTSA) services into one convenient platform for everything from driver's licenses to vehicle registration. Huawei had also made conspicuous commitments to the social engineering aspects of *Vision 2030*, according to which a new generation of technologically skilled Kenyans was needed to achieve the transformational goals of the plan. With initiatives like Seeds for the Future (a global internship program designed to select young students for Huawei's own talent pipeline), participation in the Presidential Digital Talent Programme, collaborations with technical colleges and universities, or programs like DigiTruck (ICT training in rural areas), the company had positioned itself as the government's key ally for the human-upskilling ambitions of *Vision 2030*. A memorandum of understanding in 2014 even nominated Huawei as a partner for the country's future digital master plans.

Huawei's impressive strides in Kenya should be read against what was happening at home in China. As a digital champion, the company benefited from a few important policies of the Xi-Li administration, which had taken over the seemingly less brazen leadership of Hu-Wen in 2012.[85] Li Keqiang's 2014 Internet Plus (*Hulianwang jia*), for example, strategized collaborations between the government and an emergent ecosystem of platform companies across focus areas like manufacturing, finance, and e-government. For many commentators, one of the architects of the policy had been the founder of the WeChat/Tencent empire, Pony Ma. A year later, Made in China 2025 (*Zhongguozhizao erlingerwu*), issued by the paramount leader Xi Xingping, promoted a novel industrial plan designed to increase China's prominence in the production and innovation of high-value, high-tech products.[86] Most vocally, Made in China 2025 bludgeoned the need for delinking China's capacity to manufacture microchips from foreign patents into policy (a goal that was embraced by Huawei). These programs also dovetailed with other overarching initiatives. On the domestic front, the 2014 Mass Entrepreneurship and Innovation (MEI) campaign sanctioned the centrality of IT-related entrepreneurialism, ranging from the small start-up to the tech giant to the government office, as a vehicle to rejuvenate the nation. With MEI, writes Lin Zhang, Beijing sought "to entrepreneurialize problems of development, social equity, and national technological independence."[87] Despite all their contradictions,[88] policies like MEI blended developmentalist ambitions of GDP growth and global technological dominance with residual socialist rationalities that pledged to offer every citizen the possibility to participate in China's digital ascendancy.[89] In the following pages of this book, we will indeed encounter many Chinese entrepreneurs whose temper and personal mobility had been shaped by the shibboleth of mass innovation.

Meanwhile, on the foreign front, in 2015 Xi also inaugurated the IT component of the Belt and Road Initiative (BRI), the so-called Digital Silk Road (DSR), a program that, despite its vagueness, offered government support for Chinese technology companies to reach overseas markets. Just like the broader BRI, the DSR promised a new kind of "inclusive globalization," predicated on principles of cooperation and mutual benefit.[90] Despite its limited documented achievements, the DSR confirmed that the MEI-with-Internet+ shift toward mass innovation and more high-valued industries needed to happen not just internally but also in the global outreach of the national champions.[91] For example, at the 2018 Central Economic Work Conference, the term "new infrastructure construction" (NIC) was coined to describe a new mode of development driven by innovation in IT and not just by the traditional infrastructure that had come to dominate BRI loans and China's bilateral finance.[92] Then again, many players other than Huawei, the owners of platforms like WeChat and Pinduoduo, were more than ready to go global. And giants like Alibaba, which by then had become all-inclusive platforms, were perfectly suited to provide the infrastructure for twenty-first-century digital Global China, as Hong Shen explains.[93]

Huawei's story in Kenya, while exemplary given the extent to which the company "charmed its way into the heart of Kenya's data," as the journalist Dominic Omondi of *The Standard* wrote in 2021, was not unique.[94] Several other ICT and digital companies reached the African shores—and other regions—on the back of Beijing's domestic and foreign policy.[95] We have seen how other ICT manufacturers and operators, for example, China Mobile, China Telecom, and ZTE, made their way into Kenya in the same years as Huawei, even competing with the latter. As these hardware companies focused on the backbone of connectivity, they then paved the way for other players in different segments of ICT value chains, including e-commerce giants like Alibaba, which ran its Africa's Business Heroes competition from Nairobi; media companies like Opera, StarTimes, and Tencent; financial corporations like UnionPay; affordable mobile phone makers (chapter 2); household electronics manufacturers like Haier and Synix; start-ups and individual entrepreneurs in various sectors of the platform economy (chapters 3 and 4), and, eventually, VC investors and their careful analysts (chapter 5).

Of course, this is just a partial picture of the multilayered relations that link China and Kenya. Today the former is the second-largest foreign creditor to the latter, after the World Bank. From engineering companies involved in all kinds of large-scale projects—railways, highways, bridges, airports, geothermal plants—to real estate ventures and "flying geese" seeking to relocate manufacturing capacity, China is Kenya's main business partner.[96] And given the importance of what the political economists Yongnian Zheng and Yanjie Huang call China's "market-in-state" system[97]—which affords different degrees of bounded autonomy to private and public enterprises provided they stay within the course set by state policy—these economic ties are telling of the globalization of China's investor state.[98] But if we look at ICT and platform companies more specifically, not only can we pick out the diversity of Global China,[99] but we can also catch sight of the fact that another aspirant investor state, in this case an African country like Kenya, had actively been experimenting with policies designed to foster technological emancipation and catch-up. These moves incidentally coincided with the overseas expansion of China's digital champions and with the arrival of many other companies and entrepreneurs that "borrowed the boat out to sea."[100] Ironically, the name that was given to this enthusiastic project of statecraft in Kenya, Silicon Savannah, had certainly more to do with California than with China. Yet it was at this historical juncture that the Silicon Savannah and digital Global China found one another.

FROM A SILICON SAVANNAH
TO THE SILICON SAVANNAH

An accurate genealogy of the "Silicon Savannah" moniker in Kenya is very difficult. But a few days spent in the archives of the country's main national newspapers, *The Nation* and *The Standard*, confirmed that "Silicon Savannah" had become a catchphrase for Kenya's ICT industry in the late 2000s, specifically, in relation to a project of employment creation that became much bigger than that. This was the proposal for a technology park in the outskirts of Nairobi, in the literal savannah, that would centralize the needs of a promising yet still small industry—that of IT-enabled business process outsourcing (BPO)—into a single location. The setting for this business park, initially called Malili Technopark, was identified near a small satellite village, Konza, some 70 kilometers outside of Nairobi, along the busy highway that connects the capital to the coast. As Bitange Ndemo would recall a few years later, the idea of targeting BPO industries had emerged in the early days of drafting *Vision 2030*, as a solution to youth unemployment.[101]

IT outsourcing was a silver bullet. As an industrial policy, support for BPO required a relatively smaller initial capital expenditure on the part of the government, given that it didn't need expensive equipment but just solid connectivity infrastructure. The latter, once in place, would also benefit the entirety of the population, since ICT investments would reduce the cost of internet access and improve its speed across the board. Most importantly, BPO would offer a pool of employment and ensuing social mobility for low-skilled, English-speaking, unemployed youth. Examples from other regions of the world also showed that from basic BPO services, like call centers, more sophisticated offshored solutions could spur entrepreneurial activities and nurture other IT industries. As I have discussed elsewhere, these same rationalities animated national and local governments in other parts of the continent, for example, in South Africa, where the BPO sector contributed to the emergence of Cape Town as Africa's "silicon cape," yet another regional capital of digital innovation.[102] Moreover, to accelerate the development of BPO economies, theories of industrial clustering in vogue at the time recommended a spatial strategy of agglomeration.[103]

Vision 2030 made good on these suggestions. By then, however, the technopark in Malili had become something different: from an IT industrial estate, the likes of which NESC experts had seen in Singapore,[104] the BPO strategy now featured a whole new city, called Konza Technopolis (KT), where all the most advanced forces of the nation—industries, universities, government departments, and entrepreneurs—would collaborate on the project of a Silicon Savannah. What was the project? In a nutshell, as Permanent Secretary Ndemo observed, Konza Technopolis was ultimately about "dethroning agriculture" as the main economy of Kenya and replacing it with advanced services in IT-enabled industries.[105]

In the context of *Kenya Vision 2030*, KT was framed as one of its so-called flagship projects. Flagship projects, in the words of the plan, would "set the pace for multiple vessels behind [them]," acting as bridgeheads to wider ambitions.[106] Unsurprisingly, KT featured as a project of the economic pillar of the strategy and specifically within one of the six macroeconomic areas, namely, IT-enabled BPO, identified as strategic for state investment, as mentioned earlier. Again, this was a risky bet. While *Kenya Vision 2030* followed the playbook of other developing nations that had experienced high levels of economic growth in the decade before, thanks to investment in connectivity infrastructure that had made them attractive for the relocation of labor-intensive services by Western corporations, replacing a small technopark with an entire city of 2,000 hectares was no small feat. According to my sources, it had been a back-and-forth during a 2009 feasibility study conducted by consultants of the World Bank's International Finance Corporation that gave birth to the idea for a whole new city. In any event, KT was now imagined at a scale that did not just require fruitful private–public partnerships, but a complex program of institutional and financial planning. As an emblematic centerpiece of *Vision 2030*, KT was eventually gazetted into law as a special economic zone for IT and BPO companies, included in the national spatial plan of 2014, and promoted with visionary artists' impressions of shiny skyscrapers and tree-lined boulevards.[107] The stakes for an imagined Silicon Savannah were incredibly high.

So were the critiques. The construction of entirely new cities has been a fraught matter across the continent. Unlike new African capitals in the post-independence period, designed to address questions of postcolonial national unity, critics have argued that new satellite cities like KT are less about the making of statehood and more about creating speculative real estate markets.[108] These "urban fantasies," as the late planning scholar Vanessa Watson famously labeled them, articulate frontiers of opportunity for investors, domestic and international alike.[109] They are the epitome of speculative urban development, seeking untapped markets in the swelling peripheries of large African metropolises. They have been described as "city-doubles" or "neoliberal heterotopias," because their projected spatial features are entirely detached from the urban realities that they are meant to escape.[110] Predicated on the impossibility of redressing the strains of rapid urbanization, Africa's new cities have reflected "ambitions of 'smart' and 'green', technology-driven development where corporate digital and network technologies are included in the masterplan and leveraged in the city's branding."[111]

But was all of this true for KT? Inasmuch as the project manifested as a huge speculative endeavor, was real estate the central concern of planners, bureaucrats, and politicians who had put their weight behind it? I first visited KT in 2022, with

FIGURE 2. An aerial view of the construction site of Konza Technopolis. Photo by author.

my colleague Jack Odeo, then again in 2023, and most recently on a warm, windy day in February 2024, with another colleague. For the Konza Technopolis Development Authority (KoTDA) officials who welcomed us on all these occasions, the new city was only secondarily about the value of land. Whether they worked in the ICT unit, in planning control, or in the business development department, they were all adamant about the real priorities of KT as a piece of industrial policy. For example, new construction had been allowed to hit the ground in Konza only according to a very careful order. The first tenants, state planners explained, needed to be those advanced players that would contribute to the Silicon Savannah project: IT companies, healthcare facilities, green energy firms, research centers, and universities. Only later would traditional developers be allowed to join in. Planners had even been able to enforce a moratorium on new building developments in a vast buffer zone surrounding the technopolis.[112] KT was a project of economic statecraft and industrial policy first, a speculation yes but less about land than about the entrepreneurial vision of a Silicon Savannah ferrying Kenya into a technologically bright future. Only at a later stage of the project, my colleague Liza and I were told during my last visit to Konza in early 2024, would traditional developers be allowed to invest in the new city.

Temporarily renouncing the liquid capital of real estate investors and finding the financial outlay for a state-led project of industrial policy had made the gestation of KT long and thorny, prompting commentators to describe Konza as a "failed promise."[113] Adding to the ridicule, the shiny white building destined for KoTDA and the ICT Ministry, and built by a Chinese contractor, had stood empty for many years, a white elephant in clear sight from the highway. By the time of my first trip to KT, however, not only was the building bustling with life, albeit still unfinished; it was surrounded by an immense construction site, with cranes and trucks dotting the horizon as far as eyes could see. KoTDA bureaucrats seemed tired of the project being maligned. "It took long, but it's happening," my colleague Jack and I were told while visiting the temperature-controlled facilities of the newly built national data center, which was to be commissioned in the coming days.

The national data center was where the stories of a Silicon Savannah state project and digital Global China converged. In April 2019, Kenya and China had signed project delivery commitments identifying Huawei as the contractor for the "Konza data centre and smart city project," for a total of Ksh 17.5 billion (US$172.7 million) to be financed with a concessional loan from China's Export Import bank. In record time, Huawei had delivered the new facility, a piece of infrastructure that would centralize a number of cloud-based services of various departments and ministries but also host private cloud providers, including Huawei itself. Racks and racks of brand new servers marked by the little red flowers of Huawei's logo were ready to be deployed. And as the data center was about to go live, KoTDA had issued a nationwide call to select the first users with free access to this state-provided computing power: these were to be ten civic-tech start-ups building software that explicitly aligned with the smart city goals of *Vision 2030*.

The data center, however, was only a microcosm of the broader geopolitics of infrastructure capital that KT had come to embody. The construction of the smart grid on which the entire city would rely—roads innervated by a network of large prefabricated concrete pipes carrying water, sewage, data, and electricity—had been awarded to an Italian contractor, with a loan by Cassa Depositi e Prestiti (a publicly owned investment bank that is a major shareholder of many Italian parastatals) to the National Treasury and a bond issued by Standard Bank Kenya (which, as we will see later, is partly owned by a state-owned Chinese company) and underwritten by an Italian commercial bank. Meanwhile, the Thwake dam poised to provide water and electricity to the new city had been funded by the African Development Bank, an upgrading of the section of the highway connecting Konza and Nairobi's southern end had been partially supported by the World Bank, and, perhaps most significantly, the Kenya Advanced Institute of Science and Technology (KAIST) had received technical and financial support from the South Korean government. In other words, KT had become a test bed of the multipolar geopolitical alliances of Kenya's investor state. KoTDA, officials explained, was meant to build "a platform," quite literally a stage, for a Silicon Savannah and, in doing so, for Kenya's technological place in the world.

In this sense, KAIST was quite revealing. As the centerpiece of a broader industrial transformation strategy, KT also needed to foster the demand side of the IT economy by addressing the overall technical literacy of the country. To this end, KAIST was modeled on the Korea Advanced Institute of Science and Technology, also KAIST, an institution that was initiated by USAID in the early 1970s to boost the South Korean developmental state project. Since then, the original KAIST has exported its own model, offering standardized technical curricula for institutions in countries that seek to address skill shortages and accelerate their industrial development.[114] Remember the NESC experts who had advised the Kenyan government in the drafting of *Vision 2030*? The founder of KAIST in South Korea, Professor Kun-Mo Chung, had been one of them; he was adamant that Kenya's economic future depended on its technological acceleration.[115] In KT, KAIST would eventually produce the software engineers that the new city needed to become a crucible of made-in-Africa innovation. When Liza and I visited the site in early 2024 after scaring a flock of fearful ostriches trapped in the construction site, the new university appeared as a busy construction site nearing its completion, with Kenyan and South Korean flags printed on the fence perimeter.

The example of KT, an imagined Silicon Savannah still shaping up as a satellite city of Nairobi, is useful for painting a few important details of Kenya's embrace of techno-capital. On the one hand, KT gave a name to a bigger project of economic transition that eventually took on a life of its own. From indicating a single Silicon Savannah, the moniker has since transcended KT and extended to encompass the entirety of Kenya's ICT industry. It is now Nairobi itself, its network engulfed by coworking spaces, incubators, and often international tech start-ups. Just like Silicon Valley has gone from being the geographic tag of suburban Santa Clara Valley to now including the entire Bay Area, Nairobi has become *the* Silicon Savannah. This city, as this book argues, has come to epitomize the possibility of reimaging how and where digital innovation and technological encounters take place. This goes way beyond Chinese entrepreneurs and investors.[116] "There are weddings, new babies, call centers, small manufacturing businesses, I.T. start-ups everywhere you look," wrote Wainaiana.[117]

KT also emerged out of that period of policy experimentation described earlier in this chapter, a transition moment in which state planners had attempted a blend of "investor state" and technocratic developmental state in the context of the political bargains and turmoils of the mid- to late 2000s, Africa's shift to Asia, China in particular, the speculative promises of the ICT and BPO industries, and the austerity legacies of structural adjustment that, according to my contacts at KoTDA, had at once hindered and enabled the project. Moreover, even if the Silicon Savannah took its name from California, this moment of state experimentation with ICT-driven industrial policy was inspired by different experiences—Malaysia, South Korea, Singapore, China—and the conjunctural needs of a nascent democratic state seeking to reinvent itself through science and technology.[118] Of course, my point is not that the Californian model didn't play a role: the storytelling of Nairobi as Africa's digital capital, for example, has been about producing narratives that show how technological achievements are possible *outside* Silicon Valley.[119] References matter still.

And finally, the "siliconizing" stories sketched in this chapter and epitomized by the Konza Technopolis project speak to the centrality of state action to local projects of techno-capital and to the encounters of the different rationalities that mold the meanings of technology and innovation in what I have called Silicon Elsewheres.[120] This is not an apology for state action in general. States can be violent, and it is typically through technology that violence and repression are administered and upgraded. At the same time, these stories counter both neo-liberal fantasies of state absence and the usual portrayal of African governments as failed entities or dominated by corrupt or compliance-obsessed bureaucrats.[121] China too, on the other hand, is often taken as the exceptional paradigm of an all-efficient state enterprise that, in authoritarian fashion, has been using its technological primacy to recolonize places like Kenya. We will see in the remainder of this book how these assumptions stand the test of ethnographic scrutiny. In the meantime, the state-driven encounters of digital Global China and the Silicon Savannah explored in this chapter offer a foil for reading the following pages, which center on Chinese tech companies, entrepreneurs, workers, experts, and investors experimenting with ICT and platform economies in all niches of life in Nairobi and Kenya at large. Even if many of them perhaps shared the beliefs encapsulated by Jack Ma's words in the opening of this chapter, that states should remain outside the realm of techno-capital, they too were standing on their shoulders.

2

Machines of Data Frontiers

When I first embarked on the project to write about the encounters between Chinese digital capital and Nairobi's booming innovation scene, I imagined myself rubbing shoulders with software developers, venture capitalists, coworking hosts, and business analysts. That happened, eventually. But my first encounter with digital Global China in Kenya was of a completely different kind. I had just landed in Nairobi, in fall 2021, when I realized that I needed a burner phone to use mobile money. I was already familiar with the fact that Chinese manufacturers of affordable handsets dominated smartphone sales in Kenya—and in Africa at large. But I had not realized how crucial cheap Chinese mobiles were to the multiple value chains that linked Kenya's Silicon Savannah and China's going-out digital capital. It was when I found myself on Moi Avenue, looking for a burner phone, that I understood how the ubiquity of affordable Chinese hardware was my first glimpse into a story that I uncover in the following pages.

Busy and loud, Moi Avenue separated quieter, leafy uptown Nairobi, with its highly guarded government buildings and brutalist corporate offices, from the hustle and bustle of downtown. A colleague and friend had told me to notice how even the two sides of the avenue itself felt different. The uptown side, with its grander and better-kept buildings and more airy awnings, seemed spacious and neat. The downtown side, with its smaller arcades cluttered with all sorts of signs, appeared crowded and rowdy.[1] Both sides of the avenue, in the section that leads to the statue of Tom Mboya, one of the revolutionary founding fathers of postcolonial Kenya, are dotted with dozens of electronics stores. Some of these are branded with global corporate logos, like those of Samsung, LG, Sony, Oppo,

FIGURE 3. Luthuli Avenue in downtown Nairobi. Photo by author.

Nokia, Xiaomi, and Huawei. Others bear the logos of China's best-selling manufacturers of affordable hardware that only exist in Africa and Southeast Asia: Infinix, Tecno, Itel, Realme, Oraimo, and Zanco. Most shops, however, boisterously combine multiple labels—their windows covered with stickers and decorated by custom-printed packaging tape featuring various technology manufacturers.

Where Moi Avenue bends, at the National Archives, one can walk past the colonial building and step onto Luthuli Avenue, which hosts even more tech stores along a colorful stretch of LED lights, billboards, and hoardings. Here, along a span of less than half a kilometer, dozens of electronics stores sell, buy, repair, and refurbish tech hardware, mostly from China. And it was here, between the sampled beats of Nigerian hip-hop and the tooting of motorcycles, that many ordinary Nairobians, I would later learn, had first witnessed the repercussions and possibilities of China's technological ascendancy.

Not even a week after buying my cheap Tecno phone on Moi Avenue, I sat down for a friendly conversation with Jerotich, a local business journalist who would in time become a friend. She worked for the African chapter of CGTN, the controversial Chinese TV channel that covers African news stories. Throughout her career, she had been an observer—and critic—of Kenya's economic ties with China. I was therefore interested in her perspective on the research that I had just begun.

"If you want to understand the mobile money revolution and all that's happened in Nairobi since then," Jerotich told me, "you need to look at the moment when phones became ubiquitous. We called them *chinku*. They were cheap copies of established brands like Nokia and Motorola." "Chinku," as its sound suggests, was the slightly derogatory term for Chinese counterfeited products in Sheng, the ever-changing creole spoken by young Nairobians.[2] Chinese knock-offs were so common, Jerotich explained, that another vernacular for fake, *imbo*, literally meant "imported." And while *chinku* and *imbo* had initially referred to anything fake, they had come to epitomize cheap handsets.

Jeortich's hint to begin with affordable phones to tell the story of Nairobi as a crucible of made-in-Africa innovation is a very different starting point from the account that I developed in the previous chapter, in which I traced how the Kenyan state spent a good part of the first two decades of the new millennium seeking to engineer its blossoming tech economy through both strategic and less carefully orchestrated moves. But in a way, mobile phones are the unsung material commodities without which Kenya's ambitious programs would have faltered. Undersea broadband connectivity or experiments with USSD-enabled mobile money could have done very little to the country's economy without a diffused, capillary infrastructure, namely, the terminals through which data are accessed, conveyed, and recorded.[3] After all, as media anthropologists remind us, phones are a strange kind of commodity: one that at once circulates and creates circulations—of information, money, and more.[4] So too are mobile phones the mundane ends of large ecosystems of data that from our hands operate at an increasingly planetary scale.[5] But what do phones tell us about Nairobi, and what does Nairobi tell us about the making of phones, specifically, the affordable Chinese handsets that now dominate African markets?

To answer these questions, as Jerotich suggested, one needs to go back to the moment when these devices appeared on the streets of Nairobi, at the turn of the first decade of the century. In the previous chapter, we saw how the late 2000s and early 2010s initiated a period of fast technological change for Kenya, which quickly garnered a reputation as one of Africa's cradles of digital innovation. Without a doubt, it was mobile money, M-Pesa, that more than anything else sealed Nairobi's international reputation as a Silicon Savannah. The success of M-Pesa had depended on many material systems: from the existing financial infrastructures that were used to collateralize mobile money to the haphazard kiosks and precarious human labor that enabled its diffusion.[6] In turn, mobile money had created the data ledgers on which new digital applications could be envisioned and built: lending wallets, pay-go kits, gig-work platforms, and so on.[7] But this shift, as I show in this chapter, had also been made possible by another transition: the replacement of Motorola and Nokia cell phones with more sophisticated yet more affordable Chinese devices.

However quotidian and unremarkable, chinku handsets narrate the rise of the Silicon Savannah and its data interfaces with Chinese techno-capital. More specifically, Chinese phones in Nairobi are behind the increasing datafication of urban life at the so-called frontiers, or frontier markets, of techno-capital.[8] Thinking simultaneously about circulations of hardware and circulations of information, however, this chapter questions whether the figure of the frontier is ultimately an apt metaphor for the presence of digital Global China in Nairobi.

Frontiers evoke the expansionary and colonial nature of digital economies. Just like the strides of Global China in Africa have been sometimes unproblematically analyzed under the rubric of (neo)colonialism, digital data have been scrutinized as a colonizing force.[9] The media scholars Nick Couldry and Ulises Meijias, for example, speak of "data colonialism" to underscore the parallels and continuities between the historical patterns of imperial capture and the ways in which data "colonizes" life—manipulating, processing, and commodifying its existence. Indicating the US and China as two new poles of colonial power, they explain that data colonialism refers to an emerging order for the production of economic value via data relations.[10] Ultimately, these data relations—their definition, labeling, capture, and storage—reflect the unequal, gendered, and racialized logics of colonialism that still prime the world's economy.[11]

This perspective has been vital in the study of data platforms in Africa, where new avenues of profitability are premised on the possibility to capture information—usually through phones—about urban economies that have thus far escaped techno-capital accumulation. As Abeba Birhane writes, the "algorithmic colonization" of existing social relations, driven by corporate interests, echoes older forms of exploitation while leaving African digital economies in a state of dependency on software infrastructure made elsewhere.[12] In the same vein, Michael Kwet argues that novel forms of domination and surveillance are beholden to a "new imperialism" enabled by digital technology.[13] The example of the Nairobi data workers who contributed to the labeling of violent content for OpenAI's ChatGPT platform (through a subcontractor) and were later ruthlessly laid off perfectly demonstrates the extractive nature of data economies that rely on labor made cheap and disposable along enduring historical legacies.[14]

At the same time, data frontiers are also sites of competition and agency, domination and refusal, experimentation and failure. As the economic anthropologist Janet Roitman explains, there is a lot missing in "diffusionist" models of technological transfer that portray the majority world as a mere receiver of and therefore as a terrain of exploitation for technological configurations that emerged elsewhere.[15] African economies in particular, writes Clapperton Mavhunga, have long been mischaracterized as incapable of producing innovation on their own terms and as the borderlands of technical forms defined in the metropolis.[16] Perhaps cell phones made in China, and the data held within them, are a strange entry point to refute frontierist narratives of technological expansion and one-way domination. Yet what if these material commodities were, at least in part, innovated and conceived in urban Africa? What if twenty-first-century Nairobi, where chinku phones are increasingly interwoven in the flows of data that make urban life what it is—precarious, mutable, at times sordid and exploitative, at other times just ordinary and aspirational—offers us an account of techno-capital that departs from predetermined trajectories?

To answer these questions, the chapter combines an oral history of affordable Chinese cell phones, from when they first landed in Nairobi to when they became a common fixture of life in the city, with the voices of the experts that punctuate the value chains of this commodity: marketing managers, user-experience designers, sales directors, sales agents, shop owners, phone "fixers," and software developers. I distinguish between the two—oral history and ethnography of experts—because many of the experts I engaged did not hold a historical view. Predictably, they were focused on the near future rather than the recent past. They would talk of improving specs,[17] increasing sales, accelerating repairs, and boosting downloads. On the other hand, my oral history draws on newspaper clippings, corporate materials, and the tales that were generously shared with me by a few of my interlocutors. Some were, in fact, experts. Others were simply lay observers, yet acutely aware of how phones had shaped life in the city in the previous two decades. Through their accounts, mobile phones tell a story of China in Africa, of innovation from below and from above, of copycat and ingenuity, and of the role that African cities like Nairobi play in the mutating techno-politics of digital platforms.

CHINA IN KENYA: THROUGH A TOUCHSCREEN

The polysemic meanings of Chineseness in Kenya, Wangui Kimari writes, are constantly "under construction," encompassing preoccupations about the country's economic directions, anxieties about the government's failures, and the everyday experience of deepening China–Kenya connections that escape formal geopolitical and developmental cooperation.[18] From rumors—and fears—about "plastic rice," "plastic hair," and other plastic things infiltrating everyday life as foreign objects to the messy yet awe-inspiring construction of Nairobi's brand-new elevated expressway, these shifting references to China are often embodied by material commodities and by the infrastructures that enable their circulation.[19] When geopolitical issues become a topic of debate, for example, local newspapers, magazines, and social media feeds all teem with images of the railways, the highways, and the ports that symbolize the presence of China. Yet chinku phones, perhaps the most widespread Chinese "object" in Nairobi, rarely feature in these conversations. Are they perhaps less visibly Chinese, despite their nickname? Less controversial?

During the early rainy season of 2022, I asked these questions of another journalist, Wanbua. He was interested in and had covered China–Kenya matters as a freelancer for a few years. Some of his reporting had appeared in international outlets, which is how I had eventually tracked him down. Around the time of our meeting, the last few months in office for President Uhuru Kenyatta, a series of political billboards had cropped up all over Kenya to celebrate his legacy. Each poster—I counted almost a dozen of them—featured a piece of infrastructure—a dam, a highway, an airport runway—and an unequivocal message: "Asante, Rais" (Thank you, President). Kenyatta had invested massive resources as well as his political credibility in the delivery of new infrastructures. These were meant to create jobs, better connect a fractured country, and thus realize the ambitious macroeconomic goals of *Kenya Vision 2030*. But in the eyes of Kenyatta's critics, these projects had also amassed unsustainable debt, they had expanded an already regressive system of indirect taxation,[20] and they had opened doors to more, rather than less, dependence on the benevolence of foreign lenders, whether China or the International Monetary Fund.

Inevitably, my conversation with Wanbua had turned to one of the billboards that towered above Oloitoktok road, not far from where we were having coffee, and to the linkages between the large-scale infrastructures portrayed on the political ads and the chinku phones I was interested in. For Wambua, Kenyatta's debt-fueled bonanza of megaprojects followed in the footsteps of Kenya's "Look East" shift of the mid-2000s, when President Kibaki had kindled a series of developmental and business partnerships with China. Accordingly, it was as a result of these agreements that chinku phones had appeared on the streets of Nairobi: "Kibaki's Look East was not just a beginning, it was also the end of old Kenya. We were the poster child of structural adjustment in Africa. China did not make structural adjustment. But it benefited from two things that structural adjustment did: [. . . it] created a huge backlog of infrastructure projects that couldn't be funded by Western development money without all the usual conditionalities, and it opened the borders to foreign imports. All of a sudden you could buy a real Nokia and a fake one in the same shop on Luthuli Avenue." Luthuli Avenue, not far from where I bought my burner phone in downtown Nairobi, will be mentioned many times in the remainder of the chapter. Crowded and dazzling, Luthuli is, in many ways, one of the pulsating hearts of China's digital presence in Kenya.[21] Even though Chinese contractors and equipment manufacturers had been fundamental in the development of large-connectivity systems, including the celebrated National Optic-Fiber Network, it was often Luthuli Avenue that would prompt my Nairobi interlocutors to think about Chinese tech and the increasing dominance of Chinese companies in Kenyan electronics and hardware markets.

But unlike Chinese-funded railways and highways, the emotional terrains marked by the travels of Chinese phones in Kenya were not just dominated by angst. "I remember the first time I saw a touchscreen," recalled Eric, a marketing manager who had worked on the launch of a number of cell phone models in East Africa. "It was a frankenstein phone. It looked like an iPhone ate a Blackberry. It was terrible, but the touchscreen was something new and exciting." And the exhilaration that he had felt when holding his first smartphone had made him so passionate about mobile phones that he had made a career in marketing them.

"The difference was in the specs," a shop owner who ran an electronics store not far from Luthuli Avenue told me. "With the same money you could get either a Nokia with chunky buttons or a smartphone with full touchscreen and a camera," he explained, when I questioned him about what he remembered of the first imbo phones he had laid hands on. But surprise and marvel at these aspirational commodities—which by 2015 had become affordable alternatives to more established brands—were also accompanied by frustration and disappointment. After all, some of the first Chinese handsets were suboptimal knock-offs. Cheaper, yes, but also prone to glitches and less reliable. Even the first cell phones with their own dedicated Chinese brands became known for their stubborn untrustworthiness. I have clipped dozens of hilarious memes from those years, in which chinku phones are the visual metaphor for bad relationships, dissatisfactory sexual encounters, and online shopping gone wrong, among other regrets.

Behind both the affordability and glitchiness of affordable handsets was the manufacturing ecosystem from which they originated: the so-called *shanzhai*. In mainland China, the term captured a cultural and economic phenomenon of copycatting and customization, particularly in the domain of consumer electronics. Shanzhai, which literally means "mountain camps," was the home of renegade bandits who, in Chinese folklore, rebelled against the authoritarian rule of the Song dynasty and supported the poor by stealing from the wealthy. While it is not fully clear how the word *shanzhai* came to be a synonym for "fake," many people point to the actual mountain villages surrounding Hong Kong, where small workshops sprouted up in the 1960s and specialized in light-industry products such as toys and garments.[22] Whatever the journey of the term, in the 2000s shanzhai became associated with the creative reinvention of mobile phones from Western brands, and, eventually, of a much larger phenomenon that encompassed everything from pirated goods to parodies of official cultural norms.[23] Whether through phones or fake celebrities, writes the philosopher Byung-Chul Han, shanzhai manifested a unique facet of contemporary China, whereby the "deconstruction" of originals is a form of value addition rather than diminishment.[24] In fact, copycat manufacturers, criticized by some for their brazen copyright infringements, were initially celebrated for their inventive forms of refusal to subject themselves to the rules of global capitalism.[25] While official policy sought to orient China's manufacturing capacity to the standards necessary for an export-oriented economy, a "renegade ethos" imbued the spirit of shanzhai entrepreneurs, who kept producing consumer products for the poorest segment of the domestic market.[26] But even the most radical forms of shanzhai resistance to established power, as Lin Zhang and Anthony Fung explain, teemed with contradictions.[27] Between the grassroots heroism and the rhetoric of technology-empowered entrepreneurial subjectivities, the shanzhai phenomenon both enabled and quelled promises of a more democratic digital China; in fact, the convergence of politics with consumer goods was easily recaptured by the state. And, eventually, very little remains of the antiestablishment spirit of shanzhai in today's China, where "reinvention" is the domain of large tech corporations and has almost been elevated to the level of national policy.[28]

But in their early days, shanzhai phones had not been just crude imitations. With their additional functionalities, perfectly catering to the low-end consumer markets of what Jack Qiu has described as a "working-class network society," cheap handsets landed in Nairobi and started to answer the aspirations of connectivity that, up to that moment, had been addressed by a very limited range of options.[29] The first shanzhai phones were full of bugs and obstinately fickle, remembered Eric, the marketing manager. But things were soon to change, just like Luthuli Avenue. As the signboards of brands like Nokia and Samsung were largely replaced by those of Chinese manufacturers, their phones became more reliable, more sophisticated, and more desirable—while remaining cheaper than their counterparts. This shift was a function of a larger transition happening on the mainland between 2010 and 2015, when "copied in China" became "innovated in China," and the country started to be regarded as a trailblazer of everything digital, from e-commerce to finance.[30] But it was also a result of a carefully orchestrated set of experiments through which urban life in Nairobi (and probably in other large cities on the continent) had functioned as a primer to design, make, and sell phones to the masses in Africa.

A DECADE OF COMPETITION

"At first, it was Nokia," remembered Samuel, the co-owner of a computer business on Moi Avenue, a few blocks from Luthuli. With a degree in IT, he had initially worked as a sales middleman for another electronics store while moonlighting as a computer factotum.

TABLE 1   Price brackets for smartphones in Kenya, in Kenyan shillings (Ksh), as of June 2021

Ksh 0–10,000	Ksh 10,000–25,000	Ksh 25,000–70,000	Ksh 70,000+
Featurephones (*kabambe*)	Middle-range smartphones	Upper-range smartphones	Business/executive smartphones

NOTE: Data are from the author's fieldnotes. The four price brackets are according to a shop owner.

Nokia used to be a big thing in Kenya. Then it was Samsung. But Samsung did not fully embrace the lower-tier market. Let me draw something [table 1]. The market is divided into four parts. There's the—let me say—zero cash to [Ksh] 10,000. This is the most basic phone you can have. It doesn't have internet capability. And then from 10,000 to Ksh 25,000, now this is the middle-range phone. Basic internet connectivity, touchscreen. Right now, it's touchscreen, camera, GPS, and everything. Then we have the 25,000 to 70,000, they call it the "upper range." From Ksh 70,000, we have the business or executive phones, Apple, Samsung . . . flagship phones.

In the late 2000s, Samuel went on to explain, the Finnish manufacturer Nokia had dominated the lower-tier markets with models such as the 1110. Sturdy, easy to use, and durable, 1100s had been uniquely designed for developing contexts—and, as such, they were incredibly successful. Whether you had a "real" Nokia 1100 or a Chinese replica (though both would have been made in the Pearl River Delta), this model was perfect for the needs of a growing urban population that desired connectivity. It was with these phones—often bought on Luthuli—that urban Kenyans first experienced sending mobile money to their families in rural counties, I was told by another entrepreneur. He still had a vivid, emotional memory of his first M-Pesa remittance to his mother in Kitui, a mostly rural county east of Nairobi. For him, Nokia phones and M-Pesa almost melted together in his recollection of the early days of the Silicon Savannah.

By the early 2010s, however, cell phones had become smartphones, and the technological aspirations of urban consumers had extended much beyond mere mobile connectivity. Nairobians wanted touchscreens, cameras, 3G internet access, and GPS. President Kibaki's free-trade policies, including the lifting of import duties on handsets, had opened the gates to Apple and Samsung smartphones. These expensive gadgets were out of reach for most Kenyans, yet those few that appeared in the hands of businesspeople and tourists multiplied the technical affordances that *wananchi*—ordinary citizens—expected from their handsets. "Nokia did not understand this," a former design consultant explained to me in June 2021. She had worked in Kenya for several years, delivering user-experience trials for mobile phone companies and network providers. Over a long and insightful Zoom call, she elaborated that Nokia managers had become obsessed with competing with Apple and forgot to innovate what they were doing best. In 2013, they launched a color update of the 1100 model, the 105 series, which turned out to be one of the best-selling phones of all time but did not have any of the features that had become aspirational: no 3G, no touchscreen, no camera. Barely a flashlight.

In the meantime, a new set of mobile commodities had begun to appear in the streets of Nairobi. These were not just imbo copies anymore but Chinese phones with their own dedicated brands: Tecno, Itel, and, later, Infinix. They all belonged to the same Shenzhen-based manufacturer, an elusive company called Transsion, which had started as a shanzhai factory—a maker of knock-offs—but had then pivoted to African consumer markets.[31] With a long experience of serving the needs of the urban poor in China, Shenzhen phone makers were perfectly placed to understand that selling handsets to the African masses—to the proverbial bottom of the economic pyramid—was not a race to the bottom at all, recalled the former Nokia consultant.[32] It was, in fact, a competition for which company would get market segmentation rights.

"Tecno appeared," Samuel, the shop owner, said, while sipping black tea in a cafeteria on a narrow lane near his shop, "and they targeted this market." He pointed to the middle-range box he had drawn on a black page of his notebook (see table 1). While Nokia kept offering featurephones for the bottom tier of the market,[33] "Tecno would give you a 3G smartphone with maybe 2GB RAM, 3GB RAM, 32GB ROM, 64GB ROM. Whatever features Samsung was giving you here," Samuel pointed to the top two boxes in his drawing, "Tecno would give you here," he went on, moving his finger back to the middle-range segment.

> The screen might have not been of good quality but these guys were not interested in screens. They were interested in RAM. They were interested in performance and storage. And was it 3G? So they got hold of this middle-range market. And of course with time technology improved. They started making better screens at a cheaper cost. Storage increased. You now get 128GB at a low cost. You could get 4GB, 6GB. So they started producing different combinations of, say, a good screen with better RAM, a good camera and better ROM, but at the cost of 25,000, 30,000. So that's how Transsion ended up with a 60 percent share of total sales. Nokia didn't embrace that strategy, so they were eliminated from the market.

This was, obviously, just the initial snapshot of a decade of explosive competition, even among Chinese brands. Transsion launched Itel, which targeted the entry-level featurephone markets with new specs, including WhatsApp. After a successful campaign in India, Realme arrived in Kenya as an alternative to Tecno. Samsung too diversified its offering to compete on the lower-tier markets, with its A series. Oppo entered the battle at its upper echelon, with high standards and still relatively affordable phones. Infinix, another Transsion line dedicated to younger consumers, was challenged in its dominance by Xiaomi, which, at the time of my conversation with Samuel, was the true up-and-coming brand in Nairobi.[34] Huawei itself, a company otherwise focused on network equipment, had briefly been a contender for the mid-upper-range smartphone market, before its ambitions were quelled by the US ban.[35] Eric, with his obsession with trying new devices, even remembered some short-lived brands that were the offshoot of other Chinese companies. "At some point, I bought a StarTimes phone," he chuckled, amused by the fact that StarTimes was not known as a phone manufacturer but as a PayTV company specialized in serving rural households in sub-Saharan Africa (yet another story of a Chinese tech company dominating frontier markets in the continent).

One of the interesting facets of this fierce competition was the outlining of very detailed sociological contours for elusive sociological categories, those of the African urban middle and lower-middle classes. As the geographer Claire Mercer argues, while these social formations are not coherent economic and political groups, they nonetheless shape the material expansion of cities in very distinct ways.[36] Similarly, they also shape the algorithmic practices of platform companies, for which highly price-sensitive consumers are an imagined target and a driver of new logistical configurations, as I explore in more detail in chapter 3. In competing with each other for very specific market segments, phone makers too had contributed to delineating the meanings of both social mobility and social stagnation, even in the absence of deeper, broader changes in Kenyan society.[37] "Somehow," Eric observed, referring to his role as marketing strategist, "these machines say something about who you are, and that's my job, filling the blanks." In other words, the social life of Chinese handsets in Nairobi had become imbricated in the material qualities of prosperity, edginess, and coolness in the city. Often in ambivalent ways. In fact, while there remained suspicions and "xenophobic" biases against Chinese handsets, Samuel noted, drawing on his experience as a retailer, Chinese phones were not just chinku anymore. Some of them embodied the tangible aspirations of mobility, social and otherwise.

How did this happen? One explanation was that African markets resembled those of China a decade earlier. So Chinese hardware companies had the right experience to understand what kind of phones people wanted, as well as the marketing and sales strategies necessary to capture mass frontier markets. Rumor had it that Transsion had even poached former Nokia strategists, both in Nairobi and in Shenzhen, to inform its bottom-of-the-pyramid innovation drive.[38] But more importantly, I would argue, Transsion and other companies, such as Xiaomi, had made Nairobi into a real-life test bed of new phones, new features, new specs. And in turn, Nairobi's urban life had shaped the technological affordances of these new commodities.

EXPERIMENTED IN NAIROBI, MADE IN CHINA

Two of my interlocutors, Mike and Osama, had worked for Transsion in the early days of the company in Kenya. Both recruited when they were students, Osama's stint had only lasted for a few months, while Mike had climbed the managerial ladder and stayed for several years. Through the stories of their time at Transsion, which they generously shared with me between winter 2021 and fall 2022, I was able to capture a glimpse of how the company had come to dominate cell phone sales in Kenya (and in Africa more broadly).

Mike recalled that a friend had informed him about a new cell phone company whose research department was recruiting people "interested in statistics." He was about to complete his degree in economics at the University of Nairobi, so he immediately jumped on the opportunity. It was Mike's first job, and it came with decent pay. Osama remembered he had heard about Transsion from other students who were working for the company part-time, to make some money on the side. "All they wanted was people who could handle a spreadsheet," he told me when I questioned him about the job requirements. In fact, at the entry level, there was little statistics but a lot of manual data work.

Over the years, Transsion had recruited hundreds of graduates to conduct in-depth market research in order to inform sound manufacturing decisions. The most basic kind of research involved customer satisfaction surveys. Each new employee would be provided with a call log of people who had bought a particular phone model and left their number with the sales agent. "What we used to do is call them," Mike explained, "and there was a survey. Generally, it was about getting feedback about the model—what they liked about the model and what they didn't like about the model—and getting suggestions about what they would want for the next model in the same series." Mike speculated that Transsion had perfectly understood the aspirations of social mobility that were embodied by smartphones in the early 2010s. Customer loyalty was built on the promise of offering bigger and better at a fraction of the price of an iPhone. He observed how each successive model would incorporate the desires and the critiques he had listened to over hundreds of phone calls. Users would complain about a camera not taking good pictures at night. Six months later, Tecno would launch a new model with a better camera and even use the new camera specs in its advertising. Then again, shanzhai manufacturers were known as a prime case of a business with rapid, market-responsive product iteration. In the meantime, the management at Transsion Kenya had taken notice of Mike's keen eye for research and promoted him to a managerial position. For almost a decade, right before our conversation, Mike had directed hundreds of trials.

Customer satisfaction, Osama further explained, was just one of the data points in a much wider experimental system. Another type of test, the so-called central location tests (CLTs), involved sending small teams to find customers of competing brands in the streets of Nairobi. Luthuli Avenue, obviously, was a favorite location, but so were the streets around the university. During a CLT, testers would administer questionnaires about certain functionalities of certain phones, especially competing brands. Questions were so specific, Mike told me, that he could often gauge the direction that the mothership was taking with their subsequent models. Similarly detailed were what Osama called "in-depth surveys." These involved paying users of a particular Transsion phone model to allow them to be tracked for a certain period: At what time did they wake up, how often did they listen to music, how much battery did they use on a web browser, and how many photos did they take in a day? For Mike, the years spent at Transsion's R&D department had made him realize the importance of not treating the lower end of the phone market as a single segment. Students wanted good cameras and good speakers. Their parents wanted a long battery life. Millennials wanted two SIM slots, to spread the cost of data packages across different mobile providers. Likewise, street vendors wanted multiple SIM slots, so that they could use more than one M-Pesa account. Instead of satisfying each of these demands in a single phone, each model sought to strike a unique balance of different specs.

Experimental practices did not stop at users, however. Mike recalled, for example, the time when Transsion sought to improve the AI of phone cameras. One of his colleagues "was tasked with [labeling] ten thousand photographs each month."

> At the beginning, we didn't have any idea. We were sending data to Guangzhou.[39] You know, all the data collection is done here, but most of the designing, development is done there. We didn't even have Chinese bosses here, they would come for one or two weeks only when we had some sensitive event, but most of the jobs, we would just send material back. . . . What used to happen, you were given a specific task, probably to take a thousand or five hundred photos of people eating, another two hundred photos of people in a class setting, photos of people in a matatu [minibus taxi].

The first cheap, camera-enabled smartphones, according to the recollection of another friend, were terrible when it came to portraying faces with high-melanin levels. Cameras would not even focus on dark-skinned people, she told me. You couldn't tell facial features. Then, all of a sudden, Transsion cameras were doing a better job. "Selfies [became] glowy and snatched," she recalled, "better than other more expensive brands." When asked about the ethics of taking photos of ordinary Kenyans without consent, Mike explained that local teams had developed ways around it: "They also wanted photos of, um, mixed-race photos. So what we did, we just went around the office, and captured Chinese [people] with a bunch of friends. So most of the photos we sent back were actually Transsion employees. And in that way we solved the consent issue."

These small acts of ethical adaptation, obviously, did not address the bigger questions raised by facial recognition practices that essentialize ethnicity and race as matters of skin pigmentation. Neither did they really challenge the issue of what facial data are ultimately used for, including the global overpolicing of Black bodies. In their study of Transsion's patents, for example, Miao Lu and Jack Qiu have noted that the company partnered with the Shanghai municipal government to build an AI database containing "billions of dark-skinned images."[40] Essentially, the "empowerment narrative" of a more inclusive camera AI was about sales and, potentially, surveillance.[41] And, as Osama remarked, there was a deep asymmetry in the flows of information that he himself had enacted.[42]

But the forms of strategic refusal described by Mike, however small, do show the oft-forsaken agency of those who collect data and, more importantly, experimentalize data collection practices. As Seyram Avle has argued (also writing about Transsion), Africa is not just a passive frontier of Global China's technological expansion.[43] Osama and Mike had ambivalent feelings about their time at the company, but they were adamant about the negotiations and friction that they had injected into the betterment of chinku phones. In their final analysis, they had not been the pawns but, at least in part, the architects of affordable handsets that perfectly suited the communication needs of ordinary Kenyans. Having navigated constraints and corporate hierarchies, they wanted me to know how Nairobi life had shaped a story that many told as one of dominance and extraction. And that even the most hierarchical, one-way-vector data collection practices relied on what many in the field referred to as "local intelligence": a distributed kind of awareness that Kenyans working for Chinese companies were proud to possess.

Similar feelings were shared by shop owners like Samuel. He explained to me how merchants would band together to understand and create coalitions against the motley supply chains of Chinese phones. On WhatsApp groups, they would discuss if a particular brand was trying to force on their customers a suboptimal handset, if an agent was unreliable, and what strategies they could deploy as an informal collective. They had built the "entrepreneurial solidarities" that allowed them to at once collaborate and compete in a cutthroat sales market.[44] Sales too were an incredibly datafied practice.

It was Eric, the animated and fast-talking marketing consultant, who explained the data-rich sales model shared by Chinese brands. He had recently engineered the boom of Xiaomi in Kenya, after working for other manufacturers, so he knew well how crucial to success their agent-based sales model was.

> Salespeople used to submit a report. Online, they have a platform to put in the IMEI of the phone they sold and at what price but also a physical spreadsheet on which they indicate the number of phones they sold and the number of phones sold by their competitors in the same shop. At the end of the day, they send the report via WhatsApp [a photo of the physical report], to their manager. . . . And so the managers can ask you, How are these people selling more than you when you're selling devices that are probably better? It's all about maximizing sales to customers. You have to be very good to people and very aggressive. But these [sales agents] are friends. They work together. They collaborate. But when a customer comes in, it looks like cutthroat competition.

Sales data are crucial for a company to understand when a particular model or line has reached the end of its shelf life as well as to gauge the exact pricing point to shift from one market segment to another. But accurate sales data are a logistical problem. With thousands of small electronics stores scattered around the country and very few official retailers, it is very hard to aggregate sales intelligence. Not just that: While some Chinese brands, Transsion included, did have official distributors in East Africa, many stores would import devices from alternative sources. Somali stores, for example, source Chinese and other tech from the Arab gulf countries, especially the Emirates. Other stores have a direct line with African agents working in the port cities of China, especially in the Pearl River Delta. These agents buy tech from Chinese domestic distributors and organize the shipping of containers and cargo on behalf of Kenyan suppliers and retailers. If this logistical complexity wasn't enough, each single sales transaction was never the same. There was no fixed price for Chinese phones. In the same shop, on the same day, the same phone might be sold at ten different prices, I was told by another shop owner on Luthuli Avenue.

To overcome this complexity, the sales agent model described by Eric functions as the engine of a large data ecosystem that from the streets of Nairobi is wired to the headquarters of tech manufacturers in cities like Shenzhen and Beijing. But it also informs more localized decisions. Specializing in a particular brand or even a specific product line, sales agents are the prongs of a very sensitive machine. By gathering fine-grained data each day, sales and marketing teams can make immediate pivots. Eric explained that any change in sales patterns is immediately followed up to understand what is causing a slump or surge. These data are then acted on by sales managers—who might decide to retrain an agent or encourage them to change strategy, to modify the layout of their shop, to reduce prices, or do something else. In other words, marketing and sales are just as experimental as the customer satisfaction tests that Mike used to handle: measured, monitored, and benchmarked. Between competition and collaboration, as in Eric's words, a vast ecosystem of data had—from the street corners of Nairobi—nudged, perfected, and ultimately "provoked" one of Global China's technological "transfers" and "translations" in Kenya and in the Global South more broadly.[45] Yet data *about* cell phones were also accompanied by data produced and held within them.

FROM HARDWARE TO SOFTWARE AND BACK

Many rumors surrounded George Zhu—or Zhu Zhaojiang—the enigmatic founder of Transsion. According to some people, he had started his venture as a maker of phones with a small shanzhai factory in Shenzhen. Others said that he had made his money at Ningbo Bird, a company that used to make affordable handsets for Chinese consumers and had modeled Transsion on the vision to export domestic successes to developing markets. Some would say instead that a secretive deal with a Taiwanese manufacturer of microchips had been behind Zhu's business triumph.[46] Whatever the case, all these rumors seemed to agree that it was a trip to Nairobi that had sparked his decision to make phones for African consumers.

Eventually, in late March 2023, I met with somebody who actually knew George Zhu, a senior manager at the Chinese desk of an important local bank. He recalled the first time that they had bumped into each other, in the early 2010s, on a flight from Kampala to Nairobi. Ming, my contact, had heard about Tecno's founder from colleagues and collaborators. At the time, Zhu was the talk of the town: an unknown entrepreneur who had stamped out Nokia's dominance in less than three years and was now being photographed with important Kenyan politicians and businesspeople. So Ming was surprised not only to find that Zhu was traveling alone in coach, but that he was involved in the trials and fine-tuning of the design, sales, and marketing experiments that I have described. Older and more experienced, Ming had been struck by both Zhu's friendliness and his deep knowledge of East African markets.

But things changed, Ming told me, between 2018 and 2019. Zhu became more elusive. He had shifted his focus to the listing of Transsion on the newly launched Shanghai STAR, the technology-focused equity stock market that Xi Jinping had wanted, in order to nudge the return of Chinese big tech listed abroad and to create yuan liquidity for domestic tech companies. The listing of Transsion on the financial market, a business analyst told me, had coincided with a strategy to expand from hardware—the sale of phones—to software. The IPO documents I came across could not be clearer about this shift: Transsion was raising liquidity to launch a fully fledged attack on a market monopolized by Western software companies, from social media to financial services.[47] To keep the cost of mobile phones affordable, the profit margins on their sales had to be minimal. But with millions of handsets already on the market, Transsion had incidentally built a distribution channel for value-added services. Data-driven platforms could be preinstalled or delivered to millions of phones that were hitherto part of the daily lives of their African users. Even before the listing, Transsion had been experimenting with messaging, music streaming, news, and other applications, having created a small start-up called Afmobi. I spoke to one of the early Kenyan employees of Afmobi, David. As a product manager, he remembered how from the very beginning his team had worked on matching a Transsion-dedicated marketplace with local software developers working on innovative applications.

After the IPO and a partnership with another Chinese software giant, NetEase, Transsion's software efforts were consolidated into three main operations. The in-house software unit would continue to work on the native operating ecosystem of its phones. A semi-independent venture capital arm, Future Hub, would invest in Africa-based fledgling start-ups, offering them early-stage capital and an incredibly capillary distribution channel. And a software company owned by both Transsion and NetEase—Transnet—would work on a number of flagship platforms, replacing Afmobi. Transnet, for example, incorporated platforms that had already existed for some time, such as the Nigerian music streaming service Boomplay, which was initially preinstalled as a music player on Tecno phones and had evolved into "the largest online African music catalogue."[48] Combining freemium with an advertising-led business model, today Transnet platforms range from short video streaming ("Vskit, the African version of TiktTok," David told me) to financial services (though these were exclusively developed for West African markets, given the prominence of other mobile money companies in East Africa). Transnet, David explained, was pushing its developers to pepper all these apps with increasingly sophisticated AI systems. From phones, Transsion had turned to data.

As Seyram Avle writes, "Transsion's gradual shifts toward [software] emphasize how hardware [is] the entry point . . . for new forms of data collection and use. Hardware is the site of platform power."[49] The frontier markets of affordable phones are, indeed, also the frontiers of platform economies that track their users to produce new forms of profit. In fact, cheap phones reach the masses in ways that the proponents of the bottom-of-the-pyramid approach to marketing would not have dreamed of only a decade ago. However "empowering" and useful to end users,[50] the making of a hardware–software nexus for African consumers is, ultimately, about expanding the data possibilities of technological profit. Yet, in the remainder of this chapter, I want to focus on a different story of data, one that brings our attention back to the ordinary hardware cultures of Nairobi.

Transsion phones are known, and sometimes ridiculed, for their bloatware—a plethora of native applications that users would find on their phones "bloating" the memory of devices. Some of these applications are simply dupes (duplicates) of Android's standard services: a browser, a marketplace, a news reader, a few games, and so on. While it has been suggested that some of these apps contain surveillance mechanisms, one of my contacts, Bolu, simply believed that after the Huawei–US affair, Chinese companies like Transsion were preparing themselves for a post-Android time. Bolu was a popular Kenyan blogger filming reviews of tech gadgets, and he told me that bloatware was, in his opinion, a way to keep Transsion's in-house marketplace ready in case of an escalation of the US–China trade wars. Yet one of these bloatware apps, Carlcare, had a different origin story.

Carlcare is the after-sales service for all Transsion brands. In Nairobi, it operates a few shops and a light-assembly plant that are dedicated to the repair of the company's handsets. According to the shop owner Samuel, Carlcare had been one of the crucial reasons for the loyalty that Transsion's customers had developed. Cheap phones, by nature of their affordability, were prone to malfunctions. Carlcare offered fast and reliable servicing for both manufacturing glitches and damage caused by users. In Samuel's perspective, this aligned with a technological culture by virtue of which Kenyans saw value in the repairability of devices. Even the fortune of Nokia years before, I was told, had been a function of how easy it was to fix and refurbish a 1100.

Mike, the former R&D manager at Transsion, recalled that Carlcare had evolved organically from the same user-experience research that he had conducted. Initially, after-sales services were a contextual solution to what Nairobians wanted in response to the paltry reliability of their handsets and their desire for a long-lasting technological investment. Unlike chinku copies, Tecno and Itel handsets came with warranties—a first for cheap phones. But then Carlcare had grown into something bigger, a whole ecosystem of repair. The preinstalled app, among other functions, would allow users to book an appointment at a service center, monitor the repair order, or even get a loan to pay for the service if the warranty lapsed. At the same time, the app would be the interface for Carlcare's own data-driven business model and for Transsion at large.

I got a sense of how datafied this repair system was when I visited a couple of Carlcare centers in downtown Nairobi in fall 2022. With a research collaborator, I ended up speaking to the manager of one of these centers, which had the functional aesthetics of a hospital waiting room. Behind several counters, Carlcare employees would call in customers sitting on uncomfortable reception chairs to hand in their broken devices or get their repaired ones back. The more tech savvy of these customers would have booked their appointment through the app. But the app, the manager told us, was not just a data interface for users; it was a trove of metadata for Carlcare. Each phone in the repair pipeline was treated as a data point and as a data source. Information about glitches and bugs, for example, would be sent back to the mothership and fed into a quality-monitoring platform. Information about common causes of damage, on the other hand, would inform how many and what kinds of spare parts the Shenzhen factory had to ship to Kenya. And so forth.

Whether by chance or by design, Carlcare had created a data-driven after-sales system that aligned with what Nairobians, and Kenyans at large, understood as valuable. As Eric explained:

> This applies . . . to any technology in Kenya. It actually started with vehicles. That's why almost everyone has a Toyota . . . , because the maintenance and spare parts are cheap and, most importantly, easily accessible. The same now applies to tech and phones. It is very easy to maintain these phones, because the panels and every other component are also very cheap, and you don't need crazy expertise. Young people fix their phones by themselves, through YouTube, because the spare parts are easy to get. What [Transsion] also invested in are these service centers. In Luthuli, they have a huge service center. . . . So yes, in Kenya, guys think about repair. It's [about] accessibility—you don't want to wait a week to get a screen replacement—and pricing, which also needs to be low. This fits the culture of repair that exists in Nairobi beyond the smartphones themselves.

Despite Eric's observations, it is not my goal to write about some kind of uniquely "Kenyan" or "African" culture of care and repair (though others have done so). My observations are rather different: Among the many technological affordances that a hardware device begets, disparate users value each of them in a different order. Prioritizing repairability over, say, the allure of a brand-new model is a function of many techno-cultural, economic, and personal circumstances. It would be a mistake to pinpoint one. Yet these localized hierarchies of valuation do shape through data, as the Carlcare case shows, the material commodities that in turn inform life in Nairobi. In other words, the datafied circulations of spare parts and repair ingenuity are another moment of both the ordinary and the aspirational acts of valuation that delineate and negotiate the "market frontiers" of (Chinese) techno-capital in urban Kenya.

FRANKENSTEIN DEHYDRATORS, MICROCHIPPED COWS, AND THE LIMITS OF DATA COLONIALITY

"When you first reached out," I was told by Kamande, the chief data analyst of an up-and-coming start-up experimenting with a distributed platform for sustainable cooking fuel, "I thought I would have nothing to say about Chinese stuff, but then you got me thinking, and I realized how my whole career has been shaped by cheap Chinese phones." It was August 2021, and we were sitting in the yard of a small bohemian café, a leafy remnant of the colonial garden city that once was Nairobi's Westlands. All around us, the quaint mansions and lush estates of imperial elites had been replaced over time by tall blocks of apartments. Kamande went on to tell me about his personal journey, a data scientist trained as a statistician turned start-up worker. As a young man, right out of university, he had been hired by the East African office of a large multinational market research firm working for companies like Coca-Cola and Unilever. He recalled how mass market research had suddenly evolved with the arrival of cheap handsets, as calls were replaced by SMS messages; how he had witnessed an increasingly sophisticated capacity to track consumer spending; how he had left for another data company doing much more fine-grained analyses of consumer satisfaction, even for informal traders, through the integration of its platform with existing payment technologies such as M-Pesa; and how he had been poached by his current employer, which was installing ethanol ATMs across the lower-income suburbs of Nairobi, where coal briquettes were otherwise the norm. In this new role, he was managing incredibly diverse data dragnets: the cooking stoves, the fuel ATMs, the phone app, and the various payment switches all produced enormous amounts of usage data about their customers, their habits, and their profiles as economic actors. Up to that moment, Kamande had used that data to iteratively optimize the company's decentralized distribution network. But, of course, data also held the slippery promise of new possibilities of profit.[51] "I realize now how so many of the data jobs I've done have been symbiotic with these Chinese machines," Kamande said, laughing, at the end of our conversation.

Yet mobile phones are hardly the sole hardware commodities that, once imported from China, produce new data frontiers. In fact, affordable hardware of other kinds is just as ubiquitous. One evening, for example, I met a young entrepreneur who was sourcing Chinese, GPS-enabled microchips for cattle. Her business model relied on the possibility of microinsuring small numbers of cows for subsistence farmers. But perhaps my favorite story was that of another Nairobi-based agritech start-up: this one was experimenting with decentralized dehydrators that would produce cooking ingredients from the food waste of smallholding farmers. After many trials, their engineers had come up with what the cofounder ironically called a "frankenstein dehydrator": a strange, cost-saving pilot machine made of both European and Chinese components. Without cheap, easily replaceable Chinese spare parts, my interlocutor told me, the project would never have hit the ground running.

What these anecdotal examples show is that affordable Chinese phones represent only a sliver of a tech race toward increasingly datafied future economies, in Kenya and beyond. Yet the recent history of chinku phones foregrounds a less discussed and yet vital facet of digital Global China in Africa: the fact that cities like Nairobi are the test bed of mutating techno-capital that emerges from trials, negotiations, glitches, and adaptations. However, and perhaps inevitably, geopolitical readings tend to obfuscate more technopolitcal analyses of these experimental practices. So China's dominance in Africa's technological present has elicited concerns about Beijing's "neocolonial" ambitions that materialize in digital systems.[52] From a purported Chinese model of authoritarian internet sovereignty pushed on African nations to the export of surveillance hardware, debates about "Chinese digital neocolonialism in Africa" abound.[53] Often, as Yuchen Chen and colleagues have observed, these readings tend to bury different components of digital Global China in the same "black box."[54] Echoing a broader disquiet about the coloniality of digital capitalism, as Benjamin Bratton reminds us, "China is now so deeply associated with technology that anxieties about technology are projected into anxieties about China, and to an extent vice versa."[55]

In this context, both Global China in Africa and global techno-capital writ large have been critically analyzed under the category of (neo)coloniality. Accordingly, while China uses its capital-export regime to neocolonial ends—creating new forms of dependence via sovereign debt and unequal trade relations, data "colonizes" life—manipulating, processing, and commodifying its existence.[56] More subtly, "digital neocolonialism" operates through all those other forms of extraction that—through data—are adroit, indirect, and often premised on a purported final agency of the individual user.[57] In Africa, where digital economies follow the traces of previous colonial relations,[58] the troves of data captured and mobilized by increasingly ubiquitous affordable Chinese handsets, their lock-ins and dextrous capacity for market making, could be easily framed as one of the neocolonial frontiers of techno-capital. Not only do phones produce the data that make urban life extractable; they are made from rare minerals extracted from the earthly deposits that were once on the frontiers of colonial expansion.[59]

This chapter has shown how these frontierist interpretations of digital Global China are, at least in part, muddled by tracing the experiments that center Nairobi in the industrial circulations of affordable Chinese devices like mobile phones. The presence of digital Global China in Kenya is animated by the state-driven initiatives that were discussed in the previous chapter, by the alignment and convergence of different matters of developmental statecraft across the two nations but also by multiple moments of experimentation through which new markets are enacted with competing logics of technological specification and diversification. What my interlocutors shared, whether they were Chinese employees of companies like Transsion or Kenyan experts working at different stages of the inventive value chains of affordable hardware, was an optimistic belief in the technological promise of meeting the needs and the aspirations of consumers unrecognized by Western brands of mobile phones. Tied to this promise, as I hope to have shown, was less an idea of a market frontier to be conquered and more an encounter of different logics of technological world-making to be cultivated.

For this reason, frontiers are, at once, an apt and a problematic analytical category.[60] What I have narrated in this chapter, albeit anecdotal, showcases the tentative, aspirational, and ingenious experiments through which frontiers are marked—in this case the "market frontiers" of digital data and the phones that enable its circulation in urban Africa. While I do not disagree that the story of chinku phones is one of techno-capital (and of Global China) finding new terrains of profit, I have illustrated in this chapter how these economies are palimpsests of colonial traces but also forms of techno-cultural imagination that escape it. So I wish to return to another meaning of frontier: limit, edge.[61] Limits, literal and metaphorical, define the ethnographic account of how Nairobi's urban life was enrolled in the experimentation and marketization of affordable phones for mass consumers in Africa. And these limits, I argue, also apply to the analytical concepts—data coloniality and the like—through which we may make sense of the ambivalence of digital Global China, whether through hardware or, as we will see next, through digital platforms for the masses.

3

Platforms of Algorithmic Suturing

"It was the mission of opportunity," explained Chao, when I questioned him about what had brought him to Nairobi. At once energetic and poised, he was the founder and CEO of Fastlee, a booming internet service provider (ISP) platform operating in a few of the lower-middle-income suburbs of the city's northeastern periphery. He had made a new home there, after a prosperous life as a Silicon Valley "argonaut,"[1] traveling between the United States and China in the crucial decade of the great technological catch-up between the latter and the former. With an Ivy League degree, Chao had found success selling cloud infrastructure services and enterprise software solutions in Beijing, at a time when those digital economies were in their infancy. With that experience, he now exuded the typical calm confidence of that indiscernible age of start-up men in their late forties and early fifties. As for the "mission of opportunity," Chao was alluding to two things. The "mission" was finding technical solutions for underserved mass markets, the forgotten users left out by what he considered profit-hungry technology companies and austerity-constrained state entities. The "opportunity" referred to the saturation of an increasingly competitive technology market in China and the desire for connectivity that was still unmet in Kenya's digital peripheries.[2]

On the occasion of our first meeting, Chao told me that Kenya reminded him of China in the mid-1980s. And Nairobi reminded him of Shanghai, where he grew up, in the early 1990s. He recalled leaving for the United States while the Jin Mao tower was still under construction, its angular pagoda shape soon to become, albeit briefly, China's tallest building, and then moving back to his home country, a decade later, the year China joined the World Trade Organization. It was 2001.

Shanghai was unrecognizable, and Beijing was brimming with opportunities. He told me that he had become not just a witness, but an active party in the once-in-a-lifetime techno-economic boom that had ensued. Like other lucky returnees (or *haigui*, Chinese for "sea turtles"),[3] he had gotten wealthy.

> That gave me the confidence that I could use such an experience. . . . Of course, I do know that the path of development in Africa will probably be very different from that in China. Even from China, it's impossible to pinpoint a single macroeconomic recipe, at the macro level, I mean. There's nothing to copy or replicate at that level. But in a single business, or in a single sector, well, if you get down to the basics, the Chinese experience has a lot to teach. Finding solutions that can address the needs of mass markets, mass consumers. That always works.

Even the history of China's technological rise, Chao concluded, could be told as "many stories of platform business solutions that truly addressed mass markets." Yet mass markets in Nairobi, and in Africa more broadly, suffered a deeper problem, an infrastructural one. Despite all the ambiguities of China's own digital infrastructure systems, the inequalities between cities and rural areas and between western and southern provinces,[4] there was a baseline that the state had been committed to meet. Electricity was not a problem in China, for example. In contrast, most of Nairobi's suburbs experienced daily losses of electric load. Even the celebrated financial infrastructure of M-Pesa was prone to malfunctions, Chao observed. At times, for a few hours, M-Pesa's application programming interfaces (APIs) would be down, making it impossible to run a business like Fastlee, which relied almost entirely on digital cash. "At Fastlee, we are doing the last mile. But what about the middle mile? Or the first mile? They don't always work. This is where platform models from China need to be adapted; we deal with constant outage."

However reductive, Chao's words portray the unique infrastructural circumstances of African cities like Nairobi. As the settlement was planned as a garden city for its European colonists, networked services like water supply, sewers, public transport, and, later, electricity and telephone lines only benefited the areas where white settlers resided.[5] In fact, infrastructure, or lack thereof, served the precise purpose of segregating urban space along racial lines.[6] Until independence, very few Kenyans had been allowed to live in the city as permanent residents,[7] and in those marginal areas centralized public infrastructure was almost nonexistent. The rift was so deep that Nairobi could never really recover from the infrastructure backlog it inherited when Kenya became an independent nation—its state coffers left almost empty at the moment of *madaraka*, self-rule. The situation did not improve in the following decades. There were many reasons for this, including internal politics, the patrimonial interests of the governing elites, limited fiscal and financial resources, more than two decades of structural adjustment–enforced austerity, and slow bureaucratic processes (also a colonial legacy), combined with incredibly rapid urban growth, the emergence of hyperdense suburbs, and the thorny question of large swaths of urban settlements declared "unauthorized" and therefore outside the purview of state-mandated provisioning of basic services.[8] In response to this, myriad other modes of service provision exist, and have long existed,[9] to fill the gaps of partial or fractured networked systems.

The historian Kenda Mutongi, for example, describes the inventive and contested emergence of matatus, or minibus taxis, as a response to the limited services offered by colonial and postcolonial public transport networks.[10] Matatus, like other modes of what is now called "paratransit" (privately provided collective transport), complemented the insufficient capillarity of Kenya Bus Services (KBS) with a self-organized system of routes that turned out to be lifelines for Nairobi's commuters. Initially haphazard and improvised, through the second half of the twentieth century matatus became more than just vehicles, forming a whole economy of urban movement, culture, and politics. Of course, as Mutongi details, this economy existed and still exists in a strange, shifting relationship with the state, the threat of suppression always looming large, despite the criticality of matatus for life in the city. But what is more interesting for the story of this chapter is that matatus represent one of the many self-organized, informal, popular, and private modes of service provision that dominate city systems in many African cities, filling gaps in partial or fractured infrastructure and creating economic value from these hybrid configurations.[11]

Borrowing a Lacanian metaphor from the anthropologist Filip De Boeck, matatus are a collective infrastructure that "sutures" the physical and economic fragmentation of urban life in Nairobi.[12] "Suture" is a particularly apt figure of speech because it underscores the fact that these multiple acts of technological make-do are not a zero-sum game. "Sutures," De Boeck writes, "suggest the possibility of closing wounds, generating realignments and opening up alternatives, because sutures also point to new kinds of creativity with (spatial and temporal) beginnings, and therefore with new forms of interactivity."[13] After all, as Abdoumaliq Simone has argued, in contexts of extreme precariousness, there is something inventive and machinic about the ways in which urban life is reworked and made infrastructurally possible.[14] These ingenious systems, as the example of matatus reveals, are not just marginal, individual responses to the "splintering" of African cities[15]—though those responses indeed exist—but also large-scale, collaborative urban economies that involve complex arrangements of workers, commodities, mutual networks, modes of accumulation, and diverse organizational practices. And just like Chao's Fastlee, a growing number of digital start-ups has emerged in Nairobi in the past few years, with the ambition of incorporating these practices of infrastructural patchwork, optimizing them through algorithmic applications, and thereby finding platform solutions to the urban "problems" of life in Nairobi.[16]

For Adam Moe Fejerskov, who has written about the "solutionism" of techno-capital in the Global South, this rush to digital experiments that frame develop-mental problems as opportunities for profitable start-ups marks a reinvention of humanitarianism in the twenty-first century.[17] A new experimental movement, fueled both financially and ideologically by organizations such as the Bill and Melinda Gates Foundation, has recast the former "developing world" not as a destination of technological transfer but as a living lab of innovation.[18] As much as these experiments are driven by philanthropic aid and by the multiple permuta-tions of Silicon Valley ideologies in the world of development,[19] they also happen to be much more mundane, yet speculative, digital businesses that at once seek to incorporate existing urban economies of infrastructural repair, readapt business models from China, and create contextual solutions for the mass markets forgot-ten by big companies.

More specifically, this chapter delves into a particular set of platform experi-ments in Nairobi—pilots that combine technological bricolage and sophisticated practices of data capture in order to make economic life legible to digital plat-forms even when this is fragmented, haphazard, and precarious.[20] Obviously, this is not just a story of Chinese companies and entrepreneurs. In fact, business mod-els based on the platformization of informal economies abound across the Sili-con Savannah.[21] From last-mile logistics to e-mobility, from pay-go solar kits to restocking apps for small businesses, from e-commerce to crowd-work, American, Arab, Chinese, European, and Indian entrepreneurs compete for markets and for access to capital in Nairobi. But as I explain in the pages that follow, digital Global China remains an important reference point for these new platform economies. At the most superficial level, as detailed earlier in the book, affordable hardware often comes from China, and therefore it is Chinese start-ups that have a unique kind of advantage in negotiating imports and deals. Moreover, Chinese venture capital investors are increasingly active in supporting these companies, especially as their domestic investment markets are saturated. Most importantly, however, many platform experiments happening in Nairobi seek to adapt and tinker with busi-ness models and marketing strategies that originated in China more than a decade ago and made the fortunes of companies like Meituan, Pinduoduo, and Alibaba. Chao's Fastlee, for example, initially employed a technical trick that he witnessed in Beijing at the time of the WiFi boom in the city. Similarly, for many other plat-form start-ups, the trajectory of digital China offers the Silicon Savannah an alter-native path to that of Silicon Valley, especially insofar as China's digital boom in part began with and from the making of hardware and software for the masses, the "information have-less" of digital capitalism.[22]

Even though the stories of Alibaba and other Chinese giants were often told as tales of entrepreneurial heroism, for many of my interlocutors they were in fact stories of marketing prowess at what was the "bottom" of China's economic pyra-mid.[23] And while Kenya's bottom-of-the-pyramid economies may have been very

different from those of China a decade before, for Chao and for the other entrepreneurs we will encounter in the following pages, there were lessons to be gleaned
and models to be adopted to craft perfect platform solutions that optimized, and
therefore created value from, existing informal economies and, more specifically,
from the infrastructural gaps and disconnections that these economies suture
in the daily life of Nairobians. To capture these processes, this chapter deploys a
concept—algorithmic suturing—that I developed elsewhere with my colleagues
Liza R. Cirolia and Jack O. Odeo.[24]

With "algorithmic suturing," we wanted to draw attention to the "mathematics"
of collective urban life that are reshaped by algorithmic practices.[25] More than just
lines of code,[26] algorithms are abstract diagrams that allow the efficient optimization of economic processes that appear unwieldy and unmanageable.[27] In other
words, algorithmic suturing captures the work of data-driven platforms that are
seeking to produce value from precarious urban economies and infrastructures
that are fragmented and purportedly inefficient. These algorithmic business models visualize the possibilities that lie within the needs and aspirations of the lower
rungs of Nairobi's middle class, the inescapably tight margins of this demographic,
the diverse forms of value promised by data-rich environments, and the various
shades of invisible work and knowledge that sustain them. And in charting these
experiments, the following pages also trace the outline of a quiet "specter of Global
China," a model for the platformization of urban Africa that, not without contradictions, marks a unique trajectory of techno-capital in the continent.[28]

LAST-MILE CONNECTIVITY FOR THE MASSES

To reach Chao's offices, located in one of the many Fastlee hubs from which the
company delivers cheap wireless connectivity to a few hundred thousand people,
one needs to drive northeast from central Nairobi, along the impressive four-lane
road that connects the city to Thika, in Kiambu county. This piece of infrastructure, some fifty kilometers of smooth asphalt surrounded by an ever-expanding
urban footprint, forms part of the Cape to Cairo highway system and was one of
the first major projects delivered by state-owned Chinese contractors in Kenya.[29]
Cofunded by the African Development Bank, China's Eximbank, and the local
treasury, Thika Highway in part followed and in part accelerated the expansion
of Nairobi toward what used to be sisal and coffee plantations on the descending
highlands beyond the city proper. On some of these picturesque hills, a few of
Kenya's most speculative, visionary greenfield urban developments are under construction, including the middle-class utopia of Tatu City and the more exclusive
Northlands estate. Punctuated by these expensive and hyperplanned garden cities,
Thika Highway also cuts across some of the fastest-growing and densest constitu-
encies in the whole country.

FIGURE 4. A view over Githurai. Photo by author.

Plot after plot, floor after floor, Nairobi's lower-middle classes have both invested and made a home in places like Githurai, Kahawa, Kasarani, Mwiki, and Zimmerman.[30] In their densest portions, tall, multifamily buildings stand side by side separated by spaces only a few centimeters wide. A concrete maze of unpaved roads, street markets, Pentecostal churches, and lively mini-malls stretch all around Thika Highway. Only gradually, when one gets to Ruiru, at the gates of Mount Kenya's coffee belt, these dense suburbs melt away and more rural landscapes reappear. But even there, the population is growing, pushing the edges of Nairoibi's real estate "frontier."[31] Rows and rows of coffee shrubs have been left to dry out, and my interlocutors would surmise that this strategic abandonment was in part a response to years of climate change–induced drought and in part a speculative bet on the city expanding even further.

This rapid urban growth, almost unique in its pace and features, has not been followed by an equally rapid development of social amenities and public infrastructure services.[32] Aside from the road bypasses and the highway, which have certainly eased the movement between the northeastern suburbs and the Southlands and Westlands of Nairobi, where the majority of employment opportunities are concentrated, the backlog of other infrastructural needs keeps piling up, despite the state's (sometimes) best efforts. Along Thika Highway, the bus rapid transit (BRT) stations of the first mass public transport corridor in contemporary Nairobi, built by a Chinese contractor, were still waiting to be commissioned in

January 2024, the last time I visited the area, after a decade-long back and forth. In the meantime, therefore, commuters rely on the private services of matatus, which pick them up at large intersections and zip along the highway at high speed. But matatus are just one of the many gap-filling solutions to which residents resort in the absence of functioning public services. From independent solar kits and small batteries used to power phones and TVs when the electric grid fails (or when it is not there in the first place), to boreholes, tanks and jerry cans (*mitungi*) that allow a distributed, unique economy of water access, myriad technical artifacts buffer locals from the patchiness of networked supply. Such is the extent of these solutions that the urban scholars Moritz Kasper and Sophie Schramm, for example, argue that storage technologies in Nairobi ultimately form an infrastructure itself, an intermediary system, perhaps a temporary one, between individual and public access to basic services.[33]

Yet when Chao first visited the crowded northeastern suburbs of Nairobi in 2017, it was another infrastructural chasm that caught his eye. Residents in the area were using mobile phones for all kinds of digital services. But their access to connectivity was limited. On the one hand, availability itself was patchy. Densely populated neighborhoods needed a dense network of 4G cell towers. That wasn't the case there. Layers and layers of concrete and stone bricks made things even worse indoors, attenuating the already busy and weak electromagnetic waves. Ultimately, base stations were costly pieces of infrastructure. Even in China, Chao told me, where close to four million base stations had been built in the previous decade, the three main mobile operators had not yet recouped the cost of that investment. It wasn't surprising that Safaricom and Telkom alone, without a strongly enforced developmental mandate, had not been able to afford the kind of ubiquitous infrastructure needed for a seamless mobile internet.[34] This was especially true in areas where residents fell into a specific market segment for mobile operators: the users of small, almost tiny, data packages.

That was the second part of the problem. Normally, Chao had observed, the residents of northeastern Nairobi could only afford small, prepaid data bundles, those for which mobile companies charge exorbitantly high fees per byte. In fact, it was this profitable prepaid data business model that had allowed mobile operators to expand and integrate into Kenya's mass markets and informal economies in the late 2000s.[35] At heart, as the business guru C. K. Prahalad famously argued in his landmark book on bottom-of-the-pyramid markets, the ability to pay in discrete, small bits had been crucial to the very diffusion of mobile telephony among the poor of the world.[36] In what Kevin Donovan and Emma Park carefully describe as Kenya's "zero balance economy"—an economy in which individual and household savings always hover around zero and in which micro-loans allow people to buy time against unpredictable gains and losses—small payments are king.[37] Even fast-moving consumer goods (FMCGs), like soap, milk, and flour, are wrapped into tiny packages usually valued at less than 100 shillings (about half a dollar), which make purchases affordable, even though their marginal price is higher than that for larger packages. In fact, FMCG multinationals—the likes of Unilever and Procter & Gamble—and the local giant Bidco make inordinate profits from pocket portions. Kenyans have a name for this, the *kadogo* (Kiswahili for "small") economy, a slang with which they resignedly refer to the ever-shrinking purchase power of the lower-middle classes and the inevitable miniaturization of consumer staples, from data to soap.[38] Kadogo commodities also carry a much higher marginal cost than their wholesale versions.

During our first meeting, while we were served sugary Chinese tea in reusable plastic cups, Chao explained that tiny airtime and data packages were not a problem per se. They served a communication purpose and, despite their proportionally higher prices, perfectly matched the zero-balance economy of Nairobi's northeastern neighborhoods. The issue was that by 2019, when he first started exploring business opportunities in these areas, Nairobians wanted content, not just connectivity. YouTube videos, TikTok shorts, Instagram stories, and Showmax series had become aspirational commodities. Consuming digital content, however, was almost impossible with kadogo-size data bundles. After all, Chao sighed, even a few episodes of a series would chew into half a gigabyte of data. And according to market research he had conducted, the majority of people online in Nairobi's lower-income areas used less than a gigabyte per month. Usually, even less.

There was also another, related market opportunity. Scores of tech-savvy, digitally literate young Nairobians had begun offering their labor as remote data workers. Using existing platforms, or often subcontracted by specialized data processing and labeling companies, they were contributing to the future emergence of large-language models like Open AI's ChatGPT and to the training of other kinds of generative AI (or the equally manual flagging of violent content for companies like Meta). Their fees made cheaper by systemic inequalities in the global labor market, many Nairobi-based data workers saw the cost of connectivity as crucial to their livelihood and to the very possibility of being competitive labelers, verifiers, and annotators.[39]

With this in mind, Chao had gathered a small team of local software and network engineers and started experimenting. His solution was, on the surface, a radical transformation of the prepaid, kadogo business model. As an ISP, Fastlee would sell time instead of data. By joining Chao's platform, users could prepay to go online for a chosen amount of time and with no data restrictions. With only a few shillings, residents could spend a night binge-watching a series at a fraction of the cost charged by the mainstream mobile providers. Or they could doom-scroll TikTok videos filmed by Nairobi street comedians without worrying about data running out. More productively, they could now perform their gigs as data labelers and make more money from the same tasks: not only was their internet access cheaper, but they didn't need to go somewhere else with better connectivity to work. Even local businesses, the numerous small shops and parlors scattered along the narrow streets of the area, could access the same ISP platform. Needless to say, Chao's business proposition had been an immediate success. In early 2023, less than two years after his launch, he could boast hundreds of thousands of subscribers and a team of more than one hundred locally hired employees. A year later, the last time I visited him, the number had grown to 850,000 single registered users. Not all of them, of course, would stay as regular customers, but the company was still expanding fast.

In Chao's view, however, his accomplishments were more than a function of a perfect market-fit, an optimized business model, or the intuition to shift from prepaid packages of data to prepaid time slots. Behind his success, he believed, were the last-mile infrastructure itself, and the delivery model he'd crafted. As for the former, Fastlee had to overcome the patchy coverage of Internet services that plagued other players, whether mobile operators or fiber providers. To do so, he'd initially experimented with mobile antennas—an immediate failure—and WiFi bridges. His company had installed thousands of wireless routers, one on each floor of the buildings that were to go online. This solution mimicked Chao's previous experience in Beijing, where in the early days of the internet boom lower-income residents had become accustomed to most public and private spaces in the city offering network access through WiFi bridges and routers. But that model too soon turned out to be unsuited for this part of Nairobi. Users were too numerous, the bandwidth was crowded and unreliable, stone bricks dampened the signal, and too many routers were an infrastructural predicament for his network engineers. Eventually, Chao's business turned to hardwired connectivity and, during my first visit in 2022, cartons full of decommissioned routers were a common sight in his headquarters.

Fastlee had struck deals with fiber providers in Kenya, which included lighting up the unused dark fiber of the electricity parastatal, KPLC, and with first-mile providers like China Telecom. By doing that, Fastlee could rely on what network engineers call a "loop," an interconnected system in which more than one active path carries data from one place (in this case, the Nairobi data center where undersea cables have their land terminals) to another (in this case, Fastlee's points of presence in the area). A network loop ensured the kind of redundancy that other providers did not have. From each point of presence—small data centers equipped with gel batteries to provide backup in case of load shedding—Fastlee's technicians had then laid miles and miles of last-mile cables innervating the surrounding urban fabric. They had created their own middle mile, bypassing costly providers that would charge exorbitant bandwidth rents. At the time of my last conversation with Chao, sixty thousand buildings had been hardwired. In each building, cables would branch onto each floor and reach every unit, ultimately ending in small, WiFi home terminals. They had also kept some long-range routers, to create seamless access in the area as a whole. In other words, after purchasing their prepaid time bundle, Fastlee users could move around their neighborhoods and remain online, even in the streets.

FIGURE 5. A snapshot of Fastlee's digital twin. Photo by author.

It had been an incremental, trial-and-error test bed for an alternative mode of service delivery, on a large scale. For each area going online, Fastlee could now provide not just affordability but also reliability, scalability, and redundancy. To reach this diffusion, however, Chao and his team had needed to accurately map an area that was rapidly changing and create an internal dashboard to keep track of the different infrastructural components of the network, from the data centers to the terminals. They had tagged each building manually, drawing shapes over an otherwise unreliable satellite image taken from Google Maps. Eventually, they had created something that not even the city government had ever attempted: a digital twin for every neighborhood in the area, each geotagged building carrying additional metadata (e.g., number of floors, number of apartments, number of households, number of signed-in customers). The digital twin, of course, was only the visual component of a much more complicated dashboard through which Fastlee could model and monitor its services.[40] Their internal communication tool too—a digital suite provided by the makers of TikTok—was plugged into the dashboard.

Eventually, the entire delivery system had been incorporated into the digital twin-based dashboard. From the sales teams to the deployment and installation teams, as well as the after-sales customer service team, the whole operational crew had been onboarded into the purposefully designed platform.[41] In doing so, Fastlee had vertically integrated a business that is normally distributed across different players. Having tried many different options, and tracked the cost of externalizing part of this system to other companies, Chao believed that his integrated approach had been fundamental to keeping prices low for end customers.

> Operators don't even need to think about technology solutions. It's a world apart. If you're Verizon, if you're AT&T, or you're like Safaricom, or you're Airtel, your technology partners are the likes of Huawei, ZTE or Nokia or Ericsson, right? And their technical solutions are ready to use. So of course, these companies, the telco companies . . . Their mandate is to have a high profit margin. And the cost of using technology from other partners, to maintain good profits, is offloaded to the consumers. And there's little they can do about it. And add to that the cost of actually building networks. It's like a real estate developer having multiple design and building subcontractors. . . . So we [at Fastlee], we are not just an operator, even if you can describe us as an ISP, ultimately. Yes, we're operating the network to the end customer, but we are also our own design house, our installation and deployment contractor, and our network maintenance company. [In doing that,] we reduced the capex [capital expenditure] cost by two-thirds.

In addition to vertical integration, Chao and his business partner had envisioned a community-based recruitment strategy. For each area going online, salespeople and builders would be hired from among the residents of the same geographic boundaries. Their localized knowledge was necessary to knock on every door, subscribe new users, and identify and partner with building landlords, and this recruitment practice, in due course, would build trust for Fastlee even before its WiFi signal went live. "Don't expect people will just come to you," Chao smiled blithely, recollecting the early days of his start-up and how difficult it had been to market the possibility and the habit of unlimited internet access. "That's why we were so specific about hiring locally, and this was not just about sales, but about after-sales support," he continued, "because things break down every day, actually, . . . there are a lot of . . . things that can go wrong, like a lorry just passing by and destroying our power line. That's why we needed an extremely local presence, not just our data centers but also our teams."

Incidentally, having a local office in each neighborhood gave Chao and his team an additional idea for further embedding their business in each community. After all, the space they needed was only going to be busy once a week, during the training of new recruits and the strategy meetings with each squad. On other days, Fastlee offices could double as community centers, providing much needed communal space to areas of Nairobi that have very little of it. "It's all things at once," I was told by Chao, who nodded toward the large room around us, "it's our office, it's our service center, it's our coworking space, and it's our community center." Eventually, he asked me and my colleague Zhengli to visit Fastlee on a Saturday morning, to witness some of the activities that Fastlee was hosting. From prayers to slam poetry sessions, they had curated a rich calendar of neighborhood activities. During idle times, young people could use desks and free internet. Local start-ups could use the space at affordable rates. Volunteer teachers were running dedicated classes for them. Local artists were offering periodic education programs. And all these activities further entwined the business of internet access with many other facets of urban life.

Then again, Chao never lost sight of his "mission of opportunity." While he was servicing an underserved market and building local trust through welcome activities, now, with hundreds of thousands of users logging on and off the network on a daily basis, the business of selling data had become a data business in itself. As the sociologists Marion Fourcade and Kieran Healy remind us, digital companies often build personal data dragnets without a specific goal in mind, in case these troves of information may be monetized at a later stage.[42] Even without recording personal particulars and without tracking online behaviors, Fastlee was constantly gathering massive amounts of details about their users; Chao could now outline the market profiles of a segment of Nairobi's society that defied easy characterization. In turn, these market profiles could power, for example, an alternative credit scoring system to offer the small loans that Nairobians rely on to cope with the precarity of their economic lives.[43] They were sitting on so much data they had not yet figured out the full gamut of possibilities buried under the stockpile of trails that their dashboard was constantly tracing. Admittedly, Chao was thinking about the option of using proxied credit profiles to build Fastlee's own digital currency and buy-now-pay-later financing to his existing customer base. But he was actually busy with a different and much wider-ranging ambition: the creation of a "super app."

E-COMMERCE FOR THE MASSES

Through mutual connections, I met one of Chao's business partners, Daiyu, in late March 2023, on one of those clear days that precede the long rains. She had been introduced to me as somebody who was building an interesting e-commerce platform, and it was only during our first conversation that I realized how the platform in question was an additional component of Fastlee's expanding suite of digital services. Only a few months earlier, Chao had mentioned his plan to add an online marketplace to the Fastlee platform, so it was not surprising that he had found an ally in Daiyu.

Originally from the inland province of Sichuan, a region globally known for its numbingly hot cuisine, Daiyu's journey to Kenya had not been too dissimilar from other stories I had heard. With a degree in finance, she first came to East Africa to work for Stanbic, the local subsidiary of Standard Bank Group (SBK). From its beginnings on the diamond and gold fields of nineteenth-century South Africa, the bank is today one of the continent's largest financial services groups. It is also one of the most prime examples of China's first wave of going-out policy: in 2007, 20 percent of Standard Bank was acquired by the Industrial and Commercial Bank of China (ICBC), a $5.6 billion cash-for-stock deal that at the time was the biggest foreign acquisition by a Chinese commercial bank. Through the partnership with SBK, the state-owned ICBC, a bank largely focused on commercial lending, had become capable of extending credit lines to other Chinese companies operating in Africa. And to deliver on this promise, each subsidiary of SBK, including Stanbic Kenya, now had a China office, focusing on dedicated financial services for large and small enterprises entering or expanding into the local market. In that office, Daiyu had spent almost half a decade, becoming acquainted with the different shades of Chinese investments in Kenya.

Eager to learn more and expand her career, she had then moved to the United States for an MBA, only to quit soon after and return to Kenya with a desire to start her own business. This was in late 2021, the glimmer of an idea already formed around starting an e-commerce business for underserved urban markets. The collaboration with Chao, himself an entrepreneur trying to serve digitally underserved swaths of Nairobi, was a perfect match. They shared, she explained, a similar understanding of mass markets and a complementary techno-entrepreneurial ethos.

> It's an . . . e-commerce platform targeting the urban consumers who are not served well. As you can see, both myself and Chao, we believe that urbanization in Africa is the ultimate certainty. And more and more people are going to move to the city, but the infrastructure is going to take a very long time to cope. Not only roads, housing, but also traditional supermarkets. . . . It's going to take a lot of time for [large retailers] to build enough outlets to serve new urban consumers as well. That's where we feel that technology can come into play. Because we've seen how e-commerce platforms are transforming the lives of Chinese people in Tier 5, Tier 6 cities in China.

Daiyu's inspiration had been Pinduoduo, China's youngest e-commerce giant. Founded in 2015, Pinduoduo came to prominence by straddling the gap between farmers and rural artisans and their customers in secondary Chinese cities, where other e-commerce platforms like Alibaba and JD.com have a smaller footprint, their focus being on Tier 1 urban consumers.[44] Ultimately, Pinduoduo demonstrated the possibilities of so-called consumer-to-manufacturer (C2M) business models to the entire world, adapting the traditional online marketplace platform to the needs of price-sensitive consumers through two main mechanisms: the bypassing of major distribution channels and the possibility of discounted prices through peer-group purchases. These two features were especially relevant for Daiyu: if she could manage to buy bulk direct from distributors, avoiding the multiple layers of brokers, she, like Chao, could turn the kadogo economy on its head and offer locals much lower prices on staples like soap and oil.

As we spoke, Daiyu further detailed her staunch belief in the e-commerce system she was busy building, together with Chao. On the one hand, she seemed to be convinced that the retail industry in urban Africa was on a trajectory different from anywhere else. While in other contexts e-commerce had evolved from "mom-and-pop shops to large supermarkets and then online lifestyles," she told me, Africa was leapfrogging from informal sellers to mobile apps. Supermarkets were only a small part of this transition, especially at the urban periphery. On the other hand, well-known Silicon Valley–inspired start-ups like Jumia, while understanding the potential of e-commerce, were focusing on middle-class markets, "leaving out 80 percent of the population in Nairobi." They were not competitors. Moreover, Daiyu told me that through the partnership with Chao's Fastlee, she already had a powerful distribution channel to acquire customers: her e-supermarket could simply be added as a feature of the existing platform, like Pinduoduo had done in China, adding its heart-shaped "buy together" option on the WeChat app marketplace.

At the time of our meeting and only a few months after launching the prototype of the web application, Daiyu and Chao were already processing a significant volume of orders. They had partnered with both distributors and manufacturers: a few Kenyan Indian food factories and the usual Chinese FMCG and electronics importers scattered around Nairobi. Daiyu explained, "We see the sales increase, dramatically. . . . [T]hat's made us very confident that some people out there are definitely underserved. That's why we continue. . . . And the benefit to a consumer is that they get lower prices on essential commodities, so that they can reallocate their spending. If before they spent 40 percent on daily essentials and food, now they can spend more on other things that are more important. It's really hard to help them grow their pie. But you can kind of optimize how they allocate those pies better for their living standards."

Curious about their "e-supermarket," as Daiyu called it, I asked her about the logistics behind it. Her eyes gleamed with pride. "This is the most innovative part of our model," she told me. Having studied the distribution system underlying group buying in China, Chao and Daiyu had engineered a decentralized hub-and-spoke delivery network. Each area covered by their e-supermarket was anchored by a warehouse, serving a radius of about ten square kilometers. From these semi-decentralized hubs, serviced by small vans that could navigate the narrow and rutted roads of Nairobi's dense peripheries, motorcycle taxi riders—the famous *boda boda* operators (more on them later)—would bridge the last mile and deliver to widely scattered community pickup points. At the time of our conversation, they had modeled each community to be 250 people strong. It was, Daiyu explained, just an experimental pilot. Eventually, communities might need to be bigger or smaller, depending on the data that they were gathering. But most importantly, in crowded and unmarked portions of the city—no street signs, no house numbers, no door buzzers with names—these communities needed to have local motorcycle riders, whose native knowledge about the social and spatial fabric of each community rendered Fastlee e-supermarket's delivery system as accurate as possible. "It's very counterintuitive," Daiyu concluded, "because most people think centralized solutions decrease costs, but in urban Africa, it's different. It's the decentralized organization that, actually, will be the most profitable."

> It's a very on-the-ground business. It's not something fancy. It's more like great, dirty work because you're counting the flour, the maize, and sugar everyday. You're delivering this essential every day, but I and Chao feel very motivated because this is our customers' first online shopping experience. And it's life changing. It's opened a huge door for their other potentials. I'm always using my mom as an example. She had never shopped online until Pinduoduo entered our small city. Then people from the city started shopping online, watching videos, chatting, group-buying, and also selling stuff. . . . I think that's something . . . the potential that can unlock. . . . [S]ometimes it feels like we are mending a tear, but it's so rewarding.

A year later, I finally visited one of the warehouses from which Fastlee's e-supermarket operated. Ironically, it wasn't a purpose-built warehouse but a failed supermarket that the company had rented and converted into a fulfillment center, even using the old shelves to store bulk goods. By then, friends told me, Daiyu had already moved on to new business ventures in Rwanda, a move that belied her stated commitment to Nairobi's underserved market, but the e-commerce business she initiated kept running. Chao introduced me to his warehouse manager, Jeff, a tall, soft-spoken man from the area. The business, he explained, was still being tweaked and adapted, but some staple items were in high demand: nappies, soap, cooking oil, and maize. In the previous months, Kenya had experienced a deep cost-of-living crisis—owing to a mix of factors, including the enforcement of IMF requirements that had cut fuel subsidies. Jeff thought the perfect storm had arrived to expand operations, even though the uptick of online buying required careful work of building trust that was still a steep climb ahead.

An interesting fact was that, as Daiyu had told me a year before, their e-supermarket was not selling fresh products like vegetables. This was a decision based precisely on the promise of trust that Chao and its team had made to the communities that they were servicing with both affordable internet and affordable commodities. So as not to crowd out local informal vendors, whose main source of income derived from the sale of fresh produce, they had chosen to avoid competition with them. In fact, the future algorithmic iteration of Fastlee's e-supermarket was a partnership with informal sellers, whose stocks Fastlee could potentially supply with better prices than those of big distributors. After all, as Chao kept reminding me and everyone willing to listen, Fastlee was a business but a business that was trying to do well while doing good for the people it served.

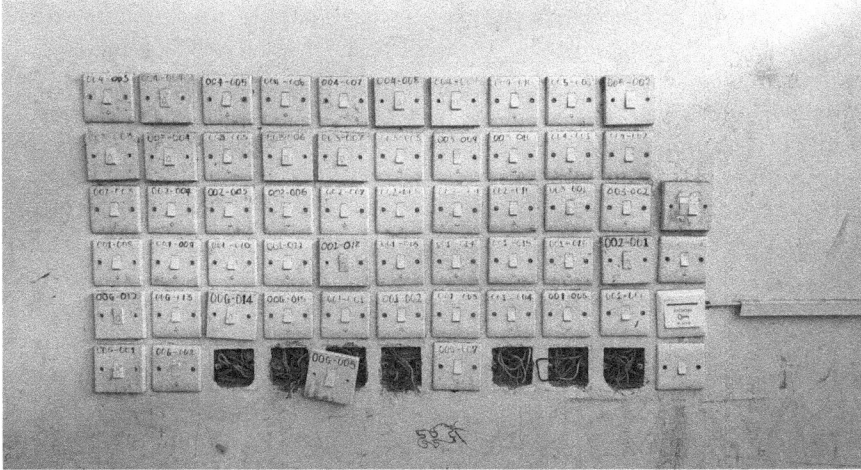

FIGURE 6. The problem of "addressability." Photo by author.

Another good example of this ethos was in yet another pilot that Chao was busy conducting when I last visited him, on an El Niño–drenched summer day in January 2024. Always the experimenter, Chao was exhilarated by his latest addition to Fastlee. His team had been working on the prototype of a water ATM. These are normally vending machines that dispense clean water filtered using reverse osmosis. In many urban contexts across Africa, these ATMs are a common sight, including in Nairobi, where their contested politics laid bare the distressing lack of basic infrastructural access in the city's poorest settlements, as well as the attempts by states, NGOs, and start-ups alike to make water access (and payment) "smart."[45]

Yet Fastlee's water ATM prototype was slightly different from those that already operated in the poorest parts of the city. As we have seen thus far, in the lower-middle-income neighborhoods of Nairobi where Chao had started his business, most people did have access to running water, mostly by means of collective boreholes that served one or more buildings. From these underground boreholes, pressure was created by pumping the water up into the large black tanks that stand tall on every rooftop. What was missing was drinkable water. Locals would buy bottles or suboptimal water jugs that promised to filter water while not doing much against heavy contaminants, a toxic remnant of Nairobi's industries that once dotted the area. Chao and his engineers had a solution: building-scale ATMs that, using technology from China, would purify borehole water at a fraction of the cost of plastic bottles. Scanning a QR code on each machine, residents could get cheap, safe water from the same platform by which they were already accessing the internet. "We are building a super app," they kept saying, using a language borrowed from the description of Asian companies like Grab, Gojek, and WeChat, tech giants that covered multiple industries and sectors.[46]

Water-dispensing machines were not, in fact, the sole infrastructure system into which Fastlee was branching. Having realized the potential of using Fastlee's digital infrastructure (and everything that underpinned it) to expand into basic service delivery, Chao was also prototyping small solar panels that, in the event of load shedding, would power a family's WiFi router as well as small appliances. The solar panels too would be sold and managed through the same Fastlee platform, possibly through an integrated payment system, further increasing the reliability and redundancy of its services in a context of patchy electricity. In fact, as Chao reminded me in many of our conversations, his ultimate goal was to forge a payment system, an M-Pesa alternative that would partially rid his customers of pricy transaction fees. All of that was on the back burner the last time we spoke, on a day Chao was especially gleeful because he had recently received a hefty investment from a Chinese venture capitalist and a development grant to pilot his ISP system in a much poorer area of the city. Now, he observed, he needed even more technological acumen for an even more splintered fragment of Nairobi. As a witness, it was impossible not to share at least part of his buoyant optimism that one could suture broken systems and make a sustainable business out of it. It was not the first time, or the last, that I would come across such promises and practices of algorithmic optimization, as the same techno-optimistic shibboleths informed several platform experiments with other "last miles," at the interface of Chinese-imported commodities and Chinese-inspired business models.

PLATFORMING THE LAST MILE, WITH CHINESE CHARACTERISTICS

Let me return, for the concluding stories in this chapter, to something I mentioned at its outset. The example of Fastlee speaks to the creation of algorithmic platforms that just like matatus fill the gaps of absent, partial, or fractured networked systems. But Fastlee is only one peculiar case in a much wider gamut of platform experiments that address the last-mile "problem" in Nairobi. Another urban economy that is increasingly the target and the object of platform experiments is that of motorcycle taxis.

From wealthy suburbs to the margins of very poor informal settlements, motorcycle taxi drivers are an extremely common sight in Nairobi. Much as in many African cities, the two-wheel taxis—called boda bodas—are used to carry people, goods, and parcels.[47] They are one of the fastest ways to move through the city and deliver small goods. As a prosthesis to splintered economies, boda bodas operate where other mobility and logistics options are too costly, too cumbersome, or simply not flexible enough to address the last-mile problem. In fact, the modal choice of the motorcycle is a practical response to the material conditions of Nairobi, where getting passengers and commodities to the outskirts or through the narrow lanes of high-density suburbs requires an affordable, fuel-efficient, and agile vehicle. Such agility of movement is likewise necessary to bypass the thick traffic clogging highways and intersections and overcome incomplete and under-maintained road networks that may be heavily rutted and unsuited for cars. As a vital and rapid undercurrent, Nairobi's boda bodas stitch together fragmented parts of the city, overcoming the brittle and enduring legacy of colonial planning, postcolonial projects of modern city building, and forced informality.

While two-wheelers were initially conceived as a solution to austerity measures (especially cuts to public transport investment) introduced by structural adjust-ment, today they are seen as an unwieldy "rogue sector," always on the brink of regulatory fights.[48] However, riders, mostly young men, also constitute an impor-tant political clientele.[49] Central and local governments have therefore pursued ambivalent and contradictory practices. In Nairobi, for example, they are banned from taking on passengers in the central business district. In general, the Kenyan government has long turned a blind eye to the boda boda sector—allowing the emergence of competing and self-regulating voluntary associations, usually in the form of collective saving groups.[50] Ultimately, whether in a small town or in the capital city, as Joyce Niairo beautifully captures, boda bodas are a marker of Kenya's postcolonial modernity, a cultural and not just infrastructural phenom-enon, and "a vehicle for laughter, outrage, (in)dignity and wealth."[51] With their adrenaline-fueled rides, their disregard for safety, and loud, ubiquitous presence, boda boda riders are the turbulent sutures of innumerable urban economies.

In this context, Nairobi's thriving tech community has been increasingly impelled by the possibility of creating platforms that incorporate motorcycle mobility, within the city and beyond. The promises of these technology experiments are many, pro-ducing data-rich ecosystems about a sector that is data-poor, retrofitting boda bodas with IoT (Internet of Things)–enabled electric batteries (the green transition story); creating asset financing options for entrepreneurial kinds of social mobil-ity; improving the quality and safety of the riders' services; and so on.[52] Along-side e-hailing (dominated by global giants like Uber and Bolt) and food or grocery deliveries (dominated by Glovo and Jumia), the invisible majority of these recent platforms are focused on optimizing the business models of companies that utilize motorcycles for last-mile, express, and on-demand deliveries, often operating as business-to-business (B2B) players.[53] It is in this niche that some Chinese compa-nies are increasingly competitive and intent on importing and adapting platform business models from mainland China. Once again, the examples that I am about to address entertain the question of affordability for Nairobi's lower-middle classes and the unique last-mile problems that arise from the creation of e-commerce solu-tions for such a shifting and elusive demographic group.[54]

My first interlocutor who mentioned the importance of targeting less-than-wealthy consumers was Li, head of marketing at Shoppist, one of the Nairobi-based e-commerce platforms that at the time was already active in Kenya and Uganda. It was mid-2021, and the city was still under recurring curfews and the occasional, seemingly unexpected bouts of COVID-19 cases. I met Li in the aesthetically bare offices of Shoppist, which he had joined only a few months before, after a stint as head of marketing for another Chinese retailer selling fast-moving consumer goods in Nairobi. Unlike his previous employer, however, Shoppist was a rather unusual example. The company had not actually come from China but had been founded in Kenya in the mid-2010s by a Chinese expatriate, a former Huawei executive whose fame in the tech scene preceded him.

The inspiration for Shoppist was obviously Alibaba, and the rags-to-riches story of its founder, Jack Ma. Alibaba's success, Li told me, was a function of its capacity to experiment with and diversify its business models, from drop-shipping to consumer-to-consumer options. For Shoppist's founder, Alibaba and other Chinese giants like Jingdong (JD.com) had something valuable to teach Africa's fledgling e-commerce sector: reaching the customers who were usually left out of online shopping platforms was not just about marketing prowess but also about last-mile logistics, both financially and geographically. However, Li explained, "e-commerce in China is very unique. . . . In Kenya, we [could] not just copy Alibaba or Amazon. And so that's why it was important to have local intelligence." Local intelligence, he later elaborated, meant more than hiring a team of locals for the operations team. It entailed relying on their understanding of the Kenyan market, on their knowledge of specific urban economies of logistical distribution (specifically, boda boda networks), and on an iterative, cumulative process of data-powered learning.

From the very beginning, these experimental processes translated into a series of small adaptations of and tweaks to more traditional e-commerce models. The first of these changes was the integration of M-Pesa. This was no small feat, given the risk attached to foreign currency purchases. But with M-Pesa, Shoppist had become one of the first online retailers where Kenyans could buy affordable phones made in China in the same way they used to do in a physical shop: with a one-off, fully paid, cash-like transaction. Only a few months after Shoppist, Li told me with a hint of pride, AliExpress (Alibaba's retail platform) too had eventually implemented a Lipa na M-Pesa (Pay with M-Pesa) option.

The other change in the business model stemmed from the intuition that Shoppist did not need to function completely as either a drop-shipping company (i.e., one with no warehouse) or a stockist (i.e., one with large-scale warehousing facilities). Shoppist's hybrid model was based on a central warehouse located close to Nairobi's international airport (in an area that was more and more densely packed with this kind of logistical facility) and pop-up warehouses in Mombasa and Kisumu that would become available during peak order periods, such as Christmas. A three-tiered product taxonomy thus ensued: things that were already in the warehouse (which never stayed for more than a month), things that were sold by other stockists in Kenya (and were in third-party warehouses), and things ordered directly from China (which stayed briefly in the Nairobi warehouse before being dispatched).

FIGURE 7. The warehouse complex where Shoppist operates. Photo by author.

For this carefully orchestrated supply model, Li argued, coordinating the last mile was as important as understanding the suppliers. In fact, managing the supplier side depended on last-mile data and coordination. For goods to move quickly to their end customers, two motorcycle-enabled solutions had to be crafted to resolve two addressability issues. The first difficulty was that Nairobi addresses may or may not be accurately geolocated or even have a specific house number. Boda boda riders knew the city well enough to fill this gap, already acting as sutures of otherwise incomplete logistics configurations. The second problem was the total lack of an address for those Shoppist customers who lived in parts of the city that for one reason or another are unaddressable (including the neighborhoods that Fastlee operated in). In this case, the last-mile solution consisted of little delivery hubs called Shopposts. These hubs were fulfilled daily by boda boda riders, and they had the double function of providing a delivery address for people without one and for those customers who could not receive deliveries at home during working hours. As Li explained, Shoppist customers were mostly young people who didn't belong to the upper-income brackets of Kenyan society; consequently, delivery options on Amazon or other e-commerce platforms were prohibitively expensive. The Shoppost option was essential for this type of customer because, according to the company's research, they were less addressable than middle-class households.

While Shoppist employed a small number of riders directly, the majority were subcontracted through B2B last-mile logistics platforms. The reason for this choice was that specialized two-wheel delivery companies had developed more efficient distribution algorithms, and they did a better job of optimizing delivery routes across the urban center, so the riders had much stronger performance indicators than could be achieved with in-house operations. At the same time, keeping a few riders on the payroll meant that Shoppist had a degree of flexibility and could adapt to unexpected market fluctuations, particularly in Nairobi. Such a system, Li concluded, had not happened by chance but evolved organically using the last mile itself as a data source, constantly monitoring and experimenting with feedback loops to improve the final leg of logistical coordination while ensuring that small tweaks to the dispatch system would not affect the affordability of Shoppist's e-commerce offering.

These were small but crucial aspects of Shoppist's business model that attest to the ways in which platform algorithms seek to mend disjointed urban fabrics. By framing the goal of selling affordable products to its target customers (the urban lower-middle class and youths) as a problem of addressability and by formulating incremental and iterative data-driven experiments, Shoppist was making Nairobi a real-life test bed for future African e-commerce, a market aided by the platformization of existing mobility networks like the boda bodas, whose riders' intimate knowledge of the "unaddressable" city had been enrolled in the functioning of platform-powered last-mile logistics.[55] This was often a very speculative endeavor, as the next example reveals.

To find a specialized last-mile company that supported e-commerce platforms like Shoppist, one didn't need to travel very far from Shoppist headquarters. At the southern end of Mombasa Road, Nairobi's main traffic artery, stands a growing cluster of depots and other logistics operations, attracted by the proximity of Kenya's main international airport, the terminus of the newly built standard-gauge railway, and access to the country's busiest highway. At the crossroad of these networks, Dasher occupied two large warehouses painted in bright colors, one the distribution center and the other a sorting facility.

Dasher was one of an increasing number of small last-mile companies that offered logistics services through a network of boda boda riders across Kenya. Unlike bigger platforms like Uber and Bolt, Dasher only operated in the B2B market, offering a plug-and-play delivery service to e-commerce businesses, explained Jenny, a petite, animated young woman who was head of sales for the company. Started by a small team of Chinese expatriates in late 2020, Dasher was the subsidiary of a conglomerate already active in half a dozen African countries, as well as, more recently, the Middle East. These subsidiaries all reported to headquarters in Shanghai, but, as Jenny elaborated, they only did so once a year, and Dasher was an independent business unit operating as a start-up.[56] The seed investment had come from one of China's leading express delivery companies, a logistics firm that had made its fortune on the heels of e-commerce giants like Alibaba and JD.com. Handling a staggering volume of more than ten million parcels a day, the mother company's expansion into the African market was replicating the model that had been used in China, with a growing cluster of subsidiary start-ups that gradually formed a comprehensive network of logistical services, from line haul first-mile to express last-mile solutions.

In Kenya, Dasher was spearheaded by Kevin, a tall young man who had cut his teeth as a logistics manager in southern China during the heyday of the e-commerce boom, ten years before relocating to Nairobi. Sitting with Jenny and my colleague Jack Odeo in a small office separated from the sorting facility by a glazed wall, Kevin described for us how Dasher's network worked. At the center of the network stood the warehouse complex in which they welcomed us. Parcels coming in from overseas, for example, would be scanned in the sorting facility. This was a mostly manual operation, augmented by technological equipment imported from China and by in-house software that Dasher had built to automate its logistics management. In the future, Kevin planned to import a fully automated sorting belt, but at the time the volume of parcels did not warrant a large-scale machine. From the sorting facility, items would move across to the distribution center, where parcels were assigned to trucks and vans of various sizes that would head out to smaller distribution hubs across the city and in most of Kenya's other counties. The latter distribution hubs were either small shop fronts with loading bays or, in some cases, other businesses acting as franchisees. From these hubs, boda boda riders would bridge the last-mile gap, delivering parcels to end customers on behalf of Dasher's B2B clients. These hubs were also drop-off points for domestic deliveries: once an item was scanned at one of these hubs, it traveled to the main distribution center in Nairobi, from where it would be line-hauled to the destination hub and eventually delivered by local boda boda riders. This centralized system responded to the need to optimize the interface between the middle and the last mile, Jenny explained, pointing to the second warehouse building: "Everything goes through this DC [distribution center]. So, for example, between Meru and Mombasa trucks would be half full. But because they all go through this DC, we make sure that all the routes are optimized. . . . In logistics, the most important thing is the network; the more a network is capillary, the bigger your abilities." The ultimate capillaries of this network were indeed boda bodas, she went on to explain, showing us the algorithmic system that rendered each rider and each parcel as a discrete data point thanks to the barcodes scanned at key points of a delivery.

Unlike other large on-demand labor platforms offering parcel services, Uber included, Dasher did not rely on a casual workforce. The riders were all formally employed, although their wages were still piece based. Only during peak periods such as Black Friday would temporary riders be added to the base team, which, after just one year of operation, already comprised some two hundred members (ranging from seventy-five in Nairobi to just a couple in smaller cities). While casual labor would be a cheaper option, Kevin had realized that to ensure a good service—and that their riders were indeed data collectors (as well as couriers)—he needed to employ and train them. After all, boda bodas had a rather bad reputation in Nairobi.[57]

The ways in which Dasher understood its last-mile network offer us a glimpse of the patient, often quiet, even if quickly moving speculations of Chinese companies that see in the future of African cities a present past of China's own trajectory. Both Kevin and Jenny were adamant that Dasher's aim was to become Africa's "number one last-mile service provider" dedicated to e-commerce. This was the tagline they had memorized, something of a pipedream, as they admitted, since e-commerce in Africa was still only taking its first steps. But they were playing the "long game," said Kevin, arguing that it would only take two ingredients for e-commerce to finally boom: a functional, diffused online payment system and effective last-mile logistics.

> If anyone can solve these two things, online payment systems and last-mile logistics, e-commerce will be pumping. . . . No country can escape e-commerce. I don't know who will be the last winner. In America it's Amazon, in China it's Alibaba, and in different countries they have their own. I don't know who will be the winner in Africa. But whoever it is, they'll need us.
>
> So why did we come here? At this phase, we are building the night work. We've connected every county, trained our team, taught them how to be ready. We are waiting like a crouching tiger.

In playing this long game, performing the "night work"—the invisible preparations that make things work—in the hope that African e-commerce would truly bloom, Kevin was already thinking about the distributed infrastructure that an explosion in the demand for last-mile delivery would mean for a city like Nairobi.[58] He had ordered twenty smart cabinets from China. These cabinets, which were to be distributed across the city to shopping malls and large corporate offices, would function as the last-mile endpoints to Dasher's delivery services. Enabled with IoT technology and fully automated, the cabinets sported the same bright colors as the company's brand and were equipped with small lock-boxes. Every day, boda boda riders would fill and take from these cabinets across the city—attending to the same issue of addressability that Shoppist was trying to solve with its Shoppost model.

The prototype of one of these smart cabinets, soon to become a new fixture of e-commerce in Nairobi, sat just outside the office where Jenny and Kevin were talking to us. As a fix to problems of last-mile coordination, in Dasher's business model motorcycles contributed to a unique hub-and-spoke logistics model in which the gap-filling capacities of the boda boda sector were visualized as both capillaries of a larger distribution network and the data-gathering terminals of this network. Then again, what we have called "algorithmic suturing" is always more than just software-based "tricks," as Matteo Pasquinelli explains, writing more broadly about algorithmic rationalities.[59] The platform-based optimization of mundane systems, in this case networks of last-mile logistics, entails riders, motorcycles, cabinets, warehouses, and so much more, all in an effort to mend the social and spatial fragmentation of an unaddressable city. What is also worth noting—which Dasher illustrates even better than other examples in this chapter—is the speculative nature of these platforms; not only was the start-up operating at a loss, a "crouching tiger" waiting for an e-commerce boom that may or may not materialize, but it was doing so by experimenting with a spatial network of distribution that was in the making but not there yet.

PRECARIOUS LIVES AND NEW EXPERIMENTAL TERRAINS

It is hard not to admire the operations of Fastlee, Shoppist, and Dasher for their speculative ingenuity. These fledgling companies were promising to service underserved markets, to produce algorithmic optimizations of inconvenient urban economies, and they were doing so with inventive protocols that adapted business models from China's homegrown platform ecosystem to the unique infrastructural configurations of Nairobi.[60] It is also clear that Jenny, Chao, Kevin, and Li (as well as other platform creators and attendants with whom I interacted over time) shared a similar kind of technological optimism about a China-inspired platformization of society in Africa. As the media scholar Julie Chen writes, digital platforms have indeed become "an imagined stage, on and through which China continues to participate in the global capitalism for the sake of development."[61] This is a state-driven narrative that frames algorithmic platforms as "connective forces" that "shake and improve the conditions for social changes," in and beyond China.[62] It is the underlying discourse of a benevolent globalization produced by going-out Chinese digital giants like Alibaba.[63] But it is also the manifest, ambitious mantra of start-up founders and managers, people like Chao, who combine a certain kind of Silicon Valley–inspired technological solutionism—one directed to the "developing" world—with models and formats emanating from China's digital trajectory.[64]

But beyond the inventiveness of these businesses, platform experiments modeled on the mass-consumer market reach of Chinese super apps are not without shadows.[65] In Nairobi, these experiments copy, rely on, sometimes bypass, and sometimes enroll existing informal economies that already act as sutures for the spatial and social fragmentation of the city.[66] Such economies are, because of their existence in gray legal areas, already precarious, expendable, just as much as the livelihoods that they sustain. Boda boda riders, for example, live at the edge of survivability in a city that is rarely kind to them. Digital platforms may not make their lives worse off; in fact, they often do not. But they do seek to tap into this pool of workers whose labor is made cheap precisely by their structural precariousness to produce profit and convenience for others.[67]

In fact, these *others* are often precarious too. The lower-middle classes that Fastlee and Shoppist wanted to serve, these elusive sociological groups turned into a potential mass market, are also made up of urban populations that live on the threshold of subsistence. Often indebted, caught between the illiquidity and volatility of a zero-balance economy, the survival of these Nairobi lower-middle classes is contingent on meager salaries or, more often, vacillating income streams.[68] And platforms that promise them inclusive convenience are never too far from offering instead predatory inclusion, whether it is through the optimization of last-mile connectivity or the mirage of affordable online shopping.[69]

This wasn't necessarily the case of Chao and his cohort of deft yet declaredly moral entrepreneurs, but I did encounter digital platforms that were, without a doubt, exploitative and rapacious. In 2021, I spoke to an employee of one of the several dozen lending wallets (many of them operated by Chinese entrepreneurs) that became a matter of national panic when Google banned many of them—deus ex machina—from its Android Play Store in January 2023. In whistle-blower fashion, my informant met me on a Zoom call wearing a theater mask to remain anonymous. He described how his job consisted in enforcing repayments through debt shaming, thanks to the call logs and SMS logs that the lending app had gained access to leveraging their users' unwitting authorization. He would make intimidating calls to the relatives of debtors who were late on their repayments. He would send baleful SMSs to their employers and friends. All the while, the lending app was sharing personal data with other wallets, and they were doing the same, forging a wily racketeering scheme of vicious credit. No wonder that in time the Central Bank of Kenya would intervene through the hands of Google, with the 2023 Android ban.

In addition to whether (or to what extent) platforms that seek to algorithmically suture an unaddressable and fragmented city rest on the widespread precarity of life, labor, and economies that makes Nairobi what it is, the question that remains to be asked is what kinds of city these platforms imagine. Was it just a city whose patchy infrastructure is fixed by tech businesses that have learned a lesson from China's digital ascendancy, as Chao put it? Was it just a city whose untapped markets could be patiently opened up to China's transnational techno-capital, as Kevin seemed to suggest? This chapter shows that different technical logics and rationalities animate the experiments that cast Nairobi as a test bed city, as a terrain of trials and pilots that belie the optimistic promise of algorithmic suturing.[70]

On the one hand, it is easy to recognize how these datafied processes, tentative as they may be, enroll what Neferti Tadiar has called the already existing "vital platforms of techno-social reproductivity."[71] After all, economic systems like that of the boda boda already—without digital augmentation—provide respite from both the purposeful and the arbitrary precarity of life in a fractured postcolonial city. And yet, whether it is a WiFi provider, an e-commerce business, or a logistics operations, the combined efforts of these and other platforms are also experiments in the "pluralization" of the concerns, as Isabelle Stengers would write, that shape the making of techno-capital in Nairobi.[72] Addressability, affordability, convenience, optimization, and other matters, together with optimistic promises of profit, were given a technical form in such experiments.

Challenging simplistic visions of neocolonial domination and leapfrogging, the speculative platforms described in this chapter foreground the place of Nairobi's urban economies in a multipolar, diverse world of techno-capital, where digital Global China acts as a source of human and literal capital but also as a model of diversification. We will see even more of these logics of pluralization in the next chapter, as I turn to the making of standards for cross-border payments.

4

Microgeopolitics of Standards

Earlier, we briefly encountered Bolu, a popular Kenyan blogger and YouTuber who built his niche celebrity unboxing and reviewing mobile phones and tech gadgets, mostly from affordable Chinese brands. What he started as a small personal project was by the time we met in June 2021 the go-to website to learn about the launch of new devices and get trusted assessments of prices and functionalities. Beyond reviews, the website had become a much bigger blogging platform about everything digital, from news about start-ups and venture capital investments to opinion pieces about cryptocurrencies and how-to guides for micro trading. But for many, Bolu remained the "online guy" who had introduced them to Chinese phones, with his meticulous reviews and reliable advice. I knew that his perspective on the ascendancy of China's hardware industry in Kenya would be insightful, so I contacted him, and he generously agreed to meet me at a café on the rooftop of a popular shopping mall in Westlands. Over coffee and *dawa*—Nairobi's beloved lime, ginger, and honey drink—our conversation inevitably turned to Transsion, the Chinese manufacturer that dominated phone sales in the country and to the scramble over operating system standards.

Operating systems, Bolu told me, were "a new geopolitical field." In 2019, the Trump administration had placed Huawei on the US "entity list" and thus forced Google, a US company, to revoke the Chinese tech giant's Android license. In response, Huawei had soon unveiled Harmony (Hongmeng in Mandarin), a new operating system partly based on the Linux kernel of the Android Open Source Project, the basic Android architecture, but devoid of any of Google's proprietary applications.[1] This speedy switch to a new operating system confirmed speculations that Huawei had been secretly working on an Android alternative for almost a decade, both as a plan B in case of a Sino-US trade war escalation and as a techno-nationalistic challenge to Google's and Apple's hold over the technical standards that prime the interfaces of mobile connectivity.[2] In Kenya, however, the removal of Google's application marketplace from Huawei smartphones had temporarily taken the wind out of its aspirations to compete in the local cell phone market. The retreat of Huawei had further entrenched the dominance of Transsion and Xiaomi, which could still run on Android and provided access to Google Play. Cell phone buyers, Bolu observed, "wanted just the standard Android apps and stopped buying Huawei," even though, he admitted, Huawei smartphones remained "some of the best machines on the market."

In the meantime, Bolu had also taken notice of how Transsion phones, while still operating on Android, were jam-packed with dupes of Google Play services: a browser, a news reader, and so forth. Transsion phones even had their own marketplace.[3] These preinstalled services were sometimes subfunctional. While they provided an alternative channel for app developers to the more expensive and harder to access Google and Apple marketplaces, they also unnecessarily crowded the storage space of devices that, by nature of their affordability, had very little. In tech jargon, these native apps were thus called bloatware. As discussed in chapter 2, low-cost Chinese phones were often ridiculed for their bloatware, even though some of these memory-bloating apps were functional to the economies of care and repair that had been introduced to retain customers in African markets. And while some journalists had speculated that bloatware was in fact spyware, a backdoor to surveillance,[4] Bolu simply believed that after the Huawei-US affair, Chinese companies like Transsion were preparing themselves for "a post-Android time." He told me that bloatware was, in his opinion, a way to keep Transsion's in-house marketplace ready in case of a further escalation of a tech war between the US and Chinese tech giants.

For Bolu, this was a war fought on many fronts. Something as unassuming as export controls, like the placement of Chinese companies on the US entity list, operated across many domains of the tech industry, from hardware manufacturing to the provision of network equipment to digital services. The example of Huawei was telling: not only had the company been cut off from Google's Android marketplace, but it had also lost its access to the most advanced semiconductor chips, which usually contained US-made components and US-copyrighted software. Microchips are, after all, the blood cells on which many innovative industries depend, from large AI language models to self-driving cars. The economic historian Chris Miller even suggests that semiconductor technologies have become the world's most critical and essential resource.[5] And indeed, after the lesson learned in curtailing Huawei's global dominance, the United States redeployed its microchip export control strategy on a much larger scale in late 2022, fundamentally creating a "silicon blockade" against the entirety of the Chinese internet industry, as *The New York Times Magazine* put it.[6]

While more openly aggressive, US techno-nationalist stratagems were also a response to China's unequivocal ambitions to become a standard-bearer, not just a standard follower, of digital technology. A broader version of this goal, explains the geographer Ding Fei, became clear already during the 2012 18th National Congress of the Chinese Communist Party, which paved the way for initiatives like "Made in China 2025," a set of industrial strategies designed to foster manufacturing independence both at the level of the supply chain and at the level of research and development.[7] In the meantime, on the international stage, China's presence in standard-setting institutions such as the International Standards Organization (ISO) also grew significantly in the 2010s. In this way, many technological fields that were and are yet to be fully standardized, from drones to AI languages, from data security protocols to electric vehicles, have seen an increasingly hefty presence of Chinese companies and experts on international panels. Take, for example, the mobile communication 5G standard, which features thousands of technical specifications. According to a recent report, no single company has had more technical contributions to the 5G standardization process than Huawei at the 3rd Generation Partnership Project (3GPP), the international panel that develops and oversees protocols for mobile telecommunications.[8]

In the global arena of internet governance too, namely, in organizations such as the International Telecommunication Union (ITU), the Internet Engineering Task Force (IETF), and the Internet Corporation for Assigned Names and Numbers (ICANN), Chinese delegations have been more and more active in the outlining of new protocols for the future of internet infrastructure, which was historically dominated by the United States. However, far from imposing the authoritarian goal of a fragmented, multilateral internet,[9] as many critics suggested, China's visions for internet governance have reflected both its standard-bearing ambitions and the contradictions of its own digital economy path,[10] caught between the willful integration into the most competitive forms of transnational techno-capital and domestic agendas inspired by socialist notions of development. Then again, just like the "Chinese internets" have been plural and never merely the outcome of a monolithic, centralized state capitalism, as Jack Qiu and colleagues write, so too the geopolitics of China's push for technical standards in the digital economy have been diverse and multifaceted.[11]

But against the backdrop of what *The New York Times Magazine* described as an emerging "tech cold war," these geostrategic moves felt both impalpable and distant in the streets of Nairobi.[12] Even the then ICT secretary, Joseph Mucheru, had scoffed at journalists' questions about Huawei-gate. "We pick what is best for us," he declared at a press conference in July 2019.[13] A year later, he solomonically explained that the decision to use or not to use Huawei's equipment and technical support essentially rested in the hands of telecommunication operators like

Safaricom.[14] Overall, the Kenyan government seemed so unconcerned that, despite international pressure from the West, it followed through with an agreement that identified Huawei as the sole contractor for a critical piece of digital infrastructure, the National Data Center. Several of my Kenyan interlocutors too were rather ambivalent or even cavalier about the politics of US-China technological rivalries.

Yet, as Bolu pointed out during our meeting, these fights over technical standards ultimately determined which mobile phones people bought, which apps people downloaded, what personal data users were asked to forgo, and so on. Although operating systems were just one fragment of a much wider terrain, featuring embattled technology giants and foreign governments, they revealed in a very tangible way how large geopolitical movements had repercussions at much smaller scales. The scale of our hands. Bolu was adamant about this point: If I was to understand the influence of Chinese techno-capital on Nairobi's Silicon Savannah, I needed to look at those small experiments, like Transsion's half-baked bloatware, that were piloting new technical standards for a less US-centric global digital economy. More explicitly, I needed to search for those speculative experiments that were imagining a new world of technical standards in and from Nairobi. Even though I had just started my research journey, I soon realized that I was already surrounded by these test beds. Some were incredibly wide ranging, like the user-experience tests discussed in chapter 2. Others were bootstrapped and tentative, though not less sophisticated. Of the many experiments that I encountered during my field research, the following pages are dedicated to two fintech start-ups that, in their own way, were using digital technology to rewrite the existing standards for cross-border payments between Africa and Asia. But what did they mean by "standards," after all?

MICROGEOPOLITICS OF STANDARD MAKING

Standards are usually defined as sets of agreed-upon rules.[15] They describe, specify, orient, guide, and define the criteria for a dazzling number of the technical things that surround us. Ultimately, standards ensure some sort of material or semiotic consistency across the qualities of products and processes and the way we define and measure these qualities. Their maintenance depends on a variety of organizational forms: from the professional guilds of the European Middle Ages to the national standards bodies of the early 1900s to the thousands of international Standard Developing Organizations (SDOs) that today develop and issue industry-specific rules across almost every sector of the world economy. The best known of these SDOs is probably the Geneva-headquartered International Organization for Standardization, or ISO, which Keller Easterling evocatively describes as "a quintessential parliament of 'extrastatecraft,'" a polity that supersedes national states and primes global infrastructure systems by calibrating their uniformity.[16] But ironically, definitions of standards are not standard themselves. Even the ISO offers a vague depiction of standards as the "best ways of doing something," and "the distilled wisdom of people with expertise in their subject matter."[17] In a way, therefore, it is easier to describe standards according to what they do and how they act (and are acted on) in the world, as the science and technology scholars Geoffrey Bowker and Susan Leigh Star suggested in their landmark study on classification.[18] If standards are hazy, then *standardization*, the making and enactment of standards, is perhaps a better entry point.[19] Standardization allows us to see that the construction of technical uniformities is always a techno-political project of making "things work over distance or heterogeneous metrics."[20] In this perspective, standard making is also an economic project—or to use Louis Thévenot's famous phrasing, an "investment in forms."[21]

Building on these insights, this chapter charts precisely the making of new standards. I delve into two attempts at standardization in the domain of China–Africa cross-border transactions enabled by new financial technologies (fintech). Albeit tentative and exploratory, these attempts were explicitly described and promoted by my interlocutors as alternatives to existing standards. It goes without saying that these experiments contained and articulated a clear geopolitical program. But it wasn't grand narratives—the Chinese century, the tech cold war, or the like. Rather, it was a minor, pragmatic kind of geopolitical project, which I describe as "microgeopolitical" for two reasons. First, these technological experiments sought to offer modest, run-of-the-mill solutions to cross-border payment inefficiencies that were linked to much bigger and intractable geopolitical misalignments.[22] Second, these solutions were encapsulated in something as small as a digital application running on a cheap smartphone. But however small, the microgeopolitics of standard making for cross-border payments do shed light on important ways in which Nairobi's urban economies had become test beds of competing technical imaginations. In other words, the microgeopolitics of standards are another window onto the key empirical argument of this book.

But let me return briefly to the definitional question. Lacking a uniform definition, standards existed, in the words of my research interlocutors, across different meanings. Standards captured both the official specifications of financial regulators and the informal rule systems of illegal remittance markets. Standards were something viewed as negative (i.e., the inefficient status quo) and as an aspiration: the common ambition of the two start-up experiments was indeed to set *new* standards. So standards manifested as financial protocols to be challenged for their power imbalances but also as opportunities to create uniformity in economies that were hard to grasp and measure.[23] Ultimately, my interlocutors saw their experiments with standardization as a process of rethinking the operating protocols of international payments from a more plural set of rules in the world of technology and finance. Through their testimony, I realized that the power of standards did not only rest in making "things work over distance," but in their capacity to exist across different registers, from the critical to the aspirational. It is for this reason that in the following pages the word *standard* appears in the multiplicity of its meanings, starting from the story of Easytransfers, a nestling fintech start-up led by a young Chinese entrepreneur named June.

FRICTIONS OF FINANCE

June and I met for the first time on a cloudy day at the beginning of the rainy season, in fall 2022. By the time we sat down for our first conversation, I had come to realize she was a prominent member of the Chinese tech community in Nairobi, a respected and active network broker who used her connections in a very deliberate yet graceful manner. Not a single WhatsApp group about Nairobi's international tech scene would be started without her being invited to it. In time, this would generate jealousies and rumors, as it often happens with people who seem to stand out in the crowd without being pushy in any obvious way. I return to this part of the story later.

With a creative background in marketing and advertising, June's first foray in the African continent took place in her early twenties, through a student volunteer organization. Once in Tanzania, for a six-month humanitarian program, something unexpected happened and forever changed her journey. "Yes," thinking about how her marketing skills could be used "at the bottom of the economic pyramid" was an interesting endeavor, she told me. But what was even more interesting was to observe how the many Chinese people living in Tanzania had adapted to life in a new, foreign geography. Many of them had come with large state-owned enterprises in the mining and engineering sectors. Some had eventually left those companies to start their own businesses: restaurants, grocery shops, small construction contractors working in the value chain of bigger Chinese-funded projects. All of them, June remembered, had learned survival in conditions of extreme precariousness. With no Kiswahili, very little English, deep uncertainties about their medium-term futures, and a lot of eating bitterness (*chi ku*), they had made a home in Tanzania.[24] And yet, because of their isolation, much of their talent and much of the potential of these business connections had remained idle, she explained to me. Since then, forging solutions to imagine China–Africa connectivity in more productive ways had guided June's resolution to stay in the continent.

Her path had not been straightforward. In order to remain in Tanzania, she took a job offer at a large Chinese state-owned company working in the energy sector. "Things were changing, at the time," she recollected. "They were setting up the first-ever public-private partnership [PPP] with the Tanzanian government, and the Chinese company was going to become a long-term investor in the plant.[25] They needed help in the communication department, and with someone like me who spoke English and could manage their public relations. So I figured, if I can get the experience of successfully implementing my first PPP project, I will be very very grateful." Little did June know how challenging that job would turn out to be. "Mostly, the challenges were with me. I couldn't survive the culture of the company," she explained with a chuckle, referring to the harsh, competitive, and hierarchical corporate environment of the overseas units of Chinese state firms. A lifeline came in the form of a job offer from a Kenyan boutique investment bank.

"A bank! I thought nothing could be more boring than banking, but I had no options, I wanted to stay in Africa, and so I said, well, banking it is!" In hindsight, it was the right move. The Nairobi-based bank needed somebody for their sales department, a relationship manager who could interact with important Chinese companies that had set up business in Kenya, companies like Transsion and Huawei. The bank had a suite of dedicated capital market consulting services and targeted financial products, which they had developed over the previous decade, when Kenya entered a second wave of World Bank–backed privatization of parastatals.[26]

Over five years, June specialized in offering these banking products and consulting services to other businesses. She then left the bank for a brief return to her earlier humanitarian work, but she soon realized that it was hard, too hard to make a living working in a social enterprise. She also started to question the very ethos of humanitarianism. Her skepticism eventually brought her back to the banking sector, this time with an Islamic institution. "They wanted to tap into Chinese businesses too," she told me. "It didn't turn out to be very successful. I left after six months . . . but . . . it was a very interesting learning curve for me." She later elaborated that at the time the bank was "trying to shift from traditional Islamic management to a modern one." For June, the lesson gleaned from that experience was almost an epiphany: finance and its underpinning infrastructure systems were not universal protocols. They reflected different cultural, legal, and religious worldviews about how money ought to move and be stored.

June's intuition about the diversity of finance was confirmed by her next job: a marketing position at a roaring Kenyan start-up, Mamapay, which was at the time being celebrated in the news for being the first Africa–Asia payment platform of its kind.[27] From the beginning, however, she had doubts about these claims: "But I said to myself, 'Let me just try and see.' And then that's how I got into the start-up ecosystem." This new world, she went on to explain, turned out to be "amazing." "Amazing both in a good and in a bad way," she told me with a hint of irony, as it started pouring rain all around us, and our conversation briefly took a turn to what June believed to be the flaws and perils of overvalued and overhyped African start-ups in the fintech industry.[28]

At Mamapay, despite her short stint, June became aware of two insights. First, behind the glossy celebrations of African fintech start-ups in the media often stood venture capitalists overvaluing the companies in which they had invested. I return to this point in chapter 5, but in short, June had become convinced that rather than raise huge sums of capital to burn, a better way forward was to proceed in small, strategic steps. "Crossing the river by feeling the stones," as the mantra popularized by Deng Xiaoping goes. This guarded incrementalism was the opposite of what June had observed at Mamapay, which she had decided to leave soon after taking the job.

Her second insight confirmed her earlier observations that financial systems were not universal. Different legal and cultural practices created frictions in the movement of money. And these frictions were mostly felt by ordinary people. "Banks or wealthy players never have problems moving money," June remarked with a smirk, somewhat belying the techno-solutionist spirit that permeated many Africa-centric fintech companies.[29] Mamapay's business model was based on exactly that mission—taking care of the frictions, at a less expensive rate than what legacy financial institutions charge. Despite not liking the ways in which the start-up was operating, June had come to believe that it was the right time for the smooth China–Africa payment infrastructure foreshadowed by Mamapay's promise.

Her own cross-border payment platform had recently become a reality as Easytransfers. She had cofounded the enterprise with her husband—an experienced fintech entrepreneur in his own right—and two other team members. But before moving on to June's venture with Easytransfers, a brief digression about financial standards for cross-border transactions is in order.

BETWEEN SWIFT AND HAWALA

The early 1970s were a time of turmoil for commercial banks in the West. Not only had the United States unilaterally ended the gold standard, one of the key monetary underpinnings of the Bretton Woods system, but the looming Latin American debt crisis had exposed how globalized lending operations had become, with a growing number of US and European institutions holding credit and transacting in foreign jurisdictions.[30] The internationalization of banks had been accompanied by a burgeoning of technological solutions: with early computers, Telex networks, and other proprietary intranets, several electronic data interchange (EDI) systems had cropped up to manage, standardize, and partly automate both domestic and international payments. In turn, this technological shift had generated the need for a global communication protocol to reduce the redundant back-and-forths implied by the existence of competing systems and related risks.[31] In 1973, after a few years of planning, 239 banks formed the Society for Worldwide Interbank Financial Telecommunication (SWIFT), a Belgium-headquartered cooperative bestowed with the mandate to create a shared infrastructure for international payments.

Four years later, in 1977, the SWIFT service went live in full, with a dedicated messaging platform, a routing system, and, most importantly, a set of message standards. Developed to seamlessly exchange data across linguistic and technical differences, the SWIFT message standards have since become *the* standard for cross-border payments, not least because they were retroactively made into an ISO standard (ISO 20022) of which SWIFT is a registration authority. In other words, SWIFT is both the promoter and the custodian of its own financial communication protocol through the ISO. Today, even non-Western clearing and settlement systems, such as the People's Bank of China's Cross-Border Interbank Payment System (CIPS), utilize a version of the SWIFT syntax for its messaging, though they do not travel through the SWIFT platform itself.

Far from being the neutral, invisible "plumbing" of international financial exchanges, as the political scientist Marieke De Goede writes, SWIFT has often been drawn into geopolitical tussles, especially since the start of the war on terrorism, with SWIFT being weaponized to impose economic sanctions on Iran.[32] The 2022 Russian attack in Ukraine is another recent case when cutting access to the SWIFT system for Russian banks was advocated as a possible punishment and eventually implemented for a small number of Kremlin-linked institutions. Despite this, Russia could still rely on its very own interbank messaging system, which, ironically, mostly aligns with the SWIFT-inspired ISO 20022 standard. Put differently, as De Goede suggests, infrastructural standards have a life of their own, an agency that at once escapes and shapes geopolitics.[33]

Yet June's and her Easystransfers' challenge to SWIFT was imbued with a different kind of geopolitical flavor. Though SWIFT standards are widely used, SWIFT itself has not been immune to the criticism of experts and lay users, first and foremost for its high cost on small transactions, lack of fee transparency, and lengthy settlement process (even if SWIFT is not in itself a payment system but just a semicentralized messaging platform that in turn requires separate clearance and settlement).[34] In response to these disadvantages, the Belgian cooperative released a number of updates to accelerate and streamline the algorithmic steps required by its own standard, with a new protocol called SWIFT gpi (global payment initiative), ensuring faster transactions and end-to-end transparent tracking. These improvements were also made necessary by the emergence of competing payment technologies, driven by a handful of fintech companies through which cross-border transactions have been able to partly bypass SWIFT.

The most popular of these platforms was undoubtedly Transferwise, later rebranded as Wise, a company started in London by one of the original founders of Skype at the beginning of the fintech boom in the early 2010s. Wise's intuition was to target the overseas remittance market with a solution that eluded legacy banks' systems for clearing cross-border payments. Without getting technical, a simple explanation of Wise's business model is that money sent abroad does not actually cross borders. Wise manages accounts in different currencies in each of the jurisdictions in which it operates. In this way, a sender who wants to remit money pays with local currency into a local Wise account. Once this transaction is verified, the receiving account is credited with the fee-deducted sum from another Wise account registered in the receiver's country. This is a slight oversimplification, but it gives an idea of how platforms like Wise have managed to partly bypass SWIFT's standards and its lengthy processing.[35] A foreigner living in Kenya, for example, would know that Wise is one of the quickest ways to withdraw M-Pesa from an overseas bank account. In my experience, with small enough amounts, the transaction is almost instantaneous.

The reason for dwelling on Wise's model is not just that June's start-up belonged to the same batch of companies seeking to upend legacy cross-border payment systems with "float management," but that Wise replicated another existing standard currently in use in Africa to settle payments in China and vice versa (though this is a rarer occurrence).[36] After all, Wise not only updated the peer-to-peer cross-border infrastructure pioneered by Western Union with its agent network: as a *Business Insider* journalist observed in 2015, "London's $1 billion finance startup TransferWise [operated] just like an ancient Islamic money transfer system."[37] The money transfer system in question was the hawala.

The hawala, or xawalaad, is a person-to-person value transfer system that predates modern banks by more than a thousand years. It allows long-distance transactions without money actually traveling geographically, thanks to different varieties of honor-based bonds between hawala dealers. The latter are usually small businesses or individuals who have sufficient availability of cash to operate as money agents within a kinship network. Such is the trust that the hawala does not usually include notes payable but relies exclusively on the brokers mutually honoring the obligations they accrue.

The hawala is hardly the sole informal value transfer system that exists in parallel to legacy and new, digitally enabled cross-border payment platforms, such as the one provided by Wise. The Chinese equivalent of the hawala—the *feiqian* (winged/flying money)—is, for example, a capillary international web, even capable of converting gold in one country to currency in another. Despite restrictions imposed by both Chinese and Western financial regulators, the feiqian is still a vital underground channel to remit money for low-income Chinese migrants.[38] The hawala, however, is a much more discussed system, perhaps for its purported—and often racialized—linkages to terrorist funding in the wake of 9/11.[39] The global epicenter of the hawala is in the Arab gulf states: in Africa and in Kenya in particular, Somali brokers dominate this market, even for payments directed to China.

"The trust system is quite incredible," June noted during another one of our meetings, without concealing her admiration for the hawala institution in Kenya. "And it responds to a very real need. China is still the factory of the world for African traders. Everybody buys things from there, and all these trades need to be settled somehow," she elaborated, pointing to the fact that while every other continent's financial corridors to China were saturated with solutions, from PayPal to Airwallex and Lianlian, Africa did not have any such provider. It was, she explained, a function of perceived risk: "It's not necessarily that there's a lion behind the bush, but it's a lack of knowledge about the market; when you don't have a map to navigate, every risk is automatically *high* risk." June's words echoed a long-standing trope concerning why capital—whether in the form of lending or foreign investment—does not flow into African infrastructures and financial markets as easily as in other geographies.[40] Yet June's point was also more specifically about the different shades of unknowability that are attached to money practices. Take, for example, her description of the way in which the hawala reaches China from Kenya: "The heart is Dubai. The money goes to Dubai, from Dubai it goes to Hong Kong, from Hong Kong it gets into China. I mean, there is something there that the western corridor [people] or we may not ever understand. But the Somali or the Islamic community just makes it work. And it works. It actually works very well."

Eventually, our conversation returned to the friction between different financial processes. With the tightening of the compliance environment in China and with the choking of illicit financial channels dictated by Xi during his second mandate, the hawala system, June explained, had started rubbing against the highly regulated currency requirements in the mainland: "Over the past three years, China has crushed many illegal money bureaus. And even those big guys like WeChat Pay and Alipay have been fined, so now they are quite conservative about overseas money flows."[41] As a consequence, she concluded, the risk of relying on hawala networks to settle payments in China had become too high. The bonds of trust could not ensure that faraway partners would not be hunted down.

Were bank-sanctioned payments the safest option then? Provided a person had a bank account, something not necessarily common across small traders in Kenya and in other parts of East Africa, SWIFT-enabled transactions did have the benefit of a much higher degree of certainty. At least in theory. In practice, frictions between different financial systems did not make the movement of money from Africa to China easy. On a very high level, the onshore renminbi (the CNY) is only traded in a very narrow band, often making it necessary to purchase offshore renminbi first (the CNH). This generates discrepancies in the value that is finally cleared, as well as additional difficulties because there is a compliance process to convert any tradable currency into a CNY bank account, namely, following an additional protocol to identify the nature of the transactions through a standard of the China National Advanced Payment System (CNAPS2). On a more practical level, although the SWIFT messaging system had embedded CNAPS2, June had anecdotally observed a very high rate of bounce-back in the Africa–China payment corridor.

> The basic problem with SWIFT is low efficiency and [high cost]. But then, you add the issue of errors, because of the name-surname swap in Chinese. The system is quite rigid. It doesn't really accommodate the different naming system. I can be Liu June, I can be June Liu, it depends on how I put it in Chinese. Also, you're learning Mandarin, right? You know that one pinyin word may correspond to different characters. This kind of thing also causes errors. So you wire the money, and the money disappears for weeks before it gets back to you, deducted of all the bank fees anyway.

Put differently, SWIFT standards are what the historian of science Lorraine Daston would call a "thin rule."[42] Unlike "thick rules," which are detailed, dense in specifications that make them applicable with a degree of discretion, thin rules are inflexible algorithms. They do not easily bend to accommodate use cases that depart from the norm. Conversely, the hawala system is governed by thick rules couched in the kinship bonds of the agents. A misspelled surname, for example, would not cause a payment to bounce back but probably just a WhatsApp or WeChat message between the dealers.

For June, this is where the competitive edge of Easytransfers materialized: at the interface between China's hardened compliance environment and a network of trust between banks, tech companies, and wholesalers. Designed with Chinese rather than Western standards as the basic model through which they had reverse-engineered their payment platform, Easytransfers was not just a piece of technology, but a layered, incremental lattice of partnerships. "It's never just about the tech," June quipped. "It's not like you always need to deploy the most advanced AI technology or whatever. It's more about creating partnerships, and then managing risk." How she and her three cofounders had achieved that, in a very short time, speaks to the multiple shades of Global China's capitals that interact in a city like Nairobi, and their competition, mimicry, and collaboration across practices of innovation.

MICRO-INNOVATION

After our first meeting, June and I kept bumping into each other. The reason was simple. Like many fledgling start-ups, Easytransfers did not have a fixed office. June and her team worked from one of the many coworking spaces scattered around Nairobi. Incidentally, I had bought a number of passes to the same coworking space, to get some respite from the chaos of house sharing and, admittedly, because that particular shared office was a perfect vantage point to observe the international community of techies that clustered in the city.[43] Located in a 1970s villa, fashionably dilapidated but equipped with state-of-art technology, the coworking space was surrounded by a lush garden of towering crotons and African olive trees. Under their canopy, little office pods, a cafeteria, and several shared desks dotted the grounds of the estate. It is there that I met Danny, one of June's cofounder colleagues, and learned more about the linkages between the much-discussed presence of Chinese state-owned companies in Africa and small start-ups like Easytransfers.

A Singaporean of Chinese descent, Danny had been in Kenya for only about a year. Unlike June, who had changed jobs many times before landing in the world of tech start-ups, he had come to Nairobi precisely for that reason: to invest his time and expertise in the booming African fintech industry, after a few years

FIGURE 8. A leafy coworking space in Nairobi. Photo by author.

of corporate jobs in China and elsewhere. Danny's first stint, however, had not been a success, at least immediately. He had cofounded one of the asset-financing start-ups that were seeking to tap into the boda boda industry, one of the largest informal economies in the country, offering platform-enabled pay-as-you-go and rent-to-own financing schemes to the young men who make up the bulk of this ubiquitous urban economy.[44] He soon realized that with high numbers of defaults and repossessions, this fintech sector was ridden with ethical compromises that he was not willing to make. He witnessed how in order to make a profit some of his competitors were turning into loan sharks. He immediately liquidated the company, he told me, and moved to payment technologies.

On the occasion of my first meeting with Danny, when June introduced us in the garden of our coworking office, neither of them could hide their excitement about Easytransfers. A few days earlier, the app had gone live, after a period of beta testing, and was already processing hundreds of transactions. Danny unlocked his phone and proudly showed it to me, quickly starting a fake payment. Moved by their enthusiasm, I remarked that the app looked just like Wise, meaning that it had the same smooth, easy-to-use look and feel. June smiled coyly and Danny laughed. "Yes, we copied the interface; it's a Chinese copy," he said, jokingly. The obvious reference was to the shanzhai phenomenon discussed in chapter 2 and to the fact that many Chinese software giants had cut their teeth by unapologetically emulating app solutions from elsewhere, as Lulu Chen narrates in her account of the early days of Tencent's messaging platforms.[45]

Weeks later, Danny and I discussed precisely this transition moment in the Chinese tech industry, the early 2010s, when China had shifted from being an oft-ridiculed market of knock-off phones, subpar gadgets, and copycat apps to an advanced innovator of all things digital.[46] It was around that time that Danny lived on the mainland and became interested in the ways in which, as the Singaporean *enfant prodige* venture capitalist Yinglan Tan wrote, "made in China" had become "innovated in China."[47] Not incidentally, Tan was one of Danny's inspirations, along with Kai-Fu Lee, another admired figure in the Chinese internet sector. A venture capitalist too, Lee boasted one of those almost-legendary profiles in the tech industry, having been at the helm of both Microsoft's and Google's foray into China in the late 1990s and early 2000s. Most importantly, Danny credited Lee with introducing him to the concept and practices of micro-innovation via his highly followed blog. "When I was in China in 2011, the term 'micro-innovation' was used everywhere, basically. Kai-Fu Lee was the guy who had evangelized it," he explained.

Silicon Valley evangelism is one of the cultural engines through which the making of techno-capital takes shape in other geographies.[48] Innovation mantras and managerial fads travel across continents in the form of books, how-to guides, and blogs. As immutable mobiles, these texts are cultural products that do much more than inspire fictional expectations of profit, though this is one of their fundamental functions.[49] They are technical guidelines that inductively formalize how the tech industry produces value. They define the steps and the boundaries of what constitutes innovation. One might say that the narrators of Silicon Valley capitalism are also the curators of its standards.[50] At the very least, they circulate the vocabulary and the grammar of venture capital as well as the corporate techniques that underlie it.[51] In the specific case of Danny's champions, Yinglan Tan and Kai-Fu Lee had also actively translated and repurposed the language of disruption to capture the purported uniqueness of China's digital innovation practices. It is not a coincidence that Tan's best-selling book is titled *Chinnovation* and that Lee's VC fund is called Sinovation. More specifically, as Danny elaborated, Lee's writings had inspired him to think about different registers of technological change.

As he explained, for many Westerners micro-innovation—or more broadly, the notion of "innovation with Chinese characteristics"—had been a euphemism for the often-brazen copyright infringements that had multiplied in China in both the hardware and software industries before and around 2010. If shanzhai stood for poor-quality copies of tech from elsewhere, however, it also captured the innovative potential of small, incremental changes targeted to the unique needs of a working-class network society.[52] It foregrounded the serendipitous ingenuity of customization practices, which were later enshrined in the modus operandi of companies like Transsion, as discussed in the previous chapters. More importantly for Danny, micro-innovation outlined somewhat of a practical *disposition*, a method if you will, that had implications beyond the making of duplicates. Incremental iterations belied a morality of waste avoidance, as well as the notion that things that worked needed not to be broken (or disrupted) but improved. Not incidentally, in those same years Silicon Valley was taking stock of a decade of wasteful practices that had contributed to the dotcom bust, as argued by the start-up guru Eric Ries in *The Lean Startup*.[53] The focus on waste was so prominent that the adjective *lean* was borrowed from management scholars who had described the system enacted by Taichi Ohno to minimize discards and delays in the manufacturing of cars at Toyota, from the 1950s on.[54] In China, the equivalent of the lean start-up had indeed been the fascination with micro-innovation, which dovetailed with a much broader, nationwide program of state-led mass entrepreneurialization—the mass entrepreneurship and innovation program of the fourteenth Five-Year Plan—and even framed reinvention at the level of industrial policy, through Xi-Li initiatives such as Made in China 2025.[55]

In the specific case of June and Danny, this piecemeal work of reinvention meant that Easytransfers featured a user interface whose wireframe had striking similarities to its trailblazing competitor.[56] A "Chinese copy," as Danny put it, self-effacingly. "Why waste time on something that already works?" he asked me. After all, Easytransfers did not have any employees at that time, and the four cofounders doubled in many roles to run the bootstrapped enterprise. Hiring designers to develop their own interface would have contradicted the no-waste goal of micro-innovating. But, more significantly, all their efforts had been channeled into a deliberate, carefully orchestrated prototyping and sales strategy—one that linked to different, layered shades of Global China in the African continent.

FROM STATE-OWNED COMPANIES
TO AFRICAN TRADERS

In the start-up jargon popularized by books such as Ries's *Lean Startup*, innovation processes are codified into steps that move from market research to beta testing and revolve around the release of a so-called minimum viable product, or MVP. The latter is much more than a prototype: the MVP is a functional version of a product or service, stripped of all superfluous implements except for the bare functions. Designed to act as experimental devices, MVPs gather and measure data that can be leveraged to compound information about user behavior, to gauge pricing points and revenue models, to attract investors, or even to simply recognize failed ideas. As Ries puts it, the *Lean Startup* triune rule is "build, measure, learn."[57] Unsurprisingly, June and Danny had made this language their own.

"We are in the learning phase, with a public beta of the service, " June explained, noting that the MVP served multiple purposes at once. On the one hand, the first release of the Easytransfers app coincided with the goal of testing a market hypothesis: namely, that there was, in fact, an opportunity to be seized in the Kenya–China payment corridor, starting with what they knew best: Chinese expatriates living in the country. Both June and Danny had dug into data from the Chinese embassy and discovered that on average 300,000 Chinese nationals had resided in Kenya over the past years and that even at its lowest point, during the peak of the COVID-19 pandemic, this population had only dwindled to 100,000. This was still a sizable target to test and refine their fintech product, as well as a sign that, despite a freeze in Chinese loans to the country, economic interests and connections were still lively.[58] Danny's research had also provided him with monetary quantification of this opportunity: "Currently, . . . if you look at the difference between exports and imports, Kenya imports from China two point something billions. But if you look at the Chinese government data, they say China's exports to Kenya amount to four point something billions. Then you know that there are two billion US dollars moving informally. There's our market." In response, I asked him how he thought those two billions missing from Kenyan data were being settled. "Through hawaladars [hawala brokers]," Danny replied, "or through people who say they are a fintech operation but behind the scenes use hawala traders." He was undoubtedly referring to his competitors, but I decided not to probe his statements and ask him more about how they envisioned their market.

As discussed in chapter 2, market segmentation, or the accurate division of customers into subsets with similar characteristics, was something that larger Chinese tech firms operating in Kenya had perfected to a great degree of finesse. A deeply attentive observer, Danny had not missed this, and he had given a lot of thought to how as a product manager with limited resources he could replicate the same level of accuracy. Despite being a Singaporean national, he had spent the previous months rubbing shoulders with members of the mainland Chinese community in the country and trying to understand their sociological layers and contours. He had observed what he called three "leagues of entrepreneurialism." At the top were the "big guys," "doing large-scale stuff, big factories, big FMCG, big construction companies." In this league, both state-owned companies and private players were active across what C. K. Lee has called different "varieties of capital."[59] These were the "big bosses," managers and business owners quietly making money and amassing fortunes in their overseas endeavors. They were the wealthy surface of Global China. They were also a shifting demographic group: one year they may have been in Kenya, another in DR Congo, and another back in China.

Below them, a much less mobile group of Chinese people were deeply embedded in the Kenyan economy. "It's another league, a middle layer. They are the ones who provide business outsourcing, they help import Chinese stuff for all the big firms, they handle all the local stuff for the big companies, and work in their value chains." He noted further that big Chinese corporations relied on this middle layer for their knowledge of Kenyan politics and regulations, for their local networks, and, even more pragmatically, to simply save costs when subcontracting business services. Finally, "at the very bottom," Danny continued, "are those who work for all these people. And they are also always trying to do something; they are always exploring. If you look at all these businesses in Chinatown, a lot of the owners used to be from ZTE, Huawei, etc. They came here as the bottom league. And then they partnered among themselves, they started a small shop. And then a small shop became a big shop and then a big shop became five shops, and then it became a whole street." What Danny described as the "bottom league" of Chinese nationals in Kenya encompassed both the current employees of larger companies and those entrepreneurial former staff who had left to start their own restaurants, shops, and other small businesses. These renegades were, according to what June had told me a few weeks earlier, the target of Easytransfers' MVP.

To explain this bottom layer, June listed a number of use cases they had developed through market research: somebody sending money to their Chinese savings bank account to pay their mortgage or student debt; somebody with relatives living or studying in China; or small business owners or private customers buying something on a very small scale, for instance, on an Instagram shop. "All in all, anyone buying a bit of something here and there from China," she explained. Put simply, they had started with remittances. Not only was this sphere of offshore payments immediately familiar to their experience as expatriates, but small peer-to-peer remittances also fell under a leaner Know Your Customer (KYC) compliance system. "China has a specific program for . . . what do we call it? *Geren waihui* [personal foreign exchange] through which everyone has a quota of US$50,000 that can be easily settled as forex [foreign exchange]," June told me.

Bigger payments implied a more complex due diligence system. In any event, for heftier payments, banks were much more willing to facilitate cross-border operations. "We are not competing with the banks; we are using them," she said, adding that they had partnered with UnionPay, the state-owned financial corporation that owns the largest card scheme in mainland China, as well as a forex licence to settle CNY under the authority of the People's Bank of China. This contract entailed a form of dependence on the Chinese state, but June saw it as a strategic maneuver to carve out a space of legitimacy. As a result of the partnership, Easytransfers had automated and modeled its KYC requirements on UnionPay's own standards, which in turn had been developed according to the Chinese regulatory framework for foreign exchange. June and her team had created a prototype MVP using the highly modulated compliance environment of mainland China rather than legal loopholes and regulatory voids, a common practice across fintech start-ups globally.[60] This was a function of their partnership-based strategy, Danny elaborated, but not the only one.

After peer-to-peer payments, which fell under the less risky category of remittance payments, Easytransfers was planning a suite of additional products, most importantly, a B2B payment option, foreign payments into digital wallets such as WeChat Pay and Alipay, and mass payouts, a product that would allow companies to pay multiple recipients at once, automatically. The latter obviously catered to the needs of Chinese companies operating in Kenya, for example, contractors on infrastructure projects.[61] Registered as Kenyan companies, the overseas units of large construction state-owned enterprises (SOEs) in China, for example, pay part of the salary of their Chinese employees into mainland bank accounts. Although these companies mostly employed Kenyan workers, Danny's research had revealed the significance of the Chinese workforce as a potential target market. For Easytransfers, working with SOEs was another low-risk partnership: as highly controlled environments, state companies would force them to design their service in a scrupulous manner. It was also easy to verify the legitimacy of an international transfer. "It's like salary processing," June explained. "You go to the company, one of the contracting companies, they have x amount of workers. Say, this company is building the new airport in Kampala, okay? This you can verify. It's a big project, they need three hundred Chinese workers. All this you can verify. They are doing the work. And then you can even estimate the range of how these workers—the reasonable amount that these people are able to send home, if they are also remitting money." Chinese SOEs in Kenya and in Africa more broadly were a test bed for Easytransfers products in that they made it possible to quantify market size as well as manage risk through accurate data, across salary payments and remittances. "It's very precise," June concluded. "We can cross-verify things and make sure all transactions are genuine."

As for B2B payments, this was a much riskier and more complicated fintech product. Compared to the Chinese diaspora (peer-to-peer remittances) and to Chinese companies (salary processing), traders of Chinese commodities constituted a lesser known and slippery market. "Especially the small guys, how do you verify that their payment is authentic? That the trade is real?" June asked, in a tone that was both rhetorical and genuine. This was as much of a problem on the Kenyan side as it was a lack of trustworthiness on the Chinese side. Danny explained that many agents working in Chinese ports were "crooks." They would not respect the specifications of an order. They would sell suboptimal versions of what had been requested, neglect promised deadlines, disappear with the money, and so forth. To understand these circumstances, June had turned herself into an amateur ethnographer. Around the time I first met her, she had recently immersed herself in Luthuli Avenue in downtown Nairobi, spending days among Kenyan small shop owners to understand the difficulties they faced when trying to buy commodities from China and settling the related payments using the hawala system. She had been on the phone with their agents and observed how small their average transactions were. She had helped them submit orders and settle forex.

Her research revealed that Kenyan traders of Chinese tech usually held very little stock in their stores. This was not just a consequence of the dearth of space, but of their very low margins. "They're trying to be as liquid as possible," June had noted. Merchants would order stock every week to keep transactions small because their availability of cash was limited and fluctuating. This was an opportunity for Easytransfers. Then again, as both Danny and June kept saying, the bigger the transaction, the more willing banks were to help. And bigger transactions were also riskier for a start-up that was just cutting its teeth on cross-border payments. Focusing on small deals, however, was arguably not the most relevant part of their marketization strategy. In fact, the trust-based network of the hawala system had something to teach Easytransfers. What if, they thought, they could build a list of Easystranfers-trusted agents in China, merchants they had vetted to ensure they were legitimate and solid business partners? What if the Easytransfers app included a list of these reliable brokers and dealers with whom Kenyan traders could interact without the risk of being ghosted or defrauded? These were the questions that June and her team were busy answering with the upcoming iteration of their MVP, at the time of our first meeting. And for this strategy, she argued, she had learned a lot from embedding herself with Kenyan merchants but also from observing how M-Pesa had become so successful: "M-Pesa started small, they realized it's always the small fish that struggle to send money. In their case, it was urban migrants sending small payments to their relatives in the countryside. In our case, it's Kenyan traders who have little cash to fill their inventory."

For his part, Danny, who of the two was the more ambitious and determined to speculate on the future of Africa–China financial channels, was also entertaining bigger plans for Easytransfers. In the long run, as a Kenyan banker told me during an interview in fall 2022, payments were never the end goal of fintech business models. Payments, especially if start-ups were competing with legacy institutions, had tiny profit margins. To stay competitive, fintech platforms needed to offer fees that were barely sufficient to cover the fixed costs of their operations. So the gains were in the data, in the ever-growing amounts of transactional data that were beholden to the facilitation of money flows. If, as the anthropologist Bill Maurer has written, payments exist as an infrastructure that is perpendicular to money, so too must they produce information that is perpendicular to the use of money.[62] They build financial profiles for individuals and businesses. And in turn these profiles can be risk profiles; they can be leveraged by fintech companies to offer more profitable financial services, such as credit and insurance. In the case of Easytransfers, Danny explained, this might consist in business credit to traders, provided by a third-party (micro)credit institution: "And why would this be appealing? With credit, if you are a business, you can increase the stock you can buy. Research shows that this leads to a 3 to 5 percent increase in your revenue. But credit for Kenyan traders is prohibitive. Kenya's minimum interest rate is 13 percent, because of forex hedging, compared to a 6 percent I would get in Singapore. And if we, as Easytransfers, mediate this loan, we can negotiate a better interest rate for businesses here, because we have data about their risk profiles based on their transactions."

This was, at once, a pipedream and a carefully calculated project. It mirrored the business model of many start-ups that were tapping into the business of restocking and inventory management of small businesses and informal traders, including some of Kenya's up-and-coming unicorns, data companies that merged last-mile logistics with financial services. But while these companies were operating within national borders, Danny imagined these same operations on a much larger scale, across continents and currencies.

BOMBASTIC COMPETITORS

On a crisp morning in June 2022, an off-putting meme spread across the Twitter and WhatsApp sphere of Nairobi's tech community. The image featured June and her husband in a doctored police mug shot. "Wanted," the caption read, portraying the two of them as financial criminals. A few days later over coffee, Danny told me that he had no doubt that their competitors at Mamapay, June's former employer, were behind the meme. And that anti-Chinese sentiment went in waves. At times it intensified, and we were in the middle of a tall wave, perhaps owing to a BBC investigative documentary titled *Racism for Sale*.[63] From my fieldnotes I cannot discern whether the documentary preceded the meme or came right after it, but I remember that both happened in a short span of time, and all of a sudden uncomfortable conversations about racism—both anti-African racism and sinophobia—multiplied around me.

Surrounded by these conversations, my research colleague Jack and I met with Annie, Mamapay's chief financial officer (CFO). With a master's degree in finance and accounting, Annie was deeply knowledgeable about the nuances of China–Africa payment channels and the different regulatory hurdles that fintech start-ups were facing, but she was also an acute observer of how perceptions of China and the Chinese presence in Kenya had evolved and continued to shift, often in very sudden ways. Overall, she noted, the meanings of Chineseness in Kenya oscillated—President Kibaki's "Look East" strategy of the mid-2000s was an example of a swift geopolitical realignment—but always eventually returned to one key factor: "the notion that if you get something from China, you cannot get it at a better rate anywhere else."[64]

"I think," Annie continued, "they've tried to curve all African minds to think China is the hub of everything you can get. And by doing that, you have a lot of traders now partnering with China so that at least they can get goods and sell them in our local markets. You never hear us talking about America or the US or any other country. It's always about China." Her words echoed many of the conversations that inform this book, especially those about the affordability of Chinese hardware. As we have seen in chapter 2, many people identified the success of Chinese goods in Kenya not just as a function of their affordability but also as a function of a broader understanding that affordability was not a one-size-fits-all strategy. "Curving" Kenyan minds, after all, had been about making less expensive stuff but also about creating the logistical and marketing channels that would allow less expensive stuff to reach consumers. This was a story of commerce and ingenuity, of Kenyan traders and overseas agents, of Chinese FMCGs and their increasingly capillary distribution networks. But as June from Easytransfers had noted and Annie from Mamapay confirmed, despite the growth in trade, the available payment corridors between Kenya and China were either illegal or cumbersome. In any case, they were unjustifiably expensive and slow. Having worked in the digital financial sector for a decade or so, including for important Chinese fintech operations in the continent, the Kariuki brothers had noticed this gap and had started Mamapay as a cross-border digital payment start-up around 2019. Annie had joined a few months later, as their CFO.

Unlike June's team, with their quiet demeanor and discreet manners, the Kariuki brothers were not just vocal and well-known members of Nairobi's tech community, but celebrities in their own right. Allegations of assault, public brawls, marriages to television personalities, and highly mediatized divorces make it really hard to use pseudonyms for them. I even considered removing the Mamapay case from this chapter but decided that it offered important insights into the contested micropolitics of standards and their making. In fact, as June herself had observed, while Easytransfers was proceeding in small, incremental steps—feeling the stones—Mamapay's cofounders were exuberantly cutting corners and often making the headlines for their rowdy behavior. Then again, they embodied two different entrepreneurial ethe. Suave and well dressed, the Kariuki brothers personified another way of experimenting with payment standards and building connections with the Chinese financial and corporate ecosystems. Whether accurate or not, it is not surprising that Danny suspected they were the instigators of the distasteful mug shot portraying June and her husband as criminals.

At the time of our conversation with Annie, who proudly told us about the complexity of being the CFO of a start-up operating in multiple financial jurisdictions, Mamapay was already a booming fintech platform company, offering several services, including API integrations, virtual wallets, and global payments products for individuals and businesses. Headquartered in Singapore and only secondarily in Kenya, Mamapay had benefited from an important move of the island state: in mid-2019, the Monetary Authority of Singapore (MAS) had signed an agreement with the Central Bank of Kenya (CBK) for the development of basic digital infrastructure and KYC protocols based on a common set of standards between the two countries. After all, Singapore was already an important financial partner of many African nations, and many local entrepreneurs saw Singapore as a regulatory stopgap to accessing bigger Asian markets.

On the other hand, setting up shop in Singapore, and partnering with MAS-licensed payment system providers, had allowed Mamapay to start transacting without the burden of first formalizing its own licenses. Eventually, the company had applied for licenses in Singapore with MAS, in Kenya with CBK, and in other jurisdictions like Uganda and Nigeria. In time, Annie explained, owning its own licenses would expedite the so-called TAT (turn-around time) of Mamapay's cross-border transactions, one of the key performance indicators of a successful fintech business. This had been possible thanks to a hefty pre-seed venture capital ticket from a group of Chinese and Japanese investors, a one-of-its kind financial bet that underscored both the belief in Mamapay's promise to create a one-stop payment platform for Asia-Africa transactions and the staggering monetary value that venture capitalists attributed to this promise. Investing early-stage money in compliance, a fintech expert had told me in an earlier interview, was rare. It only happened for very promising start-ups.

Mamapay had been using Singapore's strange financial geography—its deliberate positioning at the crossroads of East and West—to trial cross-border payment options much beyond Kenya and China and to create proof that this market was valuable for high-risk capital. Their operations already included other East Asian countries like Vietnam, seen as an alternative manufacturing hub for cheap products, and other African countries, like Uganda. Mamapay had also become one of the first African companies to go live on the Tencent Remittance Services platform, WeRemit, allowing payments to WeChat-linked accounts across Asia. Annie also mentioned that a partnership with Alibaba's payment wallet Alipay too was in the making.

As opposed to Easystranfers' prudent, incremental approach, Mamapay had started big, navigating in legal gray areas and deploying a multipronged strategy that intersected the many authorized payment-service providers that already had links with and within Asia. Instead of focusing on a few, carefully orchestrated moves and partners, the Kariuki brothers had built their success on a gargantuan plan. This "creative" way of dealing with licensing had horrified June during her brief stint in the company and convinced her to move along a different path. Even so, Mamapay eventually managed to become registered as a payment service in many jurisdictions, demonstrating that its plucky experimentalism yielded results. As Annie explained, after only a couple of years of operations, the suite of services was already very diversified.

> What we came to do is to make traders more confident and appreciate the use of digital payment systems. We've had some quite good caliber of people. Like Chinese companies that operate in Kenya paying their salaries back home, because, apparently, they're required by the government to pay I think 70 percent of their wages in Kenya back to their home country. We do a lot of mass payments. . . . So salaries, we call them "mass payments." And we also have businesses that are paying each other. We have customers who are paying businesses. And then we have P2P, like a peer just paying another peer, what falls into the remittance category.

At the time of our conversation, Mamapay had other financial products waiting in the wings of its future algorithmic iterations: the incorporation of cryptocurrencies, the development of a remittance investment option, and a trusted merchant platform (in the same way as Easytransfers). Overall, Annie observed, all these experiments would not have been possible anywhere but in Nairobi. Remittances to Kenya were at an all-time high, after a decade-long steady growth. Consumer spending had also been slowly expanding, at least up to that moment. And as one of Africa's financial capitals, Nairobi already hosted many key players: in turn, these had brought expertise and additional capital. It was easy to fund-raise and find the right people to hire. M-Pesa too, despite the monopolistic practices of Safaricom, had generated a proliferating number of small-scale experiments with payment infrastructures. In this context, the Kenyan government had been at once an attentive champion of fintech (e.g., streamlining complex CBK compliance procedures) and a deliberately permissive watchdog, only catching up with regulations in extreme cases, like the predatory lending wallets described in chapter 3. Several start-ups already handled cryptocurrencies, bypassing extant legal voids. The city was ripe for a bombastic fintech company like Mamapay.

Despite June and Danny's doubtfulness, I do not have reason to believe that Mamapay's activities were just a smokescreen. Behind the hype and the fanfare, Mamapay was a solid yet inventive project of reimagining cross-border payment standards between Asia and Africa. And Nairobi had been the right test bed for this project for reasons that speak directly to the city being an interface for China's overseas techno-capital. For example, one of the first believers and champions of Mamapay was Victor, the cofounder and managing partner of Transsion's VC arm and acceleration program, Future Hub (we will reencounter him in the next chapter). Having raised liquidity through a successful IPO, Transsion had diversified its software operations, separating its internal software division from riskier investments in start-ups like Mamapay. Through Future Hub, whose activities mainly emanated from Lagos and Nairobi, the Kariuki brothers had obtained early-stage financial support but also accessed a network of Chinese investors and venture capitalists. Their first angels had indeed been from China. And later on, as Annie told us, this had proven to be fundamental in further rounds of investments, given the relationship-based system on which Chinese VCs operated. "They only trust their lineage," Annie remarked.

Cash from these investors had in part gone to compliance, as we have seen so far, but also to the technology of Mamapay itself. Annie explained that even before obtaining its own licenses, at the stage of partnering with other licensed operators, the latter required a strong and trustworthy software backend. A solid technical infrastructure was also necessary to apply for the authorizations from central banks. Fintech start-ups need to demonstrate their capacity to handle personal data, their ability to parse suspicious transactions, and their resilience to cyber incidents, whether internal failures or attacks. To build this backend infrastructure, the Kariuki brothers had partnered with none other than Huawei. In Kenya, the Shenzhen company had already worked with Safaricom to build the highly secure data infrastructure of M-Pesa. For Mamapay, Huawei was tasked with creating something similar: a reliable, scalable, security-certified platform, capable of addressing the often patchy electric and internet networks in Kenya (and especially in other African countries), and trustworthy enough for the financial industry at large. This had entailed buying one of Huawei's extensive cloud products and annexed AI services. In turn, these optimizations had enabled Mamapay, for example, to automatically flag so-called PEP transactions. PEPs are politically exposed persons, whose transactions are at a higher risk of bribery and laundering than those of ordinary citizens. Personal details about PEPs are contained in large data sets compiled from various sources: hence, automated PEP screening at once derisks a company's operations and facilitates due diligence.

The partnership with Huawei, on the one hand, foregrounds the importance of Global China's corporate geographies for incipient start-ups like Mamapay. During our meeting, for example, Annie observed that choosing Huawei had been a no-brainer. Not only was their infrastructural presence in Kenya, including their localized customer service office, a safe bet, but Huawei's connections with the rest of Asia perfectly matched the Kariuki brothers' ambitions. Yet Mamapay's broader attempt at creating a Nairobi-based digital hub for Africa–Asia transactions, a platform independent from existing, Western-centric cross-border payment systems, also speaks to the positioning of the city as a test bed of the shifting microgeopolitics of technical standards. Of course, ISO 20022 and the power of SWIFT still loomed large, even across financial experiments that explicitly looked East instead of West. It would equally be a mistake to neglect the enduring power of the US dollar,[65] particularly in a region that is so close to the Arab gulf states. Yet if we look at the wishful speculations that animated Mamapay's founders, we also catch a glimpse of how they articulated an economy hope that explicitly linked new financial products to "a new chapter of African history," as Kevin Donovan and Chris Mizes write with regard to African financiers and fiscal experts more broadly.[66]

Attesting to these ambitions, one of the Mamapay founders wrote a lengthy essay that I clipped a few months before meeting Annie, in June 2022. The essay argued, overall, that Kenya was ready to move beyond mobile money. M-Pesa and its successful switch from a USSD-enabled offline service to a more sophisticated online financial ecosystem attested to a long future ahead for mobile money, but now the time was right to imagine a bigger transition to a more financially independent Kenya and to *undollarizing* Africa. Homegrown payment gateways, he went on to write, had a big role to play in this vision of financial emancipation. Bypassing legacy channels, steeped in high costs and idiosyncratic inefficiencies, meant possibly rechanneling these marginal gains into more productive investments, for example, government-owned, mobile money–enabled diaspora bonds that could go into infrastructure development and other forms of industrial policy, the essay agued. Perhaps a pipedream. And yet one in which new, tentative standards for cross-border money flows between

Asia and Africa were framed as microgeopolitical moves toward a financially emancipated continent.

A MORE DEMOCRATIC TECHNO-CAPITAL?

The cross-border payment protocols addressed in this chapter are hardly the sole technical standards that are being challenged, manipulated, and interfered with from Nairobi. In an increasingly multipolar and turbulent technological present, fintech start-ups like Easytransfers and Mamapay seek to reimagine the rules for transacting money between Asia and Africa by decentering the vantage point that usually informs global financial systems. They use their resources—personal knowledge, business networks, financial capital, meticulous market research—to invest in the forms of payments.[67] They aim to rethink the bottlenecks of money flows that generate inefficiencies for low-end economic actors, whether these are Chinese economic migrants or small Kenyan traders. These inefficiencies are often the function of large geopolitical alignments that cannot be addressed at their true scale, but only through pragmatic, run-of-the-mill technical fixes. Hence, these tech pilots are small, microgeopolitical moves. Still, they offer a clear, practical example of how Nairobi functions as an experimental ground for testing new technological configurations that are less and less about Silicon Valley or Wall Street, or ISO standards, and more and more about the unique economic fabric that enmeshes Kenyan street vendors, Singaporean financiers, Chinese manufactures, Beijing's state capital, and the multiple regulatory environments that exist along the money corridors of these new geographies of relations.

At the heart of these efforts, however, remained a deep contradiction. On the one hand, Easytransfers and Mamapay promised a more democratic world of finance. Even a less US dollar–dependent Africa, as one of the Kariuki brothers wrote. New payment technologies pledged to reduce costs and make international transactions more efficient for those who lacked the support of legacy financial institutions and needed to resort to risky, illegal money bureaus. In fact, the very design of these algorithmic platforms and their standards had started from the two ends of the "globalization from below" that punctuate China's global value chains in Africa.[68] In the previous pages, I recounted how June and Danny were so committed to this goal that they themselves had become ethnographers of these low-end markets in order to understand the nuances of international payments. But while promising more horizontal, accessible rules for sending money between Asia and Africa, they still needed to comply with the Chinese state-mandated regulations and also sought to become the obligatory gateways of these new financial corridors.[69] In doing so, the creators of Easytransfers and Mamapay imagined a plethora of additional ways of monetizing payment standards as proprietary data dragnets, from offering credit to creating trusted marketplaces.[70] In other words, the microgeopolitics of payments that this chapter has explored reveal one of the tensions inherent in the optimistically more democratic techno-capital imagined by June, Danny, Annie, the Kariuki brothers, and others. Undoubtedly, they all were confident that these new standards would benefit Kenyans (and African economic actors) at large. But as disruptive as their technological proposals were, their premise remained couched in the same aspirations of enclosure and accumulation that characterized the legacy systems they sought to disrupt.

Labors of Investability

I ♥ NBO

During the early rainy season of 2022, I found myself at a small welcome party on the rooftop of a popular game-night bar. The gathering had been organized by June to greet the recent arrival of a new addition to the Kenya–China community of techies and start-up folks. A former executive at Alibaba, our Chinese guest had been recruited by a local fintech company after receiving a significant venture capital ticket (investment) to expand its operations into other African countries. Unsurprisingly, a couple of the most well-known entrepreneurs of the Silicon Savannah had shown up. The occasion, despite the low-key vibes and the quiet chitchat, felt momentous: a Chinese person, not a North American manager, had been hired by an ambitious Kenyan start-up with cash to pour into their growth strategy. Was the Silicon Savannah also changing in the realm of capital investments, traditionally dominated by Western funds, experts, and expats?[1] Meanwhile, in the background of the party, across the glistening skyline of Nairobi's Westlands, a light projection over the tall facade of the recently completed Global Trade Center read in bold characters: I ♥ NBO.

I love Nairobi. Such a statement of love and belonging obviously pertained to the broader marketing of Nairobi as a place to be—and invest—in Africa. Large speculations in real estate, like the towering complex of the new Global Trade Center, required that kind of affective promotion. Word on the street was that sales of the new apartments, catering to high-income investors, had been slow. The developer, a Chinese state-owned company, had waged a high-rolling bet on that mixed-use development, poised to host important companies, a luxury hotel chain, and a high-end mall. Yet "I ♥ NBO" was more than real estate branding. By

FIGURE 9. The Global Trade Centre in Westlands. Photo by author.

then, I realized that a stated love for Nairobi was common among my interlocutors. And that gatherings like the small party organized by June were an inextricable part of the manufacturing of this sense of belonging to a city that could be just as loveless and harsh as hopeful and welcoming. "People call it *Nairobbery*, but really [this city] stole my heart the moment I got here," I had once been told. And I do not doubt that these feelings were genuine. Still, the making of this love Nairobi trope, whether by chance or by design, was an integral part of what had rendered the Silicon Savannah *investable*.[2] This was as true for Western expats and capital as it was for the networks of Chinese investors and entrepreneurs who were my interlocutors.[3]

This chapter rests on the argument that making the Silicon Savannah possible as a terrain of technology investments from China required laborious practices

that would collectivize risk and construct a shared grammar of innovation specify-
ing the features and the qualities of Chinese techno-capital. These projects framed
Nairobi as a natural test bed for challenging the preponderance of Silicon Valley
capital as well as its modes of operation. I would often ask my contacts a less suc-
cint version of the question, "Why Nairobi?" After all, there were other English-
speaking innovation capitals in the continent. Cape Town, for example, offered a
mature, well-infrastructured innovation ecosystem, as well as sandy beaches and
an arguably cheaper expat lifestyle.[4] Lagos, on the other hand, had not only already
produced billion-dollar-valued tech companies, like Flutterwave, Andela, and Pay-
stack, but it was also the baricenter of a much bigger domestic market than Kenya.
With more than 200 million people, wouldn't Nigeria be a more obvious choice for
a fledgling start-up or for a venture capital fund seeking to monetize fast-growth
rates? It was the founder of a venture capital firm, Victor, who pointed that out to
me. "It looks like a contradiction," he explained, "Nigeria has a huge market, so
in that sense it is more similar to China. And tech stuff goes viral in Nigeria way
quicker than in Kenya. It would be natural to start off in Lagos." "But not really," he
said with a smile. "Nairobi—my impression is that it's very convenient, right? I feel
comfortable when I live in Nairobi. It's highly international. Statistically, Kenya
is relatively smaller than Nigeria, so it's a good place to try something on a small
scale. But when it comes to massive adoption or growth, then we need some other
choices." True to this belief, Victor's investment model—to which I return later in
this chapter—focused on very small seed investments for minimal equity stakes.
And while his VC fund was pan-African, Nairobi was the perfect environment to
try out digital platforms (the vertical focus of his VC) at a small scale.

Other responses to the question of why Nairobi's Silicon Savannah was attractive to both expatriate entrepreneurs and international investors ranged across
different domains. Those who had a deeper understanding of Kenya's trajectory
referred to the story I recounted in chapter 1: the experiments of a pragmatic—if
not always successful—investor state had enacted industrial policies and supply-
side investments conducive to a good innovation landscape. From fast internet
access to an already existing and incredibly pervasive financial infrastructure like
M-Pesa, helpful fiscal policies, and streamlined red tape for business registration,
successive governments had gradually built the institutional and physical scaffold
for start-ups to conduct their early-stage experiments. State regulators were so
keen to engineer a favorable environment that they had recently launched a number of regulatory sandboxes, dedicated licensing pathways for companies spear-
heading products that did not neatly fit the existing by-laws of specific authorities.
The Capital Market Authority (CMA) and the Central Bank of Kenya, for example,
had opened dedicated sandboxes for fintech businesses. This had allowed entrepreneurs with disruptive ideas in the realm of finance to enter preliminary talks
with regulators so as to avoid noncompliance and, at the same time, put eventual
investors at ease. The CBK-forced shutdown of dozens of lending platforms with a

stroke of the pen in 2022 (or, rather, with a Google Play ban) had been a warning to investors.

Others, like Victor, pointed to the quality of life in the city: Nairobi was the bars and pricey restaurants of a decadent nightlife—"a shot of whiskey," had written the novelist Wainaina in one of his essays.[5] Kenya's capital was also its verdant forests, the beautiful parks, the leafy suburbs dotted by mansions with stained-glass windows, the safe cul-de-sacs of a garden city designed for settlers to avoid the "natives."[6] Echoing the colonial portrayal of Nairobi as "the green city under the sun," this narrative was not uncommon. Once a settlers' tale of belonging, the "green city" trope had become folklore among international visitors and residents. In fact, start-up folks and digital nomads were not the first expatriates to have found a perhaps temporary home in the green city: since the establishment of Africa's UN headquarters in the late 1990s and of the UNEP and UNHabitat's main global offices, the city teemed with international "experts." Given the relative stability of Kenya compared to neighboring nations, other developmental organizations also operated from (or had recently relocated to) Nairobi. Humanitarian networks of aid workers—a "legion of NGOisms," as Joyce Nyairo ironically termed them—had become a common sight in the Kenyan capital's democratic era.[7]

Of course, these lush spaces of safety for international expats and middle-class Nairobians are ultimately zones of exception and expulsion for other Kenyans, quite literally, as they are constantly searched and frisked at every gate.[8] The green city isn't available to most, and to those who are able to access it, it can easily conceal the strident, ruinous reality of life where the majority lives.[9] Yet for some the green city trope was also a necessity. One of my interlocutors, for example, told me that the safety and ease of Nairobi wasn't really a choice for a young woman like her: "Nairobi has lots of nice things to do, but I keep hearing from Chinese women in Nigeria how harsh life is. Nairobi is, um, pretty much very inclusive in that sense." Her name was Yi, and she had been involved in the project of making the Silicon Savannah more inclusive and therefore "investable" by people like her.

Finally, when asked about their journeys, a few of the international entrepreneurs who shared their stories with me simply claimed they had come to Nairobi because of its reputation as a cradle of digital innovation for the African continent. It was a self-fulfilling prophecy: they were in Nairobi because others like them had come before. The Silicon Savannah was a terrain of founders and followers. These were not just foreigners, obviously. Kenyans too, whether local or from the diaspora, populated these expansive networks of relationships and circulations. As explained by AnnaLee Saxenian in her work on the globalization of technology workforces emanating from Silicon Valley, network effects are crucial to the making of what I've called Silicon Elsewheres.[10] These economies of scale are a function of seemingly quantitative facts—like the number of international start-ups or the value of certain investment cycles—but also of the narration thereof.[11] The riskier and more speculative the enterprise, the more an "economy of appearance" needs to be conjured for investments to take place, as the anthropologist Anna Tsing has explained.[12] In Nairobi, these performances would happen daily: from one incubator to another, from VC conventions to investor roundtables, rooftop parties and blockchain workshops, anecdotes of success, failure, deft risk-taking, and skillful deleveraging swirled around the city. At heart, the Silicon Savannah was a tale of investability too.[13]

If these were the generic features of the Silicon Savannah discourse, the stories I heard from my Chinese contacts were similar. After all, Chinese start-ups relied on the same internet infrastructure and the same legal processes as their Western counterparts. They too piloted new digital products using M-Pesa as a spring-board. And they too, like Victor, enjoyed the perks of the green city—the mild weather, the quiet forests, and the glossy bars. Often, it was difficult to pinpoint the Chineseness of these nascent digital companies. June's Easytransfers and Chao's Fastlee are good examples of this: both had local cofounders, both blended different sources of international finance, and both readapted and recombined technical scripts from China with technical matters learned in Nairobi. Their Chineseness, if anything, was in the personal and technological ties to Global China. In fact, the most relevant variation in the "why Nairobi" answer, compared to other expatriates, was precisely the reference to other players of China's going-out capital. Aaron, a manager at a venture capital fund, put it this way: "I think that due to a number of larger infrastructure projects, Kenya sits in the overall One Belt One Road plan. As a consequence, the comfort levels and understanding levels of Kenya are pretty high in many Chinese circles. And . . . that might be driving a lot of the activity as well. Obviously, from the telecom angle, you know, Huawei is doing a lot of business in Kenya. The action around early-stage tech is led by these larger corporations and infrastructures, raising the level of awareness and comfort for Chinese entrepreneurs toward Kenya."

For some of my other contacts, in addition to the general recognition generated by Belt and Road projects, Kenya was known in the Chinese tech scene because of George Zhu's story. Having founded Tecno and other affordable phone brands, as discussed in chapter 2, Zhu's well-rehearsed myth of ascendancy demonstrated that it was possible to build an empire by using Nairobi as a testing ground for an Africa-tailored and China-inspired digital economy. "George Zhu was a trailblazer of this," explained Victor. "He showed that Chinese technology [could be] not just sold, but reinvented in Africa."

More generally, several of my interlocutors had staked their hopes on the possibility of arbitraging the Chinese digital economy in a context, Kenya, that resembled that of China a few years earlier. Whether a piece of hardware or a software platform, did Chinese start-ups and investors have an edge over their Silicon Valley competitors? Was there something true and practical about Global China's narrative of South–South cooperation? Or about China's and Kenya's purported temporally displaced similarities? Aihan, a VC analyst at Transsion's investment fund, believed so, arguing that "[Chinese] capital would come not only with the money, but also the similar experiences and lack of infrastructure and how that require[d] very specific kinds of interventions."

As Aihan also acknowledged, it was impossible to separate the Silicon Savannah of Nairobi from Western investments and influences. However, she and others would argue that digital Global China, while inextricable from the broader flows of techno-capital dominated by Silicon Valley, could trace a different and more successfully transformative digital economy for Kenya.[14] A Silicon Savannah with Chinese characteristics, perhaps.

Or so the stories went. Yet, however compelling, these tales should not be naturalized. Even the green city trope was not just the result of geographic luck, as we know from the history of a settlement whose location mapped onto the needs of a colonial railway.[15] The quality of life in Nairobi, the tales of local success, the narrative of South–South mutual understanding—all required deliberate, painstaking performances and shared practices of risk management. I call these "labors of investability" to underscore how the making of the Silicon Savannah into a terrain of experimentation and investment for digital Global China was not a serendipitous circumstance but the result of purposeful calculations. The remainder of this chapter describes two forms of these labors: the creation of entrepreneurial solidarity networks and the manufacturing of VC pipelines designed to ease and derisk the flow of capital between China and Kenya. These investment-related practices are another "moment of capital," to borrow from C. K. Lee, where we witness not only difference across variety but also the production of difference itself as a mechanism of investability.[16]

These labors of investability run parallel to the work that happened at the behest of the state. Making the Silicon Savannah investable was also and fundamentally a project of the Kenyan government and a policy of going-out China seeking new markets for its ICT industry. The private sector practices that shape the digital economy go hand in hand with different matters of statecraft. Moreover, as several scholars of neoliberalism have argued, the fabrication of entrepreneurialism has also been a calculated attempt to download collective economic development responsibilities to individual subjects—often poor people in the Global South.[17] This work has been shared by global development finance institutions, the World Bank and the like, as much as by leaders and bureaucracies in many African countries. In this context, as the anthropologists Catherine Dolan and Dinah Rajak explain, the entrepreneur has become "both beneficiary and catalyst, producer and product" of a new economy of development premised on individual empowerment.[18] Lin Zhang makes a similar point about contemporary China, where aspirational entrepreneurialism promises to address the contradictions of an increasingly less redistributive state.[19] These patterns of individualism are undeniable. Still, the interface of digital Global China and the Silicon Savannah was punctuated by uncertainties and hopes that also required the intervention of collective—rather than individualized—kinds of labor, labor that created mutual forms of care, made risk manageable, and produced shared, distributed cultures of innovation.[20] Hence, together with the "passionate work" that defines individual participation in these volatile economies of innovation, the Silicon Savannah project reverbated with more molecular and collective labors of investability.[21] It is to some of these that I turn now.

ENTREPRENEURIAL SOLIDARITIES

I first met Yi at a café that was popular with digital nomads, international journalists, local artists, and tech workers. It was a good place to write, I was told. Generous wooden tables also allowed small teams to meet and collaborate in the back of the venue, which sometimes turned into an open-air theater for art-house screenings. With its funky furniture and large pots full of thriving succulents, the café was the perfect specimen of establishments that contributed to the reputation of the Silicon Savannah as a soft, sometimes indulgent, landing pad for international entrepreneurs. At sunset, laptops folded away and Afrobeats music in the background, the rooftop would turn into one of those socializing spaces where tech workers hang out after hours, building networks, hopes, and sometimes mutual enmity.[22]

Yi's journey had been, to some extent, similar to those of others whom I had met before. A haigui—sea turtle returnee—to China after college in the United States, she had been sucked into Beijing's tech scene, working for various start-ups at different stages of their endeavors. At once exhilarating and unforgiving, the start-up ecosystem in Beijing had given her the opportunity to meet a few entrepreneurs from Africa.[23] Some had come on government scholarships to study for technical degrees; others were simply there "to learn what China could teach them about innovation," she told me.

> That lasted for about two years. I was doing this parallel discovery of China's tech scene and African connections. And I think in 2019, it was the peak of the question: How do you make investments in Africa? This was now coming from the private sector. So that's how I first came to Kenya, because I'd never been to Africa before. And it was more like a personal experiment. I wanted to see if I could live here, and I also wanted to know how I could take what I had experienced in China and make it useful in these connections.

In the meantime, Yi had begun working for a media company, covering Chinese tech in English. Her main job was to produce community events, those start-up gatherings and shows where entrepreneurs share their ideas, their progress, and, often, their previous failures. After a short trip to Kenya, she decided to be more intentional about building China–Africa connections in Beijing's tech scene. She even started her own consulting firm, Bridge Builder. But then, like a bolt out of the blue, the COVID-19 pandemic had put an end to the ferment in the capital city. For Yi, now determined in her goal, there was no other option than to relocate to Africa. As China turned inward, with its zero-COVID policy, she latched onto the first chance she got: a job at a state-owned company operating in Ghana. There, however, she soon realized, like June, that the corporate environment of traditional state entities, even in their overseas units, was too harsh, too coarsened by rigid hierarchies for her to survive. Yet from Ghana it was easier to get another job in the continent. That's how she ended up in Nairobi—a city she loved at first sight—on a small consulting contract. "I'm still finding my feet here," she told me, explaining that she was now working for herself, having relaunched the Bridge Builder consultancy.

The latter was now different from what Yi had imagined it would be when she first started out in Beijing. At the beginning, Bridge Builder was meant to target the African diaspora in China, connecting them with local assets. "China has all kinds of resources for foreigners, but it is very hard for outsiders to understand the system," she explained. Yi's company would act as a facilitator of connections, and she imagined that one day Bridge Builder could even become an "accelerator," one of the programs that, inspired by the experience of Silicon Valley, link talent to capital through a fast, cohort-based training camp. "I was really inspired, I felt that there was so much to do," Yi continued. It was 2019, and "from both sides," China and Africa, the expectations were high. The previous year had been the richest ever for global VC entering China; 2019 was the year of Chinese VC's rapid expansion globally.[24] "Then COVID happened, and that excitement wilted away," Yi said. The pandemic had pushed her to rethink the model she envisioned for her company. Even though by 2022, when we first met, there was a renewed interest from Chinese investors for African and Africa-based tech companies, foreigners in China had now experienced the bitterness of a society sinking into one of its deepest crises.

> I'll give you an example. I had a Togolese friend [who] really struggled. He was in Shenzhen for nine years running a start-up, but every time he talked to a Chinese investor, they would prefer a Chinese team to work on his ideas. They would go as far as to suggest that they'd give him money for the idea but then hire some other people to [implement it]. Yeah, and then things soured even further with COVID. He experienced all kinds of xenophobia, he had to come back. And I think since he got back, he's gotten a lot more interest from investors, even the Chinese investors here. But of course, he is leaning toward European and American investors now. He was telling me how he doesn't care about Chinese money anymore. Money is money, but if you can choose, why would you go with the people who made your life impossible.

In these circumstances, there was no point imagining that Bridge Builder could work the way she initially conceived, as a stepping stone for African start-ups in China. Having restarted the company in Kenya, this time the focus was on what she had learned in Beijing: community events were the very fabric of an innovation ecosystem. If, while at their desk or at the table of a hipster café, Silicon Savannah entrepreneurs needed to focus on producing ideas, code, and profit, outside their work they also needed friendships, safety nets, and new horizons of aspiration.

Building on these reflections, Yi's consulting work had now pivoted to the "everyday life" of Chinese entrepreneurs, to their welfare in a context of uncertain future prospects. For Yi, this meant "acting as a PR agent" while building spaces of enjoyment and collaboration. On the one hand, these activities were indeed about the good things of life, the perks afforded by the "green city": forest hikes at dawn, imported drinks at dusk. But ultimately, the value of Yi's proposition was the mutual networks her company promised. These social nets would collectivize, at least in part, the burden of the many risks pegged to those working lives that had been hedged against less unpredictable futures—perhaps a more secure office job in a large tech company in Shenzhen or Beijing or even a contract at a state-owned company in Africa.[25] Of course, Yi's fellow entrepreneurs were not workers in a traditional sense. Still, their inherent precarity was undeniable. What to do in case of bankruptcy? When a much-needed investment fell through? Whom to turn to for an expedited visa? A space to work? Then there was the question of being a young woman in a male-dominated industry. Or being a Chinese person in an ecosystem where other international players were often suspicious or even overtly sinophobic. She told me about awkward encounters with older men, their predatory gazes and the side-eyes at her Mandarin accent. Precarity and the capacity to survive it were not evenly distributed. Could Yi's Bridge Builder help? Could her community events take up part of this job of social reproduction for a more inclusive and therefore investable Silicon Savannah?

Notably, Yi's project was itself a start-up. When we first spoke, she was still figuring out how she could make it work financially. Her competitive advantage consisted in her networks within the Chinese tech community. To survive, Bridge Builder focused on the different possible connections between the Silicon Savannah as a whole and a contingent of Chinese companies, start-ups, and investors that existed in its midst or at its periphery. She had consulted for large tech corporations, for example. She had hosted a few after-hours functions where new entrepreneurs had been able to ask questions to senior VC analysts. At the time, she was also running the local chapter of a start-up competition organized by the Beijing Overseas Talents Association. For this specifically, she figured out that she needed to introduce and explain the possibility of being "accelerated by a Chinese entity" to all those Silicon Savannah organizations—the venture building programs and the incubators that minted and nurtured local start-ups—that would normally consider Silicon Valley the sole destination of a successful entrepreneurial journey. Beijing was a possibility too. A lot of translation work was necessary, both literally and metaphorically. In a way, this was a version of what she had imagined Bridge Builder would be in 2019, only it was now operating from Nairobi, not from Beijing.

Despite this, her ambitions were broader. Bridge Builder remained a work of passion and care. After learning about my research, Yi suggested we should organize a small get-together where I could discuss my ongoing study with interested audiences. Her investment in the topic of this book aligned with mine, though our goals may have been very different. For Yi, this act of public storytelling, one in which I would play the role of main narrator, was one way of cultivating connections and rendering visible some of the pains and the joys of the Chinese in the Silicon Savannah as a collective experience. She was keen for me to speak about what I had observed and what we discussed over a few coffee meetings: the organizational practices that nourished the connections across innovators from China and with their Kenyan partners. I was unsure: Did I know enough? Eventually, her enthusiasm trumped my impostor syndrome. On a mild, pre-autumnal Friday afternoon, we held a small presentation in the glazed cottage of the former Iranian embassy that now served—in true Nairobi spirit—as a start-up incubator. A few dozen people showed up. I talked about some of the early insights from my conversations; at the time, I had already spoken to at least fifty experts, and the first lines of sight for this book were shaping up in my notes. I would be lying if I didn't admit that some of those ideas crystallized during the informal chats that followed my talk. In turn, the making of this book, perhaps unwittingly and certainly at a very inconsequential scale, became embroiled in the reproduction of the Silicon Savannah as a shared project of investability.[26]

If Yi's Bridge Builder was a personal and tentative endeavor, there were also more formal and institutionalized organizations in Nairobi. Some, like the China Kenya Chamber of Commerce, were spearheaded by national champions like CRBC and Huawei and acted at the highest level of government lobbying. Others, however, had emerged from the entrepreneurial grassroots of the Silicon Savannah and were led by a mix of international and local entrepreneurs. A good example was the Partnership for Africa-China Technology—PACT—an organization that featured some of the most important voices among entrepreneurs who had also become narrators of the Chinese presence in the Silicon Savannah.

In 2021, I spoke to Jessica, one of the founders of the PACT, on an online call booked on her busy calendar. She was, in every sense, an important figure in Nairobi's tech scene. Originally from China, she too had spent several years in the United States, long enough that her voice had lost all traces of her Shanghainese heritage. Nairobi was the last stop after a long journey. With a degree in neuroscience and a short stint in New York's silicon alley, she left America to move back to Shanghai.[27] Those were the years of Donald Trump's rise to power, and Jessica had become uncomfortable with how foreign she now felt in the US. As someone who had spent such a long time abroad, relocating to China had not been easy either, she would recall in a blog post. Under Xi, China too was becoming more suspicious of haigui. But ultimately, going back and then leaving a second time had been transformative: "With her idioms on my tongue, with her business attitudes in my wallet, and her ambitions in my mind[,] China scours through me like a needle, stitching every thought with yellow and red," she had written.

Having read this and other reflections she had shared on social media, I was eager to find out more about Jessica's journey. At first, I learned, she worked for a South African insurance company that had established a joint venture with a partner in Shanghai to export an innovative software product to the Chinese market. Then a serendipitous opportunity had come along.

> When I was working between China and South Africa, I was having some visa issues. I had a close friend of mine who was in Nairobi doing start-up stuff. She wanted me to visit, and I needed to stay somewhere while my visa was processed. I ended up working with her and then realizing that there was just such an interesting explosion of innovation in the entrepreneurial ecosystem here, and I just decided to stay. I mean, it makes a lot of sense that many Chinese big players are here, right? If you look at demographics and market size. And I think, in general, . . . with the Belt and Road, the Chinese government came in to lay a lot of the infrastructure, whether that is physical infrastructure, roads, bridges, SGR, whatever it might be, as well as digital infrastructure. . . . I think Nairobi, given the relatively easy political environment, as well as the living standards, all those things, makes this a very easy landing pad, regardless if you're a Chinese or an American or anything.

Unsurprisingly, her words resonated with the various shades of the green city narrative discussed earlier, including the Chinese variation of it, with mentions of the Belt and Road and national champions. Jessica's idea to start the PACT, however, had taken shape from observing a practical need. Because of her experience (she had raised capital in Shanghai), her friends and colleagues in Nairobi would ask her about Chinese investors, how they operated, and what they looked for in a start-up. With a self-effacing smile, she told me that it didn't make sense to just give individual answers to those questions: it made "more sense to start creating a community that would make introductions between Chinese investors and African entrepreneurs." Or even the other way around. She had met a few local investors who were seeking to outsource manufacturing or quality assurance for their companies in China. They too had many unanswered questions. Jessica joined forces with a handful of other outspoken and prominent members of the Silicon Savannah: not just Chinese, but also local and international entrepreneurs with an interest or a stake in the "Beijing connection"—as she called it. The PACT had taken off.

> We started off with trainings. We ran these "China trainings" all over the continent. It was Kenya, Ghana, Nigeria, South Africa, Uganda, Tanzania. . . . It was about educating local ecosystems on what working with Chinese investors was like. Why would they potentially want Chinese investors, et cetera. From my experience, African start-ups understand Silicon Valley vibes very well, the kind of Y Combinator story, but very few of them understand the money or the prowess or why you would want Chinese investors, right? And so there was a lot of education in that process in the

beginning. Then there were also the connections with Chinese companies that were doing interesting things or thinking about starting their own funds, like Transsion. Even people from Huawei, people who had been here a long time, they wanted to understand a little bit more about how their interaction with the Silicon Savannah could look or how they could engage other funders from back home.

By the time I spoke to Jessica, in 2021, the PACT was not running these training sessions any longer. COVID-19 had quelled the risk appetite that was in full swing in 2019. With travel restrictions still complicating the movement of people and commodities, 2021 had not been a good year for investments from China. Things would improve soon after, but Jessica and her fellow PACT founders had pivoted to a different set of initiatives. In truth, she told me, the PACT had been quite silent, having withdrawn into more inward-looking community building activities. After all, the PACT was meant to be a "kind of social enterprise." They had been opportunistic at the time when interest was concentrated on Chinese VC, but the ultimate goal of the organization was to build entrepreneurial camaraderie. "If there's a big conference going on, we help organize it," she told me, "or if there's introductions that we need to make, we'll take a referral fee or an investment fee. Our networks still make us very competitive. But other than that, the PACT is not meant to be something that's focused on making money. . . . Our goal is to build recognition for each other, [and] for all the difficulties, learning, and opportunities that we share."

The labors of socializing the entrepreneurial interface between digital Global China and Nairobi's Silicon Savannah were often framed by ambiguous discourses, linking semantically disparate ideas of precarity and opportunity, risk and knowledge, competition and collaboration, financial reward and pro bono gratuity. In a sense, these constructs could only be contradictory. After all, the very promise of China's techno-capital in Kenya, as we have seen thus far, seemed suspended in unresolvable discrepancies. Yet the work necessary to make the Silicon Savannah investable, in the face of these contradictions, was aligned across different players. While the PACT differed from Yi's Bridge Builder in that the former was a much more formal affair and, for that reason perhaps, less adaptable to the capricious waves of China–Kenya tech connections, they were both oriented to the same moral horizon: a Silicon Savannah that looked East and that was kind, or kinder, to its troupe.

At the same time, there were also more mundane labors of solidarity carried out by people like June, founder of Easytransfers. She would organize intimate events like the welcome party described in the first lines of this chapter. To keep track of new arrivals, she had created a WhatsApp group, to which I had been invited as well. It was meant to connect newcomers with those who, like her, had already built some kind of *guanxi* network in Nairobi. It was about creating support for a smooth landing, coddling the cosmopolitan, tech-savvy Chinese who, for whatever reason, were joining the Silicon Savannah. Even briefly so. Her focus was on Chinese travelers writ large: US Chinese, Malaysian Chinese, Singaporeans, and so on. But soon the WhatsApp group became larger. People would ask for everything, from sourcing US dollars to finding a good *huoguo*, a hotpot restaurant in the city. In exchange for access to this network, June would organize various other activities of reciprocity: from fund-raising for a person in need to showing up collectively in case of the occasional floods or other events that left poorer Nairobians in extreme dire straits.

Yi's Bridge Builder, Jessica's PACT, and June's WhatsApp group are all different examples of the labors of investability that generate communal infrastructures for the Silicon Savannah's Beijing connection. Over four years of research, I came across other kinds of initiatives, including social enterprises that facilitated the placement of humanitarian volunteers, or companies that were intent on busting sinophobic myths and renarrating China–Kenya friendship. And while my attention was directed to the presence of digital Global China, I am certain that similar initiatives of "entrepreneurial solidarity" abounded across the many communities innervating the Silicon Savannah.[28] Of course, there were more "formal rituals," as Gabriella Coleman names them, of their "technological lifeworlds": conferences, hackathons, and start-up competitions.[29] Yet social bonds were also cultivated in projects that combined collective sense-making with the need to socialize, as much as possible, the risks of individualized entrepreneurialism.[30] These projects were about hedging precarity through collective labors at once phatic and pragmatic: they created discourses of belonging to the "green city," however problematic this trope was, while also providing practical aid for the difficulties of entrepreneurial life in the Silicon Savannah.[31] And if risky lives needed such collective efforts, so too did risky capital.

CAPITAL PIPELINES

Thus far, we've seen how the circulations of people who build bridges across digital Global China and the Silicon Savannah of Nairobi are abetted by acts of entrepreneurial care and community building. Driven by individual ambition as they may have been, my interlocutors often sought shared forms of belonging and mutuality to find respite from the precarity of a diasporic, wageless lifestyle.[32] This search for kinship was a laborious, restless matter of investability, needing formal and informal organizational work. In a similar way, the circulations of capital too needed collective practices of derisking. Money flowing from China to Kenya, and sometimes vice versa, also required certain labors of investability.

One form of capital investment in particular, venture capital, epitomized the most ambitious wagers on the technology-driven start-ups of the Silicon Savannah. Described as the "backbone" of the digital economy, VC usually consists of equity investments—that is, money for ownership stakes—in fledgling tech companies that might quickly grow their customers, revenues, or profits.[33] In its current form, VC is associated with Sand Hill Road in Silicon Valley, where in the 1970s zealous investment firms like Sequoia Capital staked their bets on the nascent microchip industry of Northern California.[34] The funding model, which was later expanded to the software industry with enormous success, remains more or less the same today: given the high failure rate of early-stage start-ups, particularly in innovative fields or new markets, VC funds "burn" cash in the hope of finding the one company that, once successful, will offset all losses and produce high returns for the investors.[35] For a young tech company, the enticement of VC is often irresistible: without the possibility of raising money in other ways, whether by issuing bonds or securing a commercial loan from a bank, tech start-ups resort to VC to accelerate their growth—whatever that may mean in each specific case. In exchange for the high risk they take, venture capitalists may get significant control over a start-up's decisions, in addition to a claim over its future value.[36] Moreover, VC funds are increasingly diverse in the kinds of capital that they pool: they feature different limited partners (investors with no decisionmaking power), from wealthy individuals and corporations to pension and sovereign wealth funds.[37] In this process, writes political economist Franziska Cooiman, digital start-ups are turned into an "asset class" for those owners of capital who want to diversify their portfolio with a risky yet potentially lucrative avenue of investment.[38]

Given these features, the VC model is enlivened by a cruel appetite for failure. The unspoken yet accepted rule of every venture fund is that many invested companies will have to fail for those few that are successful enough to have a so-called "exit": either being acquired by another company or selling part of their stocks to other investors. As tacit as this truth is, the likelihood of failure was not a secret among the many entrepreneurs with whom I interacted over the years. In fact, several of them saw VC in a rather instrumental manner: as a way of injecting cash into their ambitions while buying time against their own precarity.[39] Despite this, money remains money. Even the most reckless of the speculators is not fond of dissipating capital. VC is pegged to numerous acts of derisking—of reducing, managing or buffering the likely possibility of loss.

At the most basic level, VC funds derisk their investments through careful analysis of the companies whose stakes they potentially acquire. A good VC analyst, I was told on several occasions, scrutinizes the legal and financial structure of a start-up.[40] They perform administrative due diligence but also stress test the claims that founders make to render their promises worthy of backing. Ultimately, analysts and venture capitalists also gauge the "human capital" of each invested start-up. This is where, critics argue, the supposed objectivity of the VC assessment mechanism turns into a much more subjective sieve for filtering entrepreneurs according to biographical facts. After all, race, gender, class, ability, and so forth are systems of classificatory violence that do not just determine hierarchies of human value, but also scales of human risk.[41] And if venture capital is about valuation and risk, then it follows that these funds are not immune to the broader systems that structure capital expansion and reproduction.[42] Derisking is not a neutral affair.

Neither does it happen just internally—as an operation of VC analysts and general partners. Derisking too is distributed along a pipeline of activities that select and channel promising ideas, technologies, and teams. Many venture capitalists also act as angel investors: that is, they provide seed capital and mentorship to start-ups that are not yet ready for a VC investment, which usually happens at a more advanced stage of entrepreneurial maturity. So-called seed capital also comes in the form of grants, or equity-free loans, or convertible debt from a variety of other players, even from the state. These are cash injections that pertain to more "patient" forms of speculation: they emanate from investors that do not really expect a direct return (e.g., a city government seeking to nurture a local innovation ecosystem with dedicated seed grants) or do so according to more expansive understandings of "return."[43] Yet, despite the variety of these investment forms, capital remains scarce. Competition is cutthroat from a very early stage of a company's journey, but it is not just a matter of "natural selection," the fittest start-ups surviving the unfit ones. Across these investment stages, selection is always a calculated act: from participating in start-up competitions to enrolling in so-called accelerators that train the investment-readiness potential of nascent firms, each tech ecosystem is an engine for winnowing the investable from the noninvestable.[44]

After these general reflections on the processes of VC derisking, let me turn to the setting of this book and more specifically to Chinese venture capital in the Silicon Savannah. In Nairobi's tech scene, VC is a topic of conversation ridden with anecdotes, jokes, and hyperbole. In the past five years, since VC flows started their exponential acceleration, Kenya has topped the list of African countries in terms of venture investments, climbing to the first spot in 2023.[45] Inevitably, among my interlocutors and friends, VC was a hot topic. First, there were the embellished rumors of entrepreneurs burning equity cash on the altar of a dissolute lifestyle. It was not uncommon that VC money ushered in lavish safaris or weekends in Zanzibar's posh resorts—not just for founders, but also for recently hired employees. These benefits expressed, in a way, the fringe rewards of what Andy Ross famously described as the "humane workplace": a workplace that, in these cases, traded job safety and long-term security for luxurious trips and retreats.[46]

Second, there were debates, often coated by disappointment, about the fact that international VC tended to go to international start-ups rather than local ones.[47] "Even Nigerian money," I was once told by my tech journalist friend Jerotich, "ends up funding start-ups with white people." Of course, for investors, the narrative was rather different: as a VC analyst explained to me on another occasion, she thought it was only right that VC preferred "diverse teams" over local ones. She said, "There are thirty-four tribes in Kenya alone. And yet Kenya is not a sufficiently [large] market for most VC investments." Venture capitalists, she went on to explain, needed to invest in companies that could scale across many African markets. She believed that only a truly international team could do that.

Ultimately, these conversations and anecdotes also converged to an important question. Was all VC the same? Or did American VC differ from Nigerian VC? And what about Chinese VC? My Chinese contacts believed that there were important differences. At the most elemental level, Chinese venture capitalists were not the same as other investors because they did not have the baggage of suspicions and expectations that came with Western portrayals of China. Remember Daiyu, the tech founder who briefly collaborated with Chao on his e-supermarket? On one occasion, under the dangling vine of a popular Ethiopian restaurant, she told me about her experience with these different "varieties," or origins, of VC.

> There are two types of Western investors. One type, they're super excited about our Chinese style. They feel like we have access to Chinese capital, access to Chinese supply chains. But another type of investor, they are more suspicious. They will ask questions about privacy because we handle a lot of consumer data. How are you going to deal with that? Are you going to send data to the Chinese Communist Party or whatever? Or how do you treat your local employees? Are you going to take over a lot of jobs? Are you coming here just to colonize the continent again? It's just so interesting to see those very extreme perspectives. There's no middle. Either very, very glad about our ties [to China] or very, very suspicious. And I was asking them, Why didn't you guys ask the same question to Western founders? Why don't you ask them about data privacy, employment, and the colonization questions? I would sometimes get offended. But now I'm convinced that it will take some time to change the narrative. And that work sits on the shoulders of the new Chinese entrepreneurs, who can actually do things and prove these biases wrong.

If Daiyu had come to the conclusion that challenging sinophobic prejudice was ultimately about "working" against it, a collective labor of redrafting the image of China's overseas entrepreneurs, others thought that bypassing Western investments was the more promising course of action.

This was what Esther had come to believe. She was the Chinese cofounder, with a Kenyan colleague, of an agritech company that had recently raised VC—Chinese VC to be precise. I met her in 2022, at a busy restaurant where we conversed for several hours as a spicy fish and pork broth simmered in a pot over an open fire. Her promising start-up had modeled a decentralized system for providing market access to smallholding farmers in rural Kenya. In a few years, they had become the largest independent distributors of domestic groceries in the country. To do so, an integrated go-to-market infrastructure had to be created: from providing seedlings and loans to farmers to grading, packing, distributing, and eventually finding the buyers and managing food waste in productive ways. All of that was powered by a sophisticated data dashboard that, unlike most data-enabled experiments in agritech, did not focus on a single moment of the value chain but integrated the entirety of its operations. And yet, as much as that multilayered infrastructure was yielding results, the profit margins for the company were marginal. Western VC, Esther had realized, was not interested in that kind of slow, incremental profitability. Conversely, Chinese VC was more familiar with low-margin business models based on mass adoption and couched in serving bottom-of-the-pyramid markets. That's what she believed, after several rejections from international investors and a hefty ticket from a Chinese fund that operated across East and North Africa.

A year later, I met with the chief analyst of that firm, Charles, a tall Kenyan man who had earned his stripes by working with both banks and other investment funds over more than a decade. Jovial and ironic—he had several hilarious anecdotes to share—Charles invited me to a cafeteria in Lavington, a posh and hilly neighborhood in Nairobi's western section. He told me about the structure of his VC firm, Lead Ventures, and how it integrated both small investments at the early stage and also more substantial tickets at growth stages. Given his experience as an analyst in Western funds and now a Chinese fund, I was of course curious about the differences across the two. He decided to answer my questions by foregrounding technological differences instead. It was a matter of products, he explained. In his words, there were "nice-to-have" and "must-have" technologies. His current venture firm focused on the latter, on problem-solving rather than demand-creating market devices. Such a "solution-driven approach," he went on, was "funnily enough, something that Chinese investors understand better than others." "When was China still Third World?," he asked me rhetorically. "And look at the West. They too were Third World, but when? Some of the learning, especially about problem-solving technology, is more fresh in China. . . . In the rural areas, in medical technology, in e-commerce, in logistics, we Africans have a lot to learn from China. And on the other side, it's easy for them to understand problem-solving technology."

Another aspect of this affinity, Charles observed, related to the expectations of a similar technological and economic trajectory. For many people, Kenya and Africa writ large looked like "China before China." Even the populations—some 1.4 billion each—were aligned. Accordingly, Chinese investors and entrepreneurs had started their experiments in places like Kenya based on that alignment. "They felt that some of the changes that happened in China might happen in Africa, so instead of waiting for them to happen, they've come here to make them happen," Charles quipped, after a sip of his coffee. Brushing aside political correctness, another VC partner had told me that many parts of China still "looked like Africa. [It's] still a developing country. Ninety-four percent of people don't even know how to—they don't even fly on airplanes. So there's a lot of second-tier cities, lower-tier cities there. That's why I think their product experience is useful in some way to the African market."

A few weeks later, I met one of Charles's bosses for lunch. Jian was one of the general partners of the firm, and he would make the ultimate call about Lead Ventures investing in a start-up. Over a quick lunch—it felt like he didn't have much time for academic questions—he explained that Chinese VC had two kinds of unique advantages. One was in the deliberate ethos of the investors themselves; the other was more accidental. As for the former, Jian told me that unlike Western VC, Chinese funds were laser focused on profitability (cash flow) rather than growth. In other words, they assessed new tech companies based on the marginal values created in each transaction rather than on promises of quick growth in user or sale numbers. He had observed, for example, how many blockchain wallets invested in by US VCs had faltered after growing exponentially across the continent. Cash had been squandered on enormously successful market acquisition strategies, but those costs had not been offset by a careful strategy of profitability. Jian's fund operated in a different manner. The key to a promising start-up was ensuring that each market transaction, rather than the cumulative output, produced cash flow, however infinitesimal. In Jian's view, Chinese VC had also garnered the reputation of being stingy, because investors like him didn't allow weekends in Zanzibar or team-building trips. "Our money is not free money," he told me. It had been gained, saved, and invested by his limited partners, and therefore he had an obligation to it.

It wasn't the first time, nor would it be the last, that I would encounter this discourse on the quasi-moral cautiousness of Chinese venture capital. Even in different terms. June, for example, had developed a deep admiration for a local company, Craft Silicon, and a deep distrust of Western venture capital. "Craft Silicon is a very successful Kenyan company," she told me on one occasion, "one of the fintechs of the early days, before the current boom. They initially specialized in building core systems for banks that wanted to transition to more sophisticated digital services. And one of their recent products is Little Cab." The latter was a local e-hailing platform. Unlike its competitors, Uber and Bolt, Little Cab's main offering consisted of business-to-business services, providing platformed taxi fleets and shuttles to other corporations. "The point is," June continued, "Little Cab and Craft Silicon never raised venture capital. So nobody is talking about them in the media, and if they are, they are undervaluing their incredible potential. The founder, this Kenyan Indian guy, is *so* shy. But at night, they are building a super app.[48] They already have so many services on the platform, including a wallet that allows line managers to approve expenses in real time, and they are expanding to other African cities."

June's admiration for Little Cab's quiet success attested to an ethos of investment that excluded the path of burning (venture) capital to acquire customers for the sake of growth, as both Uber and Bolt had done in Kenya, falling into a quagmire of financial stress and underpaid labor. She admired how Little Cab's founder was expanding its market through small, strategic steps—and treating drivers more fairly, so she thought. Her mistrust of venture capital, the "American way," was not uncommon. The founder of a small lending platform who had turned to fintech after creating a successful high-tech fish farm believed the same: "The American way model is focused on funding. Just raise capital. To grow. You don't care about profit, just about capturing the market. Find your product, find your market, or whatever. But in that process, you focus on growth, and you burn more money than you're making. You can be lucky, but that's a road map to default for most." He too maintained that Chinese venture capitalists were more careful about honing "profits as lean as possible."

My conversations with Jian and other general partners at Chinese venture capital firms confirmed this narrative. For instance, Victor, who spearheaded Transsion's VC arm, had built his entire investment model on such guardedness. The fund would only invest very small tickets, up to US$300,000 (but $30,000 on average), and would never want to acquire more than 10 percent of the company it invested in. After all, Transsion itself, as we have seen earlier, had been capable of building an empire based on extremely "marginal gains."[49] When I spoke to one of Transsion's former analysts, who now worked for another VC firm in West Africa, she told me that she was skeptical about this investment model: with such small stakes, the partners had very little maneuvering space to operate strategically. In other words, this VC fund did not operate as the invisible yet powerful agent described by the sociologist Benjamin Shestakofky in *Behind the Startup*.[50] Rather, as Victor admitted, they wanted their companies to independently experiment with a small inoculation of cash and at the same time enjoy the powerful possibilities offered by a mothership like Transsion: a phenomenal set of distribution channels, from the affordable phones themselves (through preinstallation) to the company's ubiquitous marketing outlets.

If one of Jian's observed "advantages" of Chinese VC over other VCs was this careful approach to investments, the second point he made to me was less about the ethos of the investors and more about practical linkages. With Chinese investment, he explained, a local start-up would gain access to a network of distributors, contract manufacturers, or even other start-ups working on similar markets in mainland China, a network that could immensely benefit a company's first, uncertain steps. Prototyping a device and producing it at scale and at cost, for example, were all areas of expertise in which Chinese investors had an incidental advantage: their limited partners, in other words, the people who had invested in their funds, formed a dense network of business relationships precisely at the interface of China's dominion in outsourced manufacturing for ICT and, increasingly, in software-related contracts like cloud services. Put differently, as Jian told me, Chinese VC "[came] with this networked access that others [couldn't] have." Even the former analyst at Transsion's VC arm, who was otherwise skeptical about their investment model, agreed that Chinese venture funding offered a unique advantage over rivals. "It's an infrastructure layer problem," she observed. "Apart from the tech itself, these start-ups heavily rely on operations. So, for example, you have Huochebang, a Chinese logistics company connecting truck owners with shippers. An incredibly successful story. And now you have that equivalent in Nigeria, and in

Kenya. Operationally, they can definitely benefit from such experience, especially if investors can link them to that operational expertise and that infrastructure."

And yet neither of the two characteristics—or "advantages," as Jian called them—of Chinese VC just *happened* by chance; they required deliberate labors of investability. That is, both the less exuberant, more careful nature of Chinese investments and their attached business networks needed to be orchestrated. Neither was the technological affinity described by Charles a simple empirical fact: that too needed to be performed in practice. All these connections wanted work—work that, as is often the case in many accounts of contemporary techno-capital, remains hidden behind the scenes.[51] Perhaps this is because accessing the choreographies of VC, even accessing venture capitalists themselves (provided that they are good proxies for their investment practices), is hard. In the next and final chapters of this book I return to the unique way I was granted access to some of these spaces. For now, I want to stay on the workings of Chinese VC that are necessary to establish its purported advantages.

As for the first feature of Chinese venture investments that my interlocutors claimed were uniquely Chinese (the focus on solution-driven technology with marginal profitability), the funds were actively training their companies to not only embrace a bootstrapped approach to digital bricolage but also understand the value of small gains. "I always tell them, if you can't build it, borrow it; if you can't borrow it, copy it," I was told on one occasion. Charles, who explained how Lead Ventures distinguished "nice-to-have" and "must-have" technologies, also observed that separating start-ups doing the former from start-ups doing the latter was not just natural selection. It was, actually, an orchestrated pipeline. First, the investment itself would weed out companies that did not align with this principle. Second, even among invested companies, the VC mentorship would be geared to outlining a key value proposition based on this mantra. Third, and Charles admitted that this was the hardest part, entrepreneurs needed to be trained to be thrifty, attentive, and patient. They needed to keep the small scale of a marginal transaction together with the large scale of their pan-African ambitions. To do so, Lead Ventures relied on an array of advisers, experts working in large Chinese companies like DiDi and Meituan who would offer their experience with mass markets and returning profits based on small transactional margins. Victor went even further: since his VC focused on novice start-ups, he would intervene in the team composition to make sure that in each company there were founders who, according to his judgment, understood the ethos of small and careful gains. Ironically, his professed hands-off approach—which manifested in allowing start-ups to experiment freely—would only kick in after a good team had been put in place. "I engineer teams," he told me, with a hint of personal pride.

Interestingly, these "teachings" needed to go both ways. For example, one of the earliest investments of Lead Ventures had been in a Beijing-based media company that produced content about African start-ups. Transsion's VC fund too had provided early-stage capital to a media platform dedicated to the same theme. This was a similar, yet more public, phatic labor to that of the PACT and Bridge Builder. Chinese investors too needed to be "trained." Charles was explicit about this.

> [These media platforms] basically produce knowledge so that the Chinese invest-ment landscape understands Africa better. And the African tech ecosystem. They publish success stories, but more importantly, they produce stories of the models that African start-ups have borrowed from the Chinese market. For example, look at fintech. There's a lot that we share with China. Be it payday loans or digital loans. Be it the ride hailing. Some of the ideas are borrowed and adapted from Chinese models. Yeah, even in e-commerce: some of it is actually born out of the question: How does China do it? And then how do we implement it? And if Chinese investors understand that African start-ups are doing this, learning and emulation, and they have the same attention to detail, then their confidence [would increase].

Ultimately, if Chinese VC operated to reshape "the world in its image," this was not an image of reckless entrepreneurialism and disruption, or "irrational exu-berance," as the Nobel Memorial Prize economist Robert Shiller calls it, but of conscientious borrowing, diligent networking, and meticulous experimentation.[52]

The result, however, was not only a shared, cautious ethos of entrepreneurial-ism and speculation. It was also a discourse that placed the present of Kenya's technological landscape, and its future, in conversation with China's past and present. "Kenya is China before China." These had been the eloquent and perhaps slightly enigmatic words of one of my interlocutors, a Chinese entrepreneur who had established an internship placement program for young Chinese people want-ing international experience outside of their country. What he meant was that Nairobi's present was akin to a moment in China's recent past that had preceded the radical transformation ushered in by its technological ascendancy. The corol-lary was that Kenya's future might be just as accelerated and exhilarating if built on similar modes of technicity and innovation. We've seen this throughout the previ-ous chapters of this book: from readapted hardware to reimagined digital business models, the stories of Chao, June, Daiyu, and others attested to the reality that China's technological trajectories could be imitated or translated into a grammar of innovation for Kenya. Digital Global China thus traced an alternative horizon for the Silicon Savannah, often imagined in a subordinate relationship to Silicon Valley and in process of futile catch-up with it, to a present that Silicon Valley is already leaving behind. And, as discussed in chapter 1, China's history too has been marked by discourses of leveling up to the purported technological primacy of the West. Notwithstanding this, the possibility of arbitraging different technological temporalities between China and Kenya was a promissory speculation, one made possible by those phatic exercises that worked on the relationship between Chi-nese investors and the ideas and entrepreneurs carrying their risk-defying bets.

What Jian described as the second advantage of Chinese VC investments—gaining access to immense networks of resources—was an equally calculated enterprise. This was especially clear with Transsion's fund. As Victor explained, their distribution channels were unparalleled in the continent, ranging from the hundreds of millions of smartphones to the capillary sales and marketing networks described in chapter 2. But other VCs too were extremely deliberate. These are the words of another analyst at yet another VC fund.

> When we invest, we are actually involved from the start. In each start-up, we place a business development manager with experience working with China. For a couple of months. Just to help them have more clients. Or sign a certain B2B deal, right? Especially for the guys that need hardware equipment. We help them source such kinds of hardware from China. I feel that the advantage that we have compared to the other VCs is this, yes. And then we also benchmark with China's tech giants. So if you have this African start-up here, we always try to organize a business trip, or at least an online meeting, with a successful Chinese company running a similar model in China. What can they learn? What mistake have they made in China? What can they do to improve the model? Just sharing experiences. And that brings another advantage. Our companies gain visibility, so it's easy for them to do another raise. Especially if they could partner, in case a Chinese company wants to expand into Africa. That's how we get exits through buyouts.

The business trip was a common practice. At Lead Ventures, for example, Charles mentioned the same. "In 2019, we took around twenty entrepreneurs from Africa to Alibaba's headquarters," he told me. "Then we organized a business trip to Meituan, and another one with Didi. We took them to the big VCs in China." At last, Charles revealed, one of the companies got a US$20 million investment, and his firm cut a finder's fee from the deal.

This constellation of anecdotes and voices speaks to the collective labors that are necessary for VC, in this case Chinese VC, to make the Silicon Savannah (and other Silicon places in Africa) investable. From "engineering teams," as Victor put it, to investment trips, entrepreneurial mentoring, and the orchestration of business networks across China and Kenya, VC relies on practices of investability that in building capital pipelines collectivize an ethos of careful experimentation and redistribute its inherent risks. Then again, the VC investment model itself is based on funding collective failure for the sake of a few successes. This is true across the board. If there were indeed specific Chinese features to Chinese VC, as my contacts argued, these were not casual or serendipitous but the outcome of the investment processes that fulfilled its appetite for new geographies of speculation, however careful and premeditated, in Nairobi's Silicon Savannah.

PERFORMING THE BEIJING CONNECTION

In 2023, I was lucky enough to get an invitation to the East African Venture Capital Association (EAVCA) annual conference. In the convention center of an upscale hotel, the entire jet set of the Silicon Savannah was in attendance. The founders of Kenya's future unicorns as well as the investors that had staked their bets on them were the headliners in the main act. Together with other players in the private equity industry of the region, they would conjure the hopes that nurture the imagination of techno-capital. Unsurprisingly, the morning wove together tales of success, failure, and the deft solutions that companies had found to seemingly insurmountable difficulties. Ultimately, as the master of ceremonies pointed out, Africa was a place of innovation that was drafting its own path, and private equity, especially if different investors banded together in organizations like EAVCA, could accelerate this course. Africa wasn't just the red tape, the corruption, the slums, or the makeshift frugality; it was also the high-tech experiments and the profits therefrom. Ironically, the location of the convention center, in Nairobi's Upper Hill, evoked a slightly different *also*. Beyond the fancy hotels, the golf courses, and the shiny new skyscrapers and the tall cranes building more of them, a dense swath of shacks in Kibera (one of Nairobi's largest so-called slums), only a few hundred meters away, spoke of the persistence of inequality and violence that venture capitalists and their start-ups promised to but most likely could not erase.

This sad irony wasn't lost on Bonny, who was Chao's Kenyan business partner at Fastlee. He was there, like other representatives of local start-ups, to pitch their ideas to potential investors. In the marbled hall of the hotel, during a short break, he told me how cynical he was about the whole shebang. Could this ruthless appetite for failure really work? Yet, in a kind of cruel optimism, he still believed in the possibility that right technologies, for instance, the digital platform for affordable connectivity he was busy building, could right the wrongs of Kenya's past and present.[53] The Silicon Savannah remains, as Alev Coban reminds us, "an economy of promises and performances about technology yet to become."[54] In that, Bonny shared the same vision of technological emancipation outlined by the emcee during the opening of the event while being skeptical about the ruthlessness of VC. Certain ambivalences remained unresolved. He could be dubious but at the same deeply involved in cultivating those exact visions of advancement that promised better futures for Kenya and Africa generally.

One of these visions of technological emancipation, this book argues as a whole, is also connected to digital Global China. In this chapter, I have explored some of the forms of labor through which the Silicon Savannah is imagined not just as an offshoot of Silicon Valley but also on a technological trajectory that is inspired, populated, and invested in by digital Global China. My argument has been that these deliberate practices of investability collectivize the risks and aspirations of what Jessica called the Silicon Savannah's Beijing connection, while creating the conditions for the emergence of shared grammars and pipelines of innovation. Returning to C. K. Lee's argument that different strategic and operational logics define the variegation of capital, I hope to have shown how the making of difference itself, whether through narrative or pragmatic work, is a productive force that renders Nairobi possible for digital China's techno-capital.[55] It is through the various labors described in these pages that Chinese entrepreneurs and investors in the Silicon Savannah would outline their networks and carve out their spaces of influence while cultivating the possibility of personal survival and of successful investment cycles in the "green city under the sun."

These labors of investability also reveal how Silicon Elsewheres are made and remade far from Northern California. In places like Nairobi, where the meanings of technology, innovation, and entrepreneurialism map onto histories, relations, and aspirations that sometimes align and sometimes diverge from the models that emanate or are purposefully exported from Northern California, viable alternatives, in this case digital Global China, need to be made into discourses and practices that are indeed investable. The Silicon Savannah was not just a place, or the narration of a place, but also an experimental project of reimagining the relationship between technology and capital at its purported peripheries. So too was the Beijing connection. Underneath both flowed a current of unflinching techno-optimism that sought to articulate some of the contradictions of technicity and capital while forcing me to question the methods and the stakes of my research.

6

Ethnographies of Techno-Optimism

RESEARCHING THE CALIFORNIAN IDEOLOGY'S ELSEWHERES

One of the first conversations that shaped the themes and arguments of this book, and stayed with me since, took place in the glazed offices of Opera News in early 2021. It was one of those unexpectedly warm and sunny days that break the monotony of the long rains. From high up in the commercial building, the construction site of the Nairobi expressway looked like a gigantic Lego enterprise, as precast girders were being rolled across the span of newly built piers by enormous bridge cranes. Only a year later, the new viaduct, funded and built by the Kenyan unit of a Chinese construction giant, would open to the public and would be the object of numerous controversies, even about the pagoda-like shape of the toll gates.[1] Opera News too, albeit less visible than a highway cutting through the city, was an interesting case of China's presence in Nairobi and in Africa. Launched in 2018, it was the largest news aggregator platform in the continent (by number of active users), and, according to my desk research, it had been the first offspring of Opera—the web browser—after the acquisition of the namesake company by a conglomerate of Chinese investors.

The story of Opera was fascinating and fraught. I remembered the first Opera browser running on my dad's desktop in the early 2000s (or perhaps even earlier), when browsing interfaces did not have the minimalist look later pioneered by Google Chrome but still carried the overstimulating legacy of the first web directories. At the time, Opera was the brainchild of a Norwegian state-owned company, and, at least according to my father, a self-taught tech enthusiast, the browser was the best and fastest available on the market (he would later switch his

FIGURE 10. The Nairobi expressway under construction. Photo by author.

allegiance to another one). Fast-forward to the mid-2010s, when Opera browsers (both the desktop version and the Mini, the data-efficient mobile version) had come to dominate the African market. In 2015, Opera had even surpassed the continental market share of Google Chrome for a few months. Today Opera is the second most used browser in Africa, with a 9 percent market share (compared to 2.5 percent globally). The reason for this success was largely technical: the browser was lean and saved data. It was perfect for the kinds of low-spec phones discussed in chapter 2 and the limited prepaid data bundles discussed in chapter 3.

In 2016, Opera's brand and most of its consumer business, including the web browser, was purchased by a consortium of Chinese investors led by the billionaire Yahui Zhou, who had only recently listed his gaming company on the Shenzhen Stock Exchange. With the capital raised in the public offering, Zhou launched into an aggressive acquisition strategy that didn't stop at Opera but included—rather contentiously—Grindr, a US dating app.[2] With the new owners at the helm and after another IPO on NASDAQ, Opera received a significant cash injection to diversify its African market footprint: in addition to Opera (the browser) and Opera Mini (the mobile browser), the company birthed or acquired shares in a number of other businesses: microlending platforms (OPay and OKash), a bank to buttress the fintech business (Nanobank), a ride-hailing platform (Oride), a classified listing directory (OList), an e-commerce platform (OMall), and the news aggregator Opera News. Some of these businesses had since faltered, but Opera News could boast millions of downloads and a massive cross-media reach through the browsers. At the time of my conversation with Thomas, head of the East African offices that overlooked the new Chinese-built expressway, the news platform held the largest feed in the continent. In Kenya, Opera News was crowned the most downloaded app in 2018.

The platform itself, with its AI-powered sorting system and a human layer of crowdsourced freelancers, followed a fascinating business model. Opera's experimentations, failures, and pivots were yet another example of the multiple varieties of China's outgoing techno-capital transforming Africa's digital landscape. So focused was the company on African users that its executives had described the business strategy as an "Africa-first approach."[3] Yet what also struck me during my conversation with Thomas, who had been one of the Kenyan architects of Opera News's success in East Africa, was his attitude toward digital technology. As much as he was pragmatic about working with Chinese owners, something he at first viewed with skepticism, he was entirely, almost bullishly optimistic about the promises of technology for a new era of more democratic, more transparent, and more accessible press. He told me that a new form of high-quality citizen journalism was awakening in Kenya, thanks to the technological possibilities of AI and to the increasing availability of smartphones and, therefore, internet connectivity.[4] Even rural areas, thanks to a distributed infrastructure of news sourcing, were finally in the news. Scores of young Kenyans were bypassing the filters of elite-dominated national newspapers, while other filters, algorithmic ones, were reducing harmful misinformation. Digital media, Thomas made clear, could save Kenya from cronyism, corruption, and inequality. I was familiar with this sanguine belief in technological emancipation. Before this book project, my work as a doctoral student had focused on how the world of development and humanitarianism in Africa had been receptive to fads and mantras coming from Silicon Valley.[5] And on how those ideas ultimately converged into a very particular kind of optimism: the creed that digital technologies could at once do good (to solve Africa's ails) while doing well, financially, for their makers and owners.[6] Fix poverty, democracy, and nature, while getting rich, through technology.

One of the lineages of this techno-optimism unsurprisingly comes from Silicon Valley. Waves of crisis and resurgence in the Bay Area—first in the late 1970s, as AnnaLee Saxenian documented, and then again in the early 2000s, with the dotcom bubble—have given rise to a collective myth of resilience and belonging that, in 1996, the cultural critics Richard Barbrook and Andy Cameron famously labeled the "Californian ideology."[7] "Promiscuously combin[ing] the free-wheeling spirit of the hippies and the entrepreneurial zeal of the yuppies," they wrote, the Californian ideology has at its core the supposed liberatory power of technological advancement and its capacity to fix social ills.[8] For Barbrook and Cameron, bohemian programmers and high-tech elites had come to share a "contradictory mix of technological determinism and libertarian individualism" while turning a blind eye to the racial and environmentally destructive pasts of techno-capital in California.[9] Such libertarian optimism is far from gone.[10] Not only is it alive and well in the United States, but it has traveled to distant places, including the African continent[11]. Here the more specific pledge of this salvific technophilia is to accelerate economic growth, to create jobs, and to address long-standing issues of poverty and economic marginality by turning them into a laboratory of innovation.[12]

Development in Africa has always been primed by deep shades of techno-optimism.[13] Both independence African leaders and the systems of expertise that prescribed modernization as a solution to "underdevelopment" held a confident trust in technical expedients.[14] It's telling that infrastructures played such a central role in modernization projects.[15] But the optimism of Californian ideologues has been qualitatively different. On the one hand, if thought leaders of the immediate post-independence period largely believed that the state ought to govern technological advancement,[16] the Californian ideology featured a strong laissez-faire libertarianism instead. And if technological advancement was, even in the eyes of staunch anticommunist modernization theorists like Walt Rostow, a collective project of statecraft, innovation for Californian evangelists is a much more individualistic, entrepreneurial endeavor.[17]

More than anyone else, as Barbrook and Cameron pointed out, the "retro-utopia" of the Californian ideology was aggrandized by the futurologist Alvin Toffler.[18] A narrator of the early Silicon Valley days, Toffler had been interested in the role of technology in the transition from industrial to postindustrial societies. In the 1970s already, his book *Future Shock* and the Orson Wells–narrated TV documentary had outlined the features of an accelerated world, overloaded by information.[19] This was the *third* wave, a wave that would push older industrial cultures aside and replace them with a new technological orientation to the future itself. Toffler's 1980 book, *The Third Wave*, returned to this theme.[20] In a society of information, he explained, the state was quickly becoming an obsolete bureaucracy. At the same time, digital technology could allow poorer countries to "leapfrog," to skip the industrialization phase dear to development economists and jump straight into the "Information Age."[21] To conjure this vision, Toffler described airborne devices that would bring connectivity to rural, remote parts of the so-called underdeveloped world. Fast forward almost forty years, and these ethereal machines have recently become a real developmental mission, with Google's helium-filled balloons bringing broadband internet to rural Kenya, in partnership with a state-owned telco.[22] While the unironically named Loon project failed, Toffler's brand of techno-optimism has had much less whimsical and farther-reaching influences. Famously, Toffler was US House Speaker Newt Gingrich's mentor and confidant during the New Right's rise to power in the early 1990s, building bridges between California and Washington, DC.

Toffler's ideas had found other unlikely adherents. Among them was former President Kim Dae-jung of South Korea, who read *The Third Wave* while in prison, and—most interestingly for this book—Chinese Premier Zhao Ziyang. As discussed in chapter 1, Zhao had promoted Programme 863 in response to Chinese scientists' concerns about China's technological sleepiness in the 1980s. While the program is well recognized as foundational for the country's economic and industrial transformation,[23] a lesser known aspect of this policy was the influence of Toffler's worldview. As the historian Julian Gerwitz explains, Zhao and other senior officials debated and developed a vision of "actionable futurism" by distilling some of Toffler's ideas into a modernization ideal that, under the banner of the "New Technological Revolution," is still prominent in "the current era of Chinese state-led investment in new technologies."[24] It goes without saying that the Toffler-inspired libertarian techno-optimism in the United States was not exactly the same as China's statist approach to technological entrepreneurialism.[25] Still, as Franceschini and others have observed using the example of the ecological civilization project (*shengtai wenming*), which has recast environmental destruction as a problem to solve through technological innovation, techno-optimism remains a crucial orientation of contemporary China.[26]

In all these replications, the Californian ideology is a uniquely malleable form of techno-optimism. In Silicon Valley, it has shaped generations of entrepreneurs. Meanwhile, in places like Nairobi and the Global South at large, digital technologies have been heralded as the fix to what older developmental interventions failed to address.[27] As the example of Kenya reveals, a Silicon Valley consensus has molded new forms of development policy predicated on digital entrepreneurialism and connectivity.[28] In China too, as the country shifted from *making* to *innovating* technical artifacts, a promethean faith in information technologies has influenced the highest echelons of policy, as well as a new social contract of national belonging for entrepreneurial citizens.[29] Across these geographies, what remains stable is the infectious optimism that technologies can do good while making techno-entrepreneurial people and states rich. Or richer.

We witnessed this orientation throughout the pages of this book, not just in the words of Opera News's chief editor. From state officials to entrepreneurs, investors, and the many experts who punctuate the digital economy, the horizon of speculation was one in which technological advancements would lead to a better, bigger future—however this was conceived.[30] At the risk of ascribing excessive validity to their performances of "unfailing enthusiasm," techno-optimism has been a central and yet not fully explicit theme of this book.[31] What is techno-optimism then? A good definition would need agreement on what constitutes technology, what constitutes advancement, and what separates standard futures from *better* futures. In other words, accounts of techno-optimism are contingent on other normative projects.[32] In the pages of academic journals, for example, scholars of science debate whether this form of future speculation implies that technology can make the world good or, simply, better.[33]

In observing techno-optimism as an ethnographic fact, both its normative and its ameliorative dimensions become evident. Attentive readers will have undoubtedly recognized that ethical and pragmatic rationalities equally infused the stories of ingenuity through which I sketched the interface between digital Global China and Nairobi's Silicon Savannah. My goal here, however, is not to define the features of techno-optimism, beyond acknowledging that it is a moral horizon of action primed by a collective desire to use technology for social improvement as well as personal gain. Neither do I want to trace a detailed lineage of the Californian ideology and its permutations across geographies that embrace, refute, and readapt this faith in the liberatory power of technicity. I want to reflect, instead, on the *tricks of the trade* of ethnographic research that, like mine, ended up being about techno-optimism more than just expertise, as I initially thought it would be.

Researching techno-optimism, playing into it, was a practical affair. It was about access but also about the ethics of research and the epistemic openings and closures that I found along the way. It was about languages and networks. It was about the stakes of complicity and the debits of scholarly privilege. The following fragments, I hope, shine some light on the practical stratagems through which this distributed, ill-defined object of research appeared in my work and, as I argue, how it was a collective discourse as much as a method of research and analysis itself.

THE SILENCE AND THE LINGO

This book, as I acknowledged in the preface, is the result of the occasional luck-with-privilege that young academics sometimes run into. I was a recent PhD graduate, an underemployed returnee in a country whose university system I did not fully understand, when I applied for the grant that allowed me to pursue the research for this book. This was September 2019. Two things had happened earlier in the year. Like any recent graduate, I had found myself without a long-term job, needing to find funding—any kind of funding—to see if I could give academic life a try. I had recently moved back to Italy, my home country, for both personal and accidental reasons—the latter being an unexpected, short-term job offer. By the time I was settled, Italy had become the first G7 country in the European Union to sign a memorandum of understanding with China on the so-called 21st Century Maritime Silk Road. In March, Italian Prime Minister Conte and China's Chairman Xi had met in Villa Madama, a Renaissance mansion built on the slopes of a hill in Rome. Surrounded by lush gardens and frescoes, the two leaders had shaken hands against the backdrop of three flags—China, Italy, and the EU—and a wall overgrown with ivy.

I thus realized that it would be strategic to craft a research project about the new Silk Roads in Africa and apply for funding from the EU at a time when so many EU countries were considering or already partnering with China and asking bewildering questions about China's long game or whether Africa had been a laboratory for China's future geopolitical moves. After all, Asia has always elicited mixed emotions in Europe, between fear and fascination, as Edward Said has pointed out in his well-known study of cultural representations of the East in the West.[34] As Xi journeyed across the capitals of the continent, those same emotions reverberated in the media, swinging between overt sinophobia and a subtler incapacity to engage Global China beyond Europe's own history of modernity and colonialism.[35]

I happened to be in the right place at the right moment. I happened to have the right questions for the European Union to fund my work. I am aware that this timeliness was less a function of serendipity than of the many kinds of privilege that life had afforded me. The reason I am disclosing this backstory is that my research started with a gamble. The gamble was China. Until then, China had never been within the range of my research. Ironically, I had been interested in Africa's digital economies through the lenses of Silicon Valley's ideas and models. I had done research on US companies like Uber and Amazon and their presence in the continent. Shifting the attention to technologies and capital from China seemed interesting enough at the time. But I was aware that the research project I had written was more about the geopolitics of research funding than a real understanding of what I was getting into. Worse still, I knew how much I didn't know about China, how easy it was to fall into the trap of orientalism/Eurocentrism, and how disadvantageous my lack of language proficiency would have been had I been successful in getting the EU grant. Forget proficiency, I didn't speak a single word of any Chinese language.

And then, early in February 2020, as the eerie images of the Wuhan lockdown circulated in the news, I received confirmation that my project, my gamble, had qualified for funding. I downloaded a language app and installed a Chinese keyboard on every device I owned. Technological optimism, it seems, is also a personal fact. A few weeks later, a colleague returning from China tested positive for the COVID-19 virus. Laura, our wonderful research manager, told us to start sheltering in place. I made one last trip to the office, grabbed some books, and printed dozens of calligraphy exercise books. Ten days later or so, the entire country entered a draconian, scary lockdown. Italy was, after China, one of the first places where the pandemic shored up in all its extremeness. Home alone, severed from my family, I started learning Mandarin Chinese.

Part of my desire to study the language was just personal curiosity; another part was, without a doubt, my deep impostor syndrome. I had used China, the uneasy idea of it, to get research funding. The least I could do was learn the basics of a language that was as far from my own as it was intriguing. With sociality reduced to a minimum, or even forbidden, over the months that followed I jumped deep into it. My tutor, a jovial Chinese South African teacher who I saw online twice a week for two years, kept reminding me of a common idiom, *ju sha cheng ta*: gathering sand makes a tower (or something to this effect). I'm still gathering sand, though not with the same tutor. My literacy is incredibly basic, but I am content with sand gathering; the tower can wait.

My point is that language was a primary concern of this work from the very start. Colleagues researching Chinese development projects across the African continent had warned me not only about how difficult it was to access the compounds of Chinese corporations but also about how important it was to master conversational Mandarin. I soon realized that this was a pipedream, especially without the possibility of full immersion in a Chinese-speaking context. Resigned to my condition of not-speaking-Chinese,[36] I figured that the best approximation to conduct a thoughtful field research was to rely on an interpreter. Kiswahili and other Kenyan languages, I admit, preoccupied me too, but they seemed less of an insurmountable obstacle. I was planning to interview state officials and planners, and their work was ultimately in English, courtesy of British colonialism. My overall perception was perhaps clouded by common narratives that portray the Chinese presence in Africa as constituted by bubbles of impenetrable Chinesenesses.[37]

It turns out, the experts, entrepreneurs, and investors who were interested in speaking to me about their work *wanted*, rather than just agreed, to use English precisely because they were navigating against the myth of the hardworking and earnest yet unintegrated and isolated overseas Chinese. Sometimes problematically, they wanted me to know that there was a difference between them and the employees of state-owned companies that, fueled by state capital, operated in all kinds of economic sectors in Kenya, much beyond the digital economy, that there was a gulf between China, the state, and what they represented and stood for. Despite all the social and economic connections that they maintained with the mainland, their belonging to Global China was ultimately couched in the technological visions that they brought forward. These technological futures inspired by China's trajectory, on the one hand, depoliticized complex geopolitical questions of dependence and cooperation (the questions that are usually asked in reference to China's presence in Africa). On the other hand, technology itself also repoliticized the entrepreneurial claims that my interlocutors had for the Silicon Savannah, by shifting the perspective from nationalistic interests and personal ambitions to a cosmopolitan "will to improve."[38] Some features of this desire to be seen as part of the Silicon Savannah's collective project of technological betterment have perhaps already surfaced in earlier pages: the optimistic promises of an investor state, the desires to fix urban systems deemed broken and fragmented, the beliefs in the possibility of bypassing Western standards and technical bottlenecks, and so on. These are all examples of the auspicious pragmatism that turned molecular initiatives into a communal infrastructure of technological experiments. Precisely because of these logics, the linguistic medium ought to be English, a lingua franca that was more attuned to the cosmopolitanism of these operations.

More importantly, however, my Chinese silence was not a problem because I shared another language with my interlocutors: tech start-up lingo. I knew what a minimum viable product was, I knew what a pitch deck entailed; I knew the meaning of pre-totyping, pivoting, bootstrapping, growth hacking, and cliff vesting; I was aware of exits, lean strategies, runways, sweat equities, churn rates, UX, and so on. I owned the grammar of a particular kind of techno-optimism: disruption-speak. That this language is the vehicle of a deep faith in the promise of technological innovation is not a mystery. For the historian Jill Lepore, for example, disruption is the ill-founded, unchallenged, "theory of change" of our time, a theory that "replacing 'progress' with 'innovation' skirts the question of whether a novelty is an improvement" after all.[39] Critiques aside, the disruption jargon is one of the mobile bridgeheads of the Californian ideology, as the techies' technical language seemingly travels unimpeded by cultural and linguistic differences. I wasn't, in fact, surprised to learn that Chinese start-uppers and investors had made this lingo their own, save for some variations (like references to shanzhai and frugality). But what I didn't realize was how much my own share of this techno-optimistic vocabulary would become a critical entry point for my research.

My literacy in this *other* lingua franca derived from two autobiographical accidents: a year-long stint in a tech company before starting my graduate studies and the subsequent decision to focus my PhD dissertation on start-ups that, as social enterprises, were trying to do well while doing good in Cape Town, South Africa. By the time I started my research in Nairobi, I had bagged more than half a decade of experience of reading and speaking the disruption lingo. This experience came with a start-up-friendly LinkedIn profile and other paraphernalia of my past; most importantly, as I was told on several occasions, it came with the trust generated by knowing what to ask and how to ask it. Let me be clear: there were many aspects of my interlocutors' work that remained obscure. I cannot code, for example, and when I was shown lines of software (this didn't happen very often but occasionally), or made aware of the NP-hardness of certain logistics problems of last-mile delivery (this happened once), I could not immediately read the technological quandaries that I was presented with. Still, I knew what to ask. I owned the lingo, at least part of it, to do so. Most relevantly, I was treated as an insider, a trusted insider, because of the techno-optimistic orientation of my questions. I had learned to center technological futures even in questions about the past or about the politics of the present. I knew how deeply the will to improve invigorated those otherwise unreadable moments of sharing. And this went beyond garnering a surprisingly immediate trust by the Chinese of the Silicon Savannah, as it snowballed to others who shared the same familiarity with the substance of my research interests.

So what does language, owning it (disruption-speak, in English) or lacking it (Mandarin, code), tell us about the ethnographic work of capturing technological optimism? I have two reflections. The first concerns the inextricably autobiographical nature of ethnography. This is not a particularly original claim.[40]

"Studying up, down, and sideways," as Laura Nader eloquently put it, requires all sorts of personal hoop jumping to master the vernaculars of technicity that define the chosen spaces of our research.[41] The more technical and arcane the cultures of expertise we address, the more access is mediated by these linguistic proficiencies, however stuttered and incomplete. Obviously, the conditions of possibility of owning a share in languages depends on various shades of privilege. But here's the rub, and my second reflection.

If the language of techno-optimism is for the ethnographer a deeply autobiographical matter, it is no less autobiographical for the techno-optimist. The appearance of a coherent gospel of innovation, the promissory fact of entrepreneurial positivism, the shared grammars of a change-oriented "actionable futurism" are all products of familiarity,[42] of certain modes of kinship that are shaped by many contingent circumstances, including historical anxieties and the thrilling exhilaration of technological leapfrogging, but also personal journeys across the capitals and the peripheries of techno-capital. Like me, more than me, the experts that have appeared in the previous pages were fluent in the lingua franca of techno-optimism in a profoundly personal and subjective manner. By tracing some of their journeys, my hope is to have done justice to the different ethical, pragmatic, and even critical trajectories of their optimism. Very few of my interlocutors, whether Kenyans or Chinese or otherwise, were just hapless believers in technology or thoughtless apostles of a globalized Californian ideology. Discursively containing their stories in overdetermined narratives of global domination would be misleading.

And yet, if ethnographic work is the re-creation of a collective "experience" that ties together readers, writers, and stories,[43] an ethnography of techno-capital cannot be anything but an ethnography of technological optimism, an ethnography couched in an ineludible language of optimization that reveals one side of its unfolding while keeping many others out of sight. Questions of labor, justice, violence, power, and so on, in other words, have only appeared in this work as instrumental problems to be solved. They are not. Still, I would argue, the "imponderabilia" of technological optimism offer us a sight of the ambivalence of techno-capital,[44] of the ways in which multiple and at times contradictory experiments and agendas are given coherence through the lingua franca of disruption.

(QUEER) NETWORKS, INSIDE AND OUTSIDE

If linguistic (in)competence was one of the ingredients of my research in Nairobi, another classical ethnographic question concerns the ways in which one negotiates access to the research "field" as an insider and as an outsider—at times both at once. Put differently, who were the gatekeepers and the network brokers of the Silicon Savannah's Beijing connection? And what has techno-optimism got to do with my access to these networks?

At the most superficial level, as I have described thus far, the more technical my conversations would get, the more trust I would experience in the demeanor of my interlocutors. A few of them explicitly told me that while they had been skeptical at first, they had decided to help me because of my diligent literacy in the start-up jargon. This would often translate into invitations to events and other kinds of gatherings (some of which I mentioned earlier) but also into a generous willingness to share contacts with me. But this is only part of the story. The possibility of asking technical questions that showcase literacy and diligence is not a given. One needs to be granted an audience first, and only then can one ask questions. In other words, there needs to be an initial moment of recognition, an opening for every rabbit hole that I was lucky enough to jump into during the four years I worked on this book. How I got there is what I want to consider now.

When in 2019 I first pitched the idea of this research to Liza Cirolia—mentor, friend, collaborator—the first thing we discussed was access to the experts that I wanted to engage. My original funding proposal, the China gamble, was ambitious and likely unrealizable. In her earnest pragmatism, Liza questioned the naïveté of my plans, which, in hindsight, must have read a bit delirious. With a much deeper research experience in urban Africa, she warned me not to discount the insurmountable biographical detail that I was, however literate in the start-up lingua franca, an outsider to Nairobi and an outsider to Global China. I agreed then, and I agree now. A couple of years later, well into the research, Liza and I returned to this question. How was it possible, we discussed, that I had been granted such unsparing access to diaspora networks that are usually shrouded in rumors of being suspicious of and impenetrable to strangers? By then, we were writing together a short reflection of the infrastructure of our research practice, an infrastructure that we linked to our queerness in worlds that were not, in any apparent way, *queer* or subjects of queer research.[45] I want to return to some of those reflections in the following lines, to make two points about the gatekeepers and the entryways that made this book possible.

Building on Lauren Berlant's expansive definition of infrastructure as "the living mediation of what organizes life,"[46] Liza and I described those networks of people and relations that formed the backbones of our methodology as "queer infrastructures." In practice, we argued, much of our capacity to do research depended on informal networks, friendly safety nets, shared tacit knowledge, and webs of word-of-mouth in cities where being queer required a special kind of "queer craft of engagement."[47] Of course, our being white, cisgendered people, foreigners in a way that granted a unique spatial permissiveness to our bodies, made our queer networks all the more powerful and privileged, despite the awkward moments of silence and unspeakability we often stumbled upon. Still, as Sarah Ahmed reminds us, our (sexual) orientations matter to how we inhabited the world but also to with whom we did so.[48] Our queer networks not only made our "being there" possible in a traditional ethnographic sense but also shaped the kinds of claims we could make in relation to the people into whose networks of care and mutuality we were welcomed. There was, in addition to a debt of gratitude that inevitably queered our perspective, an infrastructural quality, a technological mode of existence of our queerness. Ironically, while queer orientations are often layered by different shades of pessimism, the lattice of connections we recognized was full of becoming, zeal, and futurity.[49]

I don't want to belabor this point. Queerness can involve extreme homophobic violence, and my experience is anything but universal. I want to acknowledge, however, a parallel and an intersection between the privileged optimism of the queer networks of my research and the privileged optimism that I ended up studying while charting some of the appearances of digital Global China in Nairobi. Crucially, I came to see the latter through the former, as my queer network seeped into others, and more doors opened up. After all, our orientations, writes Ahmed, "are about starting points."[50] For ethnographic research on expert cultures, this is equally true.

In my case, a single contact became the thread leading toward a much bigger web of connections. It started with a few Zoom calls. By the time I landed in Nairobi, early in 2021, there was already a small cohort of people who anchored my life as researcher in a new city. I was welcomed in their homes, in their parties, in their volunteering activities, and in their working lives. My first impression of the "green city under the sun" was forged through an encounter of the professional and the personal. This queer network grew, of course, as my stays in Nairobi continued. I call it *queer* because it was less about sexual orientation and more about the queerness of our family structures, our political attitudes, our refusal to accept comprehensibility in place of multiplicity, and our work to cultivate a queer optimism and joy in an otherwise globally unfriendly environment of patriarchal normativity. To the people who helped me at first, I was an insider, precisely for these reasons. Inevitably, such a network was not a closed entity. It bordered and interfaced with the circuits of expertise that I was interested in gaining access to. At times, this was serendipitous (a random encounter at a dinner); at other times, this required pulling favors and strings. Ultimately, I am writing these lines not to "out" the usual yet often unspoken practices of gate-crashing that any research entails but to make a point about the modality of access. Was there ever a line between the researcher and the researched, friendship and collegiality, work and leisure, observation and participation? Was there ever a gate to be crossed with the help of a gatekeeper? Perhaps, but perhaps more importantly, my field of sight was bound by the ethical and practical repercussions of being always, through queerness, a little more (or much more) than a researcher to the people and the places I researched. What does one give back, Liza and I asked in our paper together, "in exchange for being part of queer infrastructures?"[51] I return to this question in the closing of this chapter.

While I was *inside* this queer network as an insider, as an outsider I ended up being, at least occasionally and fleetingly, inside the Chinese diaspora network of tech folks in the Silicon Savannah. The dynamics of access were similar. It is often one single person who brokers a favored way in. Then the list of contacts snowballs. At the end of the research, I realized I had been in contact with more than 170 people. I had shared tea, cigarettes, and *baijiu* with a remarkable number of start-up founders, workers, and investors (many more than I promised the EU's funder I would). Regardless of my way in, however, I came to understand that it was my outsiderness (together with my basic start-up literacy) that allowed me to grasp a sliver of these circuits of expertise. As a non-African person, from a peripheral country in the world of geopolitical competition for technology, I did not create skin-deep suspicions. I was the *other* other. I heard this on several occasions: my interlocutors trusted the knowledge-creating nature of my project. They wanted to contribute to it *because of* and not *in spite of* my outsiderness. Some reported having had previous experiences with journalists and researchers who had betrayed them. One outlet—I will not name it—was the object of very vocal and bitter hostility. "I love working with American entrepreneurs," I was told once by Bobby (more on him later), "but American researchers are out to get us." This was certainly ungenerous, as I met US colleagues and journalists conducting careful and sympathetic research in the Silicon Savannah and in Nairobi. But the broader context in which these statements were made, one of rising geopolitical rivalries over global technological primacy, could not be discounted. I often made the case that Italy too was a country of rampant sinophobia and racism. Still, many saw me through a prism that was devoid of enmity.

Ultimately, like my queer network, my Beijing connection network too seeped through my life in the form of friendship and mutuality, in ways that demand, as I elaborate later, certain kinds of negotiations between debts of gratitude and demands of critical distance.

BEING EVERYWHERE

Over the course of the research for this book, techno-optimism was never in a single place. Neither was it confined to single moments or performances of hope. It was instead a dispersed and decentralized moral horizon of action. For my purposes, it has also been a distributed object of analysis, often indistinct and hazy, overshadowed by technical jargon. It was only by returning to my notes over and over that I noticed this pattern of speculation. It was only by returning to my interlocutors again and again that I realized how their failures and successes kept being measured against a collective ambition of technological betterment and personal gains. What's more, techno-optimism was never confined to the field in a traditional sense. While writing, for example, I would often pick up my phone and double-check details with interlocutors who had become friends. I would receive WeChat and WhatsApp updates about their work and their journeys. I would occasionally check their LinkedIn announcements, screenshot them into my digital diary. In these short-lived connections too, a "patchwork" of life and field,[52] a technological will to improve kept appearing, however fugitively.

In a way, techno-optimism belonged to a factory without walls.[53] I conducted some of my research in incubator spaces, in coworking venues, in cafeterias and bars, in makerspaces, in convention centers, and so on. These spaces did have thresholds to be crossed. And again, my personal circumstances often made it easy to cross them. I even had a formal research permit from Kenya's National Commission for Science, Technology and Innovation (NACOSTI), a piece of paper that legitimized my access to rooms that would otherwise have been shut. But then, start-ups and venture capital firms, for example, had much more ill-defined and vague borders.[54] Most only had metaphorical walls. Even big tech companies, like Huawei and Transsion, existed across different spatial registers: they had their formal headquarters (not far from each other) but also operated through the multiple experimentations and distributed channels that we've seen in previous chapters.

As a result, my ethnographic being there in the spaces of techno-optimism was always fleeting. Techno-optimism itself was nomadic and ephemeral in its appearances. It was, after all, an ethos of experimentation as much as it was a future-oriented disposition. In turn, the gospel of innovation and disruption was not just physically displaced across many sites and relations. It was also temporally scattered across and bounded by specific and less specific moments of recognition. Some of these moments were the events, the talks, the hackathons, and the conferences that are often described as the choreographed performances through which the promissory hopes of technology are socialized.[55] Other moments were less choreographed and entailed improvised arrangements or more personal forms of sense-making. Occasionally, it was my presence that conjured technological hopes. The most banal, matter-of-fact interview would sometimes turn into a stage for the future to be presented as a trajectory of technical progress and betterment. Still, whatever the circumstances of its revelations, technological optimism remained a cursory object.

Even leaving techno-optimism aside, my broader engagement with the Silicon Savannah's Beijing connection was spatially and temporally fragmented. This raises an important question concerning the features of my ethnographic work. After all, two of the qualities traditionally associated with this codified research and writing practice are *depth* and *thickness*. Bronisław Malinowski, the putative father of ethnographic fieldwork as a method, wrote, for example, of the deep immersion required for unfamiliar cultures to become readable.[56] Clifford Geertz, half a century later, argued that while immersion in a field of action was indeed the starting point of any ethnographic venture, it was "thick description" that defined the enterprise.[57] For Geertz, thickness described not just a method of research but also an act of interpretation and, ultimately, writing. And while these definitions of ethnography have been challenged and reevaluated many times, especially in relation to the deeply colonial idea of immersing oneself in a radical otherness, they still prime the imagination of what constitutes good ethnography.[58]

Strictly speaking, neither depth nor thickness has been a characteristic of this book, or of the research that built it. My hanging out with the experts that populated the previous chapters was a staggered, inconsistent endeavor. Compared to researchers who spent months or years in single venues of technological optimism,[59] whether a start-up, an incubator, or a makerspace, my work in the field was shallow and transient—so much so that many of these spaces have not even appeared in my writing. Research consisted of brief moments, even when I returned to the same places or people on many occasions. My approach perhaps reflected what the anthropologist Ray Rist described as "blitzkrieg ethnography," replacing lengthy immersions with the intensity of an "ethnographic movement" of short blitzes.[60] Not incidentally, this mode of action was not foreign to my interlocutors. They too made sense of their context through a tireless commitment to multiple sites and moments at which the Silicon Savannah was staged, even just to make an appearance. Aaron, the VC partner discussed earlier, was explicit about what I needed to do—"be everywhere"—when I asked him what tips he had for me to dig further. He elaborated that what I was interested in researching could not be found in a single place or a momentary occasion. It was apportioned across a network of circulating individuals, companies, and ideas. To say something about the presence of digital Global China in the Silicon Savannah, in other words, I had to share the same restless and methodical dedication to the diversity and multiplicity of the encounters that my interlocutors planned, created, and attended. Overall, as acknowledged earlier, my mobility was a function of my many privileges, including my whiteness. And sometimes conversations were just simple conversations, although the overall feeling of my efforts was that I was gathering thin slivers of knowledge and not sinking into the real depth of a Malinowskian field.

Which brings me to the matter of thickness. One of the characteristics of thick description, Clifford Geertz explained in his landmark essay, is the capacity to "fix" and "rescue" objects that are otherwise perishable and mutable by lending them to "microscopic" scrutiny on the page.[61] But I'm doubtful that technological optimism, defined as a horizon of speculative action, can really be rescued through the magnifying properties of a microscope. The latter presupposes a certain distance between the observer and the observed, even if this distance is bridged by meticulous attention to the details and to the proverbial imponderabilia of ordinariness. So if thickness is the result of a rapport between distance and detail, then this book contains *thin* rather than thick description, as the anthropologist John Jackson put it.[62]

For one, technological optimism was not an external fact: not to my biography, not to my craft of engagement. Neither was it localized in a way that easily makes minute facts speak to larger concerns. More importantly, I tried to capture the stories in this book through overlapping layers that are movable pieces and not microscopic, detailed accounts of immersive participant observation. After all, start-ups pivot to new business models, new companies quickly wilt away, investments fail, phone models are replaced by newer ones, market dominance can be ephemeral, excitement turns into disappointment, and vice versa. Put differently, what remains of the ethnographic endeavor is the *fixing* part of it, the *rescuing* of sporadic instances that would otherwise be erased by the renarration of techno-logical advancement as a coherent trajectory. In writing, I cut thin slices, each with its angles, perspectives, voices, and blind spots. To what extent I was successful in doing this is for the critical reader to decide. As one of my interlocutors observed, to underscore what we had in common, my book project was itself a start-up, and as such, it required the same leaps of faith and punts that had become the object of my study.

WE ARE ALL EARLY STAGE

It was Bobby—investor, poet, astute businessman—who told me that my research, in his eyes, was "a start-up." It required rowing against the currents of self-doubt and fallibility. It demanded a certain kind of optimism and exhilaration. It was also contingent on my capacity to mirror and replicate some of the buoyancy of my interlocutors. I must admit it wasn't the first time that one of my contacts had pointed that out. Years earlier, during the first few months of my doctoral research, a social entrepreneur in Cape Town told me that I needed to get "better at net-working." He invited me to shadow him on several occasions, to show me the craft of getting access to start-ups and investors. He was methodical. After each day spent at a conference or at an investor summit, he would carefully archive business cards and new contacts, and write down the instances where he thought he had failed. It was about creating a ledger for business networks that would be otherwise intangible and dispersed, but it was also about measuring ourselves. How well had we done? How much better or worse had we performed, compared to our previous outing? When had we been too cocky or too shy? Networking, this elusive trade of the entrepreneurial self, was not innate but a trick of beguile and calculation that needed to be learned through mimicry and practice. Since then, I have had the habit of recording a log of my network for each project I have undertaken.

Networking, however, was not the only thing I had to glean from the emu-lation of my interlocutors. Aaron believed, for example, that I should embrace the fake-it-until-you-make-it attitude of start-uppers to get them interested in my work. I laughed at the suggestion but then realized he was being serious. "I hon-estly think that if you emphasize the prestige of being in a book, and the way the book becomes distributed with them—they love publicity," he added. In response, I explained that as an academic researcher, I had very little to offer to my future interlocutors. Since their stories would be as anonymous as possible, I doubted that my work could bring them into the limelight. Aaron chuckled. "Just say that [your book] will be presented at some sort of World Forum in the next few years. A bit of self-posturing never hurts." Self-posturing, I came to understand, was not really lying, but seeing this book project as inextricable from the web of techno-optimistic promises that became its narrative. It was also about acknowl-edging that the Beijing connection, or even the Silicon Savannah generally, was an experimental project of world-making. So, Aaron explained, even a book, with its lengthy publication journey and its anonymized characters, could be a contribu-tion to the overall trajectory of technological advancement to which many had tied their chances. I just had to be "smug about it," I was told on another occasion.

In response, I became more explicit about my goal. Instead of introducing my research as a project, I would talk about a "book" project. I do not know to what extent my contacts became more (or less) willing to share their stories with me because of the tangible narrative output that oriented our encounters to a shared future. But I am certain, because I was reminded of this many times, that the book tied our chances together. "What if everything disappears, all of this," asked Kamande, the data analyst, raising his Transsion phone, "will you still write the book?" As we spoke more, I understood he also wanted to know what would happen to my project if the Silicon Savannah folded and became just a historical moment of postcolonial Kenya in the transition to something different. But ulti-mately, it was the mutual orbit of my book and the Silicon Savannah as a project that aligned my storytelling with promises of technological emancipation. One of my contacts, a former Huawei employee from Kenya who had gone on to found a blockchain training school, was adamant about this: "I'm open to tell [you my story]. Because there's so much stuff happening, especially with constantly emerging technologies now. It's like we are on the forefront of tech innovation right now, looking at the fourth industrial revolution, so a lot is happening here. A lot of partnerships are happening, a lot of investment is happening from the outside world. And it's all focusing on real use cases, you know, solutions that impact lives one way or another. And transform the entire ecosystem around us. It's beautiful stuff, and your role is also pretty *exciting*." My "exciting" role, she explained, consisted in the fact that we were going at the same speed. "Unprec-edented speed," she added. The broader point was that our projects were inextri-cable, despite their differences.

A good example of this inseparability was the small conference I organized with Yi, from Bridge Builder. At first, as I explained earlier, I was uncertain about having anything to say about the Chinese in the Silicon Savannah. I texted her sev-eral times, explaining how my research was at an early stage and how I still needed to solidify my understanding of what I was going to write about. I screenshot one of her responses to my doubts. "We are all early stage," she had WhatsApped back, epigrammatically. I was already convinced by then but still surprised by how much, as Yi had revealed, I thought of my project in the language of start-ups. I like to believe that our small event, however inconsequential, allowed me to test some of the more speculative—one might say, ambitious—claims of this book, the same way early-stage entrepreneurs test their claims and their MVPs by rendering business models experimental.

More than anyone else, however, it was Bobby who saw my book project as one of the many diverse experiments of the Silicon Savannah's Beijing connection. Where to start with him? The son of a modest Chongqingnese family, he had studied to be a primary school teacher. But in the early 2000s, Chongqing didn't offer much to an ambitious young man. Though the city is now a vibrant center of the Belt and Road Initiative, it was in the backwater of China then. In search of adventure, he had moved to Shenzhen. In a turn of fate, the announcement of the special economic zone in the city, on August 26, 1980, had coincided with the day of his birth. Convinced that those kinds of coincidences need to be pursued, he had left his teaching job, moved to the Pearl River Delta, and started a new career as a salesman at ZTE. He had eventually relocated to South Africa for ZTE and traveled far and wide across the continent. I don't have space for his story here, so I'll just note that by the time we met, Bobby was the owner or coowner of a suite of different companies, from factories producing digital meters to data center businesses. On our first meeting, he told me he spent the previous month teaching himself the basics of cryptography, in order to better understand the potential of blockchain and become an investor in it.

Bobby was so animated and high-spirited that it is impossible to capture him on the page without falling into the cliché of the obsessive, bombastic Silicon Valley character with which TV series have made us familiar. In truth, he was thoughtful, self-aware, and well read, but his cheerful personality belied a different, shallower temperament. One of my contacts described him as a peacock with its tail unfurled and warned me not to believe anything he said. Still, I was eager to meet him, so when he reached out on WeChat, and despite the last-minute invitation, I joined him for drinks at a popular nightclub. He reserved a table for a group: several Chinese managers in different tech companies were going to join us. Only later did he tell me he was vetting me. Was I going to join, and how? It was Bobby who had become suspicious of journalists and researchers. Somehow, I passed the test.

After that first evening, we had several meetings over the years and started a trail of shared reflections on WeChat, where he would send me his poetry, rants, links, lines from Mao, lines from Confucius, updates about his business, and everything in between, including his pipedream to buy a soccer team in Italy one day. On one occasion, he even invited me to witness how he closed a business deal. We were having a family lunch with some key executives of state-owned ICT companies in Nairobi when he called me aside and put his phone on speaker. "I'm doing a deal, listen to this," he said. The affair was in Mandarin, so I only caught disjointed words and sentences, as well as his suddenly exacting tone. Still, this anecdote is a good example of how much Bobby deemed my book and my research experimental accessories of a bigger scheme. It didn't matter that I couldn't understand the stakes or the details of the deal. He never revealed them. What mattered was the role he embraced, in his supposedly Confucian orientation to episteme, as my mentor. "Silent observation," he kept telling me, was key. He was my guide in that process. In that spirit, the spirit of a teacher guiding a silent learner, he would invite me to both business and social events. He would school me in the rules of apprenticeship that I needed in order to succeed in a project that was mine as much as it was shared property of everyone I had encountered and engaged. The book, he believed, was the ultimate cornerstone of my learning project. It was the inevitable third step in a trajectory of personal and collective realization: "First, cultivate yourself. Be an upright man. Focus on integrity. Build your own reputation. That's number one. Number two, if you're a businessman, be a billionaire. If you're a general, win the war. Whoever you are, be the best at what you're doing. Number three, leave your words, write it down, write it down, in whatever form: an essay or a poem or literature. So those are the three things Confucianism requires of every single gentleman. You need to focus. Set up your virtue, set up your achievements, set up your works in writing."

I'm not sure where these Confucian maxims came from. I had made a decision that I would try to avoid any culturally essentialist readings of Chineseness. Bobby was an avid reader of old Chinese philosophy as much as of Smith, Mao, and Marx. He had developed his own opinions about socialism, about Deng, about Xi. He had studied their texts, even though he preferred poetry over politics. The broader point I want to make is that my research was not, for him, any different from the endeavors pursued by the young entrepreneurs he had mentored (and supported financially) in the past. Neither was it different from his own journey. We were steeped in the same commitment to entrepreneurialism, and our methods were research methods as well as methods for engaging the uncertain futures of our environs. One day Bobby told me, "I would like the last chapter of your book to be just like this, open-ended. Tell your audience that this chapter still goes, it never ends. This is only the beginning of something great." The ultimate end of our trajectories, whether a successful business or an insightful monograph, mattered less than the process itself: it was the dedication, the principledness, and the writing that made it worthwhile. At the very least, we all owed something to each other.

THE COMPLICITY OF CRITIQUE

"Are you going to criticize *me* in your book?" asked Bobby during one of our lunches, almost offhandedly. We had been talking for hours already, and I had not shied away from posing pointed questions. It was our usual back and forth: he would challenge me, and I would retaliate. We knew by then that there were many things about which we disagreed. We had been talking about nationalism, and then the conversation had veered to Jack Ma announcing that after Alibaba he was ready to become a primary school teacher again. Bobby seemed to admire this decision. Ma had recognized what "good enough" meant. He had been able to separate technological advancement from more self-serving ambitions. Having disrupted the rules of global e-commerce and forever transformed rural China (however contradictorily), Ma was now scaling back. Bobby, a former teacher himself, saw his own future reflected in the backtracking steps of Alibaba's founder. One day, he too would walk back to where everything began for him, a public school in the sprawling suburbs of Chongqing. Or so he told me. In the meantime, Bobby explained, he was going to play the capitalist game, as another research contact had called it years earlier,[63] by strategically abiding by the rules of the market for a bigger goal. In Bobby's case, this goal was ever changing: it was about Nairobi, it was about Kenya, it was about China, it was about the start-ups he had invested in, it was about Sino-African technological friendships, and it was about his idiosyncratically personal desire to buy a soccer team in Europe. Speculation can be calculating and magical at once. I remarked that it was easy, as a millionaire, to be blasé about capitalism and describe it as a contingent game in a longer match. That's when he had asked whether I was going to be critical, something he must have not thought of before, given the slight surprise in his tone.

Was I going to criticize him? As a rejoinder, I asked him another question, one I return to in the coda. Was it possible to participate in, or even just imagine, his technological optimism without turning a blind eye to the forms of destruction and exploitation of global techno-capital? He knew all too well—we had discussed it over and over—that I had a much more ambivalent and less deterministic view of the things we were invested in. "I understand," he replied, "but you are still complicit, even if you criticize me." There wouldn't be any book, Bobby explained, there wouldn't be any storytelling without the stories he and others had generously gifted me. Critique was a privilege pegged to a ledger of accountability.

My ambition is to have done justice to this responsibility, striking a compromise between critical distance and critical proximity. Ultimately, as I hope to have demonstrated in the pages of this last chapter, this was a compromise made possible by methodological and analytical care, which, through the practice of ethnography, revealed how much my journey was embroiled in the trade of technological optimism itself. Because of course I was not only *complicit*; I had become deeply tethered, even as an outsider, to the lives and the promethean aspirations of digital Global China in the Silicon Savannah.

Coda

Thinking Technology Elsewhere, and Otherwise

As I penned, or better, typed, the final pages of the first draft of this book, Kenya was catapulted into global news headlines for a slew of massive youth protests. On June 18, 2024, thousands of young Kenyans took to the streets in Nairobi, and later across the country, to challenge a controversial piece of tax legislation, the 2024 finance bill. The proposed bill, following the conditionalities of a debt-relief agreement signed with the IMF in 2021, included a number of measures that would have worsened the ongoing cost-of-living crisis, including additional excise duties on staples like bread, cooking oil, menstrual health products, internet data, and a cut in fuel subsidies. Across class and ethnicity, protesters claimed that tax increases threatened the livelihoods of marginal Kenyans and that the bill did nothing to address the cronyism and corruption of political elites. Worse still, the initial draft included generous provisions for politicians. Demonstrators also denounced, using a grammar that was reminiscent of the anticolonial struggle, the imperial presence of Western powers through the IMF and the World Bank (and the about-to-mature Eurobond that required the revenue hike) in Kenya's economic affairs.

After the first round of protests, President William Ruto—who had won a close election two years earlier on the promise of centering hardworking Kenyans, "hustlers," in the government's priorities—agreed to make some small concessions.[1] But the protests were not placated. On the afternoon of June 25, barricades were breached and the parliament was stormed and set on fire. Police violence escalated, and dozens of young people were left dead on the streets. Reports of disappearances and state kidnappings evoked a brutal past. A day later, a still-embattled Ruto withdrew the bill. With the protests continuing, he also consented to a cabinet reshuffling to create a government of national unity that included members of the opposition party. But, as of early August 2024, the demonstrators have not wavered. Although the initial trigger was a finance bill, demands for systemic change cannot be addressed by its withdrawal. Whether this rupture in Kenya's history will lead to such change, championed by what commentators described as the Gen Z protests, is the big question ahead.

Meanwhile, the finance bill and the ensuing unrest bore witness to the centrality of digital technology in the life of present-day Kenya. On the one hand, the tax legislation itself contained several measures related to digital products and services. Excise duties on data and mobile money transactions aside (which would have incurred a spike from 15 to 20 percent), the bill also contained a number of other provisions, for instance, the inclusion of all platform-enabled economies—from ride hailing to task-based crowdwork—in an income tax category that previously was mostly limited to e-commerce operators, the taxation of online creators, the compulsory extension of digital invoicing to small traders, and others. Perhaps most controversially, the bill would have created a zone of exception, outside of Kenya's celebrated and advanced data privacy regulations, for the revenue authority to use personal mobile money data to enforce tax collection.

On the other hand, protesters deployed a gamut of digital tools. From uniting under the hashtag #rejectfinancebill (and others like #occupyparliament, #tokeatuesday)—something that had already happened with the antifemicide demonstration months earlier (#endfemicide)—to livestreaming the events on TikTok to avoid, or just document, police violence, social media platforms were used to mobilize and bypass the elite-controlled mediasphere. Digital leaflets for shared rules of conduct and safety were distributed on WhatsApp. Streaming platforms circulated a recognizable visual identity for the dissidents (black tracksuits and face masks). A rudimentary walkie-talkie app, Zello, became one of the most downloaded in the country, as protesters used it to coordinate crowds in real time and get around possible shutdowns of other communication channels. Ad-hoc large language models were quickly developed to answer questions about the bill in Kenyan languages that rarely feature in official documents.

The tax bill and the mass protests, in their own ways, raise a set of age-old dilemmas: Are digital technologies weapons of control and profit-driven exploitation or tools of liberation? And can they really be redeployed for the latter when their blueprints are designed to extract value and surveil through data? Can bad tech become good tech, and vice versa? Such suspension between different ethical and political agendas could be described as the *ambivalence* of technology. But ambivalence, as I hope to have shown in this book, does not just extend across the different optimistic speculations into which technologies are enrolled, but also along the various geographies that determine their meanings, uses, priorities, and specifications. The *where* of technology matters. *Silicon Elsewhere*, starting from Nairobi's Silicon Savannah and its connection to another elsewhere of technological innovation, digital Global China, has been my way to honor the goal of provincializing the world-making power of Silicon Valley while centering other geographies of techno-capital. From Nairobi, these appear to be multiple and divergent, caught between the imperatives of accumulation and the developmental promises of more inclusive digital markets. Readers will have no doubt recognized how the techno-optimistics experiments described in this book were rife with these contradictions. If and how such discrepancies can be solved remain to be seen.

Still, *Silicon Elsewhere* offers some lines of sight to current anxieties about China's digital presence in Africa and about digital technology in general. At the most superficial level, the empirical core of this book has questioned some commonplace assumptions about China's high-tech footprint in the African continent and about Africa's purported subalternity. A city of experiments and promissory hopes, Nairobi has allowed me to renarrate the nuances and the contingencies of an increasingly multiplex digital economy and to do so from a perspective different from the overdetermined framings—"the tech cold war," the "Chinese century," or "China's data colonialism in Africa"—dominating popular debates. Ultimately, against narratives of innovation that describe the West (or now China) as the sole source of technical progress and the rest of the world as a frontier where technical things are merely tinkered with or adapted, this book urges reconsideration of the cosmopolitan specificities of technological optimism in its attempts to reconcile the contradictions of technology and capital *off* their usual map.[2]

In doing so, *Silicon Elsewhere* has explored how the contact zones of contemporary techno-capital are never just the passive frontiers of new forms of exploitation, or peripheries lagging behind digital futures that are always a step ahead. Unequal political and economic arrangements are undeniably folded into the Silicon Savannah. And yet, within this project, as much as it is tied to the rise of digital Global China and to a global Silicon Valley consensus, diverse inspirations and aspirations coexist. It would be inaccurate to consolidate all facets of Nairobi's techno-capital into a ruthless critique of the lifeworlds and the experiments of technology that form it. We have seen how decidedly moral agendas, however thin, seep through these trials, creating fragility in technical configurations that otherwise seem to be coherent engines of profit. Fragility does not equal breakage. And for many dedicated critics, this means that for all its diverse rationalities, the Silicon Savannah's Beijing connection is too deeply embroiled in the global order of techno-capital to produce any valuable alternative, either ethical, political, or even technological. However, as I explained in chapter 6, the research for this book required me to walk the line between the distance of critique and the proximity of those who generously bestowed their stories on this work. If, as Tom Neumark writes, the people we research are also *travel companions*, not just informants whose ideas and mythologies need to be dispelled, then taking some of their claims at face value is a risky but necessary move.[3]

My Chinese interlocutors had no doubt. With their platform bricolage and digital trials, even with their carefully calculated investments, they were upending the unjust technicities of Nairobi's present. Sure, they were doing it for the possibility of profit, but that was much more elusive and hazier than the promise of technological betterment that infused their optimism. As for their Kenyan colleagues, collaborators, and employees, they of course had more hesitant views. Some of the feelings and perceptions of Nairobians who were either observers of or active participants in the project of welcoming Chinese techno-capital in the Silicon Savannah are cited throughout the book. Given the focus of my research on expertise, the book obviously captured only a snapshot of the emotional landscape that surrounds China's presence in Africa.[4] Sometimes my interlocutors shared the same techno-optimistic fire. A few echoed the suspicions, whether warranted or not, that much of the Western world holds against digital China. With a mix of pragmatism and resignation, others cast doubt on the veracity of Kenya's win-win ties to China while acknowledging the desirable inevitability of new technological relations. For most of them, however, a question remained crucial. Could alternatives emerge from the unequal global systems of the digital economy, even from within configurations that promised change but seemed so likely to mirror the unforgiving imperialism of Silicon Valley? Perhaps the same question might be formulated in different terms.

Through the Beijing connection in the Silicon Savannah, one could indeed ask if innovation, specification, optimization, algorithmic suturing, standardization, infrastructural justice, and all the other technological rationalities that this book has explored could be divorced from (techno)-capital. After all, any form of capitalism, including forms that are purportedly *invented* outside the West, is linked to the ecologically destructive and dehumanizing architecture of the global economic system.[5] In a way, it is easier to recognize how much global capital is made possible by technology but much harder to imagine the possibility of undoing this relationship, or, as McElroy puts it, "unbecoming Silicon Valley."[6] Can (technological) optimism be borrowed, a suggestion that the geographer David Harvey made long ago, for an otherwise of technology?[7] My proposal is that to do so, to breathe life into this project, a good starting point is the multiple technological *elsewheres* that already, albeit partially and inconsistently, mobilize hopes and rationalities to undo the rules of the game that have long seemed immutable, as Gen Z protesters are doing in the streets in Nairobi today. Do these experimental terrains of digital technology, in a reorientation of the world or, in this case, a reorientation of Africa toward digital Global China, foreshadow more just and emancipatory techno-economic pathways? As Sharad Chari notes, "Not much, not yet. And yet the provocation is too important not to address more carefully."[8] Ultimately, to reopen the question of technology, writes Yuk Hui, "is to refuse this homogeneous technological future that is presented to us as the only option."[9] And as Bobby wanted, I end this book with an opening, not an end.

Cape Town, August 2024 (revised January 2025, Turin)

NOTES

PREFACE

1. Scott, "Intellectual Diary," 7.
2. Wasserman, "The Incompleteness of Knowledge Production."

INTRODUCTION: THE SILICON SAVANNAH'S BEIJING CONNECTION

1. Ogot and Ogot, *History of Nairobi*.
2. Dittgen and Chungu, "(Un)writing 'Chinese Space,'" 3.
3. Kusimba, *Reimagining Money*.
4. "Quick codes" are technically the USSD, or Unstructured Supplementary Service Data, protocol.
5. Meagher, "Cannibalizing the Informal Economy."
6. Guma and Mwaura, "Infrastructural Configurations"; Park, "Human ATMs."
7. Guma, "Nairobi's Rise."
8. Okolloh, "Ushahidi."
9. Nyabola, *Digital Democracy*.
10. Graham and Mann, "Imagining a Silicon Savannah"; Anwar and Graham, *The Digital Continent*.
11. Kuo, "Mark Zuckerberg." Note that by then iHub had moved a few blocks away, to another office complex.
12. Wahome, *Fabricating Silicon Savannah*.
13. Rosenberg and Brent, "Infrastructure Disruption."
14. Coban, *Performing Technocapitalism*.
15. Pollio et al., "Algorithmic Suturing."
16. Owino, "Kenya Is Africa."

17. With the "Beijing connection," my interlocutor was perhaps riffing on the notion of the Beijing consensus popularized by the journalist Joshua Cooper Ramo. See chapter 5.

18. Schindler et al., "The Second Cold War." For a critical analysis, see Heeks and He, "Analysing the US–China 'AI Cold War.'"

19. On African cities and internationalism in the Cold War, see Al-Bulushi, "Dar es Salaam"; *Ruptures*; Eldridge, "Algiers"; Roberts, *Revolutionary State-Making*. "Contact zones" is an expression I borrow from Mary Louise Pratt; see Pratt, "Arts of the Contact Zone," 34. See also Coban, *Performing Technocapitalism*.

20. Mavhunga, "Introduction."

21. Both the PRC and the ROC engaged in friendship farms. Brautigam et al., "China's Engagement." See also Brautigam, *The Dragon's Gift*.

22. Monson, *Africa's Freedom Railway*.

23. Taylor, "China's foreign Policy," 444.

24. African nations also entered the lost decades of structural adjustment. See Mkandawire and Soludo, *Our Continent*.

25. Taylor, "China's Foreign Policy."

26. For an overview of the historical debate, see Zheng, "China Debates."

27. An argument explored in depth in Brautigam, *The Dragon's Gift*.

28. Brautigam, "Flying Geese"; Brautigam, *The Dragon's Gift*. For a broader overview of Chinese FDI and bilateral finance, see Dreher et al., *Banking on Beijing*.

29. See Elyachar, "Empowerment Money."

30. Alden et al., "Introduction." On the specific narrative of infrastructural renaissance, see for example Terrefe, "Infrastructures of Renaissance."

31. It should be noted that the BRI is also a project of cultural renarration of China's rightful position at the center of global trade. Winter, *Geocultural Power*.

32. Narins and Agnew, "Missing from the Map," 810.

33. Chun, *Revolution and Counterrevolution*.

34. See Schindler and Di Carlo, *The Rise of the Infrastructure State*.

35. Brautigam, *The Dragon's Gift*.

36. Taylor and Zajontz, "In a Fix."

37. Camba, "The Sino-Centric Capital"; Zajontz, "Debt, Distress, Dispossession."

38. Carmody, *The New Scramble for Africa*.

39. Among others, Alves, "China's 'Win-Win'"; Asante and Helbrecht, "Hybrid Entrepreneurial Urban Governance"; Croese, "State-Led Housing"; Fei, "The Compound Labor Regime"; Goodfellow and Huang, "Contingent Infrastructure"; Shinn, "The Environmental Impact."

40. But for a completely different perspective and challenge to these framings, see Gagliardone, *China, Africa*; Mahoney, "China's Rise"; Qiu et al., "A New Approach."

41. E.g., Gravett, "Digital Neo-Colonialism." For a detailed analysis of this, see the report by Folashadé Soulé, *Negotiating Africa*.

42. I borrowed this phrase from Power and Alves, "Introduction."

43. The trains will potentially, in the future, connect to Lake Victoria, just like the original "lunatic express." See Taylor, "Kenya's Lunatic Express."

44. APA News, "Africa Should Take Advantage."

45. Maina and Cirolia, "Ring Roads."

46. Shen, "Building a Digital Silk Road."
47. Lee, "Introduction."
48. Others have called it China+; see Keane et al., *China's Digital Presence*.
49. E.g., Gagliardone, *China, Africa*; Keane et al., *China's Digital Presence*.
50. Franceschini and Loubere, *Global China as Method*, 8.
51. Gitonga, "Conversation #1," 22.
52. Coban, *Performing Technocapitalism*; Wahome, *Fabricating Silicon Savannah*.
53. McElroy, *Silicon Valley Imperialism*.
54. I borrow this wording from Tsing, *Frictions*, 124.
55. Steinberg et al., "Platform Capitalisms." See also Akallah et al., "History of Technology."
56. Stengers, *Cosmopolitics*. On the relationship between cosmotechnics and cosmopolitics, see Hui, "Comotechnics and Cosmopolitics."
57. Hui, *Arts and Cosmotechnics*, 9.
58. Hui, *The Question*.
59. Hui asks, "If technology has already left Europe and expanded to the rest of the world, is it still European?" Hui, *Post-Europe*, 39. In his book Hui makes the case that the relationship between European philosophy and technology is ultimately contingent and that a new political economy of technology does not need to come from European thinking alone.
60. Menon, "Changing Theory," 2.
61. Medina, *Cybernetic Revolutionaries*. See also Akallah et al., "History of Technology."
62. On writing "from," see Mbembé and Nuttall, "Writing the World."
63. See, among many others, Breckenridge, *Biometric State*; Burrell, *Invisible Users*; Chan, *Networking Peripheries*; Hecht, *Being Nuclear*; Irani, *Chasing Innovation*; Lindtner, *Prototype Nation*; Mavhunga, *Transient Workspaces*; Medina, *Cybernetic Revolutionaries*; Nemer, *Technology of the Oppressed*; Qiu, *Working-Class Network Society*; Steinberg, *The Platform Economy*; Takhteyev, *Coding Places*; Von Schnitzler, *Democracy's Infrastructure*; Zhang, *The Labor of Reinvention*.
64. Mavhunga, "Introduction." See also Breckenridge, *Biometric State*; Von Schnitzler, *Democracy's Infrastructure*.
65. Chan, *Networking Peripheries*.
66. Chan, *Networking Peripheries*, xiv.
67. Chan, *Networking Peripheries*, x.
68. Datta, "The Informational Periphery," 130.
69. McElroy, *Silicon Valley Imperialism*, 6.
70. McElroy, *Silicon Valley Imperialism*, 16.
71. Couldry and Mejias, "Data Colonialism."
72. Nellor, "The Rise of Africa."
73. I borrow this from Meagher, "Cannibalizing the Informal Economy."
74. Gravett, "Digital Neo-Colonialism."
75. Chen et al., "China as a 'Black Box.'"
76. McElroy, *Silicon Valley Imperialism*.
77. Birhane, "Algorithmic Colonization."
78. McElroy, *Silicon Valley*, 9.
79. Mavhunga, "Introduction," 7.
80. Ndlovu-Gatsheni, "Provincializing Europe."

81. Robinson, *Comparative Urbanism*, 7.

82. *Jua kali*, or informal economy, literally means "fierce sun." See King, *Jua kali*. See also Cirolia et al., "Silicon Savannahs."

83. Coban, *Performing Technocapitalism*.

84. Hence why I describe the subject of this book as techno-capital and not techno-capitalism.

85. Roy, "Ethnographic Circulations."

86. While ambivalent, these efforts are also "alternative to the current, troublesome technological global order," because they emerge from the hopes of those "who have been historically marginalized from dominant technoscientific worlds." Neumark, "Hypeful Worlds," 528.

87. Obviously, competition extends also to the domain of diplomacy. See Repnikova and Chen, "Asymmetrical Discursive Competition."

88. Qiu, *Working-Class Network Society*.

89. Soriano and Cabañes, "Entrepreneurial Solidarities."

1. SILICON STATES OF DEVELOPMENT

1. Scarfe and Cai, "Agency, Bargaining Power."

2. Brautigam, *The Dragon's Gift*.

3. Xi, *Open a New Era*. See also Taylor, *The Forum*. For a critical reading of the supposedly noninterventionist stance of China toward Africa, see Cheng et al., "Reading the Forum."

4. Transcript by the author.

5. Ferguson, *Global Shadows*; Sylla, "From a Marginalised to an Emerging Africa?"

6. For a critique of this all-encompassing framing, see Mkandawire, "Neopatrimonialism."

7. For a detailed overview of Kenya's structural adjustment period, see Murunga, "Governance."

8. Mkandawire and Soludo, *Our Continent, Our Future*.

9. Murunga, "Governance."

10. A response to the Lagos Plan, drafted by African leaders in 1980, the Berg Report was a watershed moment for the enshrinement of neoliberal policy prescriptions in Africa. See World Bank, *Accelerated Development*.

11. Merab, "How Melinda Gates."

12. For a critique, see Nyabola, *Digital Democracy*.

13. Ndemo and Weiss, *Digital Kenya*, xxiii.

14. See Chen and Rithmire, "The Rise of the Investor State." Seth Schindler and colleagues speak of the emergence of a twenty-first-century "infrastructure state"; see Schindler et al., "The New Cold War," 335.

15. Shen, *Alibaba*.

16. Mazzucato, *The Entrepreneurial State*.

17. Fuchs, "Industry 4.0"; Moisio and Rossi, "The Start-Up State"; Bunnell, *Malaysia*. On the relationship between digital infrastructure and statecraft, see, e.g., Braman, *Change of State*; Stevens, "Teleview."

18. Alami, and Dixon. "The Strange Geographies."

19. Weber, "State Capitalism." See also Dal Maso, "China as a Laboratory."

20. Wainaina, "Generation Kenya."

21. Nyairo, *Kenya@50*, 49.

22. Wainaina, "Generation Kenya."

23. Heeks, "ICT4D."

24. Ogot, *Who, if Anyone*. See also Poggiali, "Seeing (from) Digital Peripheries." Obviously, these spaces of democratic participation have also become laboratories for electoral disinformation. See Omanga and Manye, "Digital Media Politics."

25. On the Anglo Leasing scandal of 2005, see Mwangi, "Political Corruption."

26. The central argument of Branch's book is that "in the absence of redistribution, ethnicity provided a way in which Kenyans could access and protect the scarce resources of land, jobs and political power." Branch, *Kenya*, 294.

27. Republic of Kenya, *African Socialism*.

28. See Githongo, "Kenya: Riding the Tiger"; Kagwanja and Southall, *Kenya's Uncertain Democracy*.

29. See Cirolia, "Contested Fiscal Geographies"; Kanyinga, "Devolution."

30. I use this distinction here following Mkandawire, "Thinking About Developmental States."

31. See Weber, *How China Escaped*.

32. Omondi, "Darling of Private Investors."

33. Government of Kenya, *Economic Recovery Strategy*.

34. Government of Kenya, *Economic Recovery Strategy*.

35. See Nyong'o, "Planning for Policy." The developmental nature of ERS, which achieved important antipoverty targets in its implementation, also incorporated some of the policy points outlined in the Poverty Reduction Strategy Paper (PRSP) developed under the previous government. See Government of Kenya, *Status Report*.

36. Nyong'o, "Planning for Policy."

37. Government of Kenya, *Economic Recovery Strategy*, 4.

38. Government of Kenya, *Economic Recovery Strategy*, 4.

39. Etta, "Policy Making."

40. See Park, "Intimacy and Estrangement."

41. Kenya Gazette, *The Kenya Communications Act*.

42. See Nduati and Bowman, "Working from the Sidelines."

43. Kirui and Muhatia, "Universal Access."

44. Munyua and Mureithi, "Kenya."

45. See Wahome, *Fabricating Silicon Savannah*.

46. Gainer, "Planning Transformation."

47. With all its contradictions. See Bunnell, "Where Is the Future?"

48. Gainer, "Planning Transformation."

49. Fourie, "Model Students," 540.

50. Government of Kenya, *Kenya Vision 2030*.

51. Together with more introspective policies, like the digitization of land records. Datta and Muthama, "Sorting Paper."

52. Government of Kenya, *Kenya National ICT Masterplan*; Government of Kenya, *Digital Economy Blueprint*; Government of Kenya, *The Kenya National Digital Master Plan*.

53. This is how Ndemo himself would describe his tenure as permanent secretary of the ICT Ministry. See Ndemo, "Political Entrepreneurialism."

54. Park, "Intimacy and Estrangement."

55. A detailed business history of M-Pesa, and the journey from airtime-based transactions to mobile money, is in Omwansa and Sullivan, *Money, Real Quick*.

56. Although other sources put this number at 80 percent. See Camner et al., *What Makes a Successful Mobile Money Implementation?*

57. Kusimba, *Reimagining Money*. The anecdotal story of M-Pesa usage during the months of election violence is told by the anthropologist Olga Morawczynski. In fact, rather than "sending money home," M-Pesa was used by the families of urban migrants to send money *from* home to the city. See Morawczynski, "Exploring the Usage." See also Rouse et al., "M-Pesa and the Role of the Entrepreneurial State."

58. Ndemo, "Inside a Policymaker's Mind."

59. A similar view was shared by the Chinese reformers of the late Qing era. See Mullaney, *The Chinese Typewriter*. For the "learning from the West" story in the Qing era, see Wang, *China Reconnects*. For the role that technical catch-up played in Mao's era, see Andreas, *Rise of the Red Engineer*. Of course, this was also a matter of national security and military power. See Feigenbaum, *China's Techno-Warriors*. On technological orientalism, see Roh et al., *Techno-Orientalism*. On social movements and the internet, see Yang, *The Power of the Internet*.

60. Needham, *The Grand Titration*, 16.

61. Needham, *The Grand Titration*, 16.

62. Breznitz and Murphree, *Run of the Red Queen*.

63. Frank, *ReOrient*.

64. Hui, "The Question."

65. Among others, Breznitz and Murphree, *Run of the Red Queen*; Hong, *Networking China*; Mullaney, *The Chinese Computer*.

66. Franceschini and Loubere, *Global China as Method*, 20–22.

67. Gewirtz, "The Futurists of Beijing." See also Liu, *Information Fantasies*, on the role of the notion of *information* in 1980s China.

68. Hong, *Networking China*.

69. For a detailed history of this shift from political cadres to scientists and back, see Zhi and Pearson, "China's Hybrid Adaptive Bureaucracy."

70. A detailed analysis of this period is in Harwit, *China's Telecommunications Revolution*.

71. See Hong, *Networking China*, which places the formation of the Ministry of Information Industry in relation to internal politics regarding the World Trade Organization (WTO) deal.

72. See Harwit, *China's Telecommunications Revolution*.

73. The other two being "China's advanced culture" and "the fundamental interests of the overwhelming majority of the Chinese people."

74. As for the competition in the ICT space, for its WTO access in 2001 Beijing had agreed to liberalize the ICT market and adopt the internet protocol as a standard for its network switches. See Hong, *Networking China*.

75. See Wen, *The Huawei Model*.

76. Li, *Ren Zhengfei and Huawei*.

77. Wen, *The Huawei Model*, 66.

78. According to the recollection of Huawei executives, Kenya had been their second African market after Zambia.

79. See Driessen, *Tales of Hope*.

80. Wen makes the important argument that these different kinds of profit appetites and the capacity to wait for investment returns are a function of what C. K. Lee calls "varieties of capital." Even if Huawei is not technically a state-owned company, it does operate according to strategies that are not geared to immediate and high-volume returns, as other network equipment manufacturers are. See Wen, *The Huawei Model*, 71.

81. Huang and Pollio, "Between Highways and Fintech Platforms."

82. See Hong, "Safe Cities."

83. Safaricom itself uses national belonging as a marketing narrative. See Tuwei and Tully, "Producing Communities and Commodities."

84. In 2018, an investigative piece in the African edition of the French newspaper *Le Monde* alleged that computers in the African Union's headquarters in Addis Ababa were connecting every night to servers in Shanghai and that the Chinese-funded building was bugged by secret microphones. See Kadiri and Tilouine, "À Addis-Ababa."

85. Still, Hu's era was marked by important shifts in the relationship between technology and politics in China—the full implementation of the Great Firewall and the Golden Shield project being a case in point. Hu also launched the Medium- and Long-Term Programme in Science and Technology (MLP) in 2006, an update of Programme 863. See Sun and Cao, "China's Grand Experiment."

86. These policies have of course been less systematic and monolithic than it may appear, since China has a centralized yet minimalist and fragmented bureaucracy and the deployment of national blueprints is heterogeneous and contingent on their application at the local level. See Chen, *Manipulating Globalization*.

87. Zhang, *The Labor of Reinvention*, 5. See also Lindtner, *Prototype Nation*.

88. See, e.g., Zhao's discussion of the ambiguities and informal adaptations of ICT policy in China. Zhao, *Digital China's Informal Circuits*.

89. Something often forgotten in analysis of state capitalism in China. See Chun, *China and Global Capitalism*.

90. Shen and He, "The Geopolitics of Infrastructuralized Platforms."

91. See He, "Chinese Digital Platform Companies"; Tugendhat and Voo, "China's Digital Silk Road."

92. Gu et al., "Spatio-Temporal Evolution."

93. Shen and He, "The Geopolitics of Infrastructuralized Platforms"; Shen, *Alibaba*.

94. Omondi, "How Huawei Charmed Its Way."

95. See Keane et al., *China's Digital Presence in the Asia-Pacific*.

96. Brautigam et al., "What Kinds of Chinese 'Geese.'"

97. Zheng and Huang, *Market in State*.

98. In all its heterogeneity, as argued by Ling Chen. See Chen, *Manipulating Globalization*.

99. Lee, *The Specter of Global China*.

100. See Brautigam, *The Dragon's Gift*.

101. Ndemo, "Political Entrepreneurialism," 7. On the centrality of BPO to the Silicon Savannah story, see Graham and Mann, "Imagining a Silicon Savannah;" Anwar and Graham, *The Digital Continent*.

102. Pollio, "Making the Silicon Cape of Africa."

103. Most famously Porter's theories of competition and agglomeration. Pollio, "Making the Silicon Cape of Africa."

104. This was reported to me by a former NESC staff expert member.

105. Interview with Prof. Ndemo on Konza Technology City by CNBC Africa, https://www.youtube.com/watch?v=5BzgwOLdLHw&ab_channel=CNBCAfrica [5/29/23].

106. Government of Kenya, *Kenya Vision 2030*, 1.

107. Government of Kenya, *National Spatial Plan*.

108. The relocation of Nigeria's capital from Lagos to Abuja, for example, responded to the vision of an ethnically neutral and nationally united central government, bringing development to what was perceived as a less advanced region of the country. Yamoussoukro in Côte d'Ivoire, Lilongwe in Malawi, and Dodoma in Tanzania followed similar logics. Of course, there were exceptions to this, like new cities in apartheid South Africa. See Cirolia, "(W)Escaping the Challenges." See also Marcinkoski, *The City That Never Was*; Moser, "New Cities"; Van Noorloos and Kloosterboer, "Africa's New Cities"; Watson, "African Urban Fantasies."

109. Watson, "African Urban Fantasies."

110. Murray, "City Doubles."

111. On "city doubles," see Carmody and Owusu, "Neoliberalism, Urbanization and Change in Africa," 65. On "neoliberal heterotopias," see, among others, Buire, "The Dream and the Ordinary"; Cirolia, "(W)Escaping the Challenges." See also Côté-Roy and Moser, "Does Africa Not Deserve Shiny New Cities"; Harrison and Croese, "The Persistence and Rise of Master Planning." A very thoughtful analysis of the smart city narratives in KT and the coming together of local hopes and global speculations is Mu, "How Not to Define."

112. This moratorium had served the double purpose of avoiding the encroachment of informal settlements around the border of KT and forcing the surrounding county governments to enact a proper spatial plan overseen by the central ministry of land.

113. Baraka, "The Failed Promise of Kenya's Smart City."

114. See Miao et al., "Urban Entrepreneurialism 3.0."

115. Business Daily, "Shift Kenya's Economic Model."

116. Rosenberg and Brent, "Infrastructure Disruption."

117. Wainaina, "Generation Kenya."

118. Note, however, that the digitalization of the state has not proceeded at the same speed in the peripheries of Kenya's economic core. See Reyes-Carranza and Muthama, "Urban Sprawl."

119. See Coban, "Same, Same but Different"; Coban, *Performing Technocapitalism*.

120. On "siliconizing," see McElroy, *Silicon Valley Imperialism*.

121. Wai, "Neo-Patrimonialism."

2. MACHINES OF DATA FRONTIERS

1. Like other colonial cities in Africa, Nairobi was planned as a segregated urban environment to which Africans had limited access. Imagined as a garden city, Nairobi featured different quarters for what colonizers identified as different races: Europeans, Asians (mostly Indians), and Africans. The latter also had restricted access to the city. Moi Avenue bordered the whites-only central business district from the area of River Road, which functioned as a buffer to Asian and African quarters like Ngara and Kariokor. Ogot and Ogot, *History of Nairobi*.

2. *Chinku* can also have a sinophobic tone if addressed to people as an alternative to the neutral Mchina/Wachina. Sheng is a mixture of Swahili, English, and words borrowed

from other languages. It is a language of urban culture and politics. See Nyairo and Ogude, "Popular Music"; Githiora, *Sheng*.

3. See Maurer, "Mobile Money"; O'Dwyer, "Cache Society."

4. Horst and Miller, *The Cell Phone*.

5. Bratton, *The Stack*.

6. In the late 2000s, the Central Bank of Kenya ruled that each shilling on M-Pesa ought to be tethered to a "real" shilling in a Safaricom commercial bank account. See also Park, "'Human ATMs'"; Guma and Mwaura, "Infrastructural Configurations."

7. O'Dwyer, "Cache Society"; Kusimba, *Reimagining Money*.

8. Fisher and Downey, "Introduction."

9. See Lumumba-Kasongo, "China–Africa"; Couldry and Mejias, "Data Colonialism"; Pasquinelli and Vladan Joler, "The Nooscope Manifested"; Ricaurte, "Data Epistemologies."

10. Couldry and Mejias, *The Costs of Connection*, xiii, 337.

11. Benjamin, *Race After Technology*.

12. Birhane, "Algorithmic Colonization," 389.

13. Kwet, "Digital Colonialism."

14. Perrigo, "OpenAI"; for a broader analysis of digital labor in and from Africa, see Anwar and Graham, *The Digital Continent*.

15. Roitman, "Platform Economies."

16. Mavhunga, "Introduction."

17. *Spec* is tech jargon meaning "technical specifications," that is, the measurable qualities of a device.

18. Kimari, "Under Construction."

19. Meiu, "Panics over Plastics"; Zhu, "Can a Chinese Import"; Guma et al., "Plug-In Urbanism." There is a vast literature of infrastructure studies charting the technopolitics that roads, dams, and railways encapsulate. For Kenya, see Manji, "Bulldozers, Homes and Highways"; Kimari and Ernstson, "Imperial Remains"; Lesutis, "Infrastructural Territorialisations."

20. See Basil and Donovan, "Costly Propositions."

21. Pollio, "The Digital Silk Road."

22. Yang, "From Bandit Cell Phones."

23. Yang, "From Bandit Cell Phones."

24. Han, *Shanzhai*.

25. See De Kloet et al., *Boredom*, sec. 2.

26. Keane and Zhao, "Renegades on the Frontier of Innovation"; Zhao, *Digital China's Informal Circuits*.

27. Zhanga and Fung, "The Myth of 'Shanzhai' Culture."

28. Zhang, *The Labor of Reinvention*.

29. Qiu, *Working-Class Network Society*.

30. Studies of innovative Chinese companies going global in this period include Yi and Ye, *The Haier Way*; Tang, *Tencent*; Wen, *The Huawei Model*; Shen, *Alibaba*.

31. Avle, "Hardware and Data."

32. Lu, "Designed for the Bottom of the Pyramid."

33. In the industry jargon, featurephones (or feature phones) identify a class of handsets that, unlike smartphones, maintain the button-based inputs and the small displays of earlier generations of mobile phones. In Kenya, featurephones are also called *kabambe*.

34. Xiaomi also shares an interesting origin story in the shanzhai industrial culture of the Pearl River Delta. See Zhao, *Digital China's Informal Circuits.*

35. See discussion in chapter 4.

36. Mercer, "Boundary Work."

37. Cheeseman, "No Bourgeoisie, No Democracy."

38. This was reported to me confidentially by more than one informant.

39. He probably meant Shenzhen.

40. Lu and Qiu, "Empowerment or Warfare."

41. Lu and Qiu, "Empowerment or Warfare," 788.

42. Critical AI and platform scholars have made this point several times, observing that data workers, or even involuntary data practices, are often alienated from a full understanding of the ultimate values produced by the actual analysis of data. See Attoh et al., "'We're Building Their Data'"; Plantin, "The Data Archive"; Posada, "Embedded Reproduction."

43. Avle, "Hardware and Data."

44. Soriano and Cabañes, "Entrepreneurial Solidarities."

45. See Muniesa, *The Provoked Economy*; Lu and Qiu, "Transfer or Translation."

46. This might have been just a colorful retelling of the fact that MediaTek, a Taiwanese microchip manufacturer, had been behind many shanzhai phone makers, thanks to the 2005 commercialization of their white-label, single-chip turnkey solution.

47. CITIC Securities, Transsion Holdings documents (my translation).

48. Avle, "Hardware and Data in the Platform Era," 1479.

49. Avle, "Hardware and Data in the Platform Era," 1485.

50. Lu and Qiu, "Empowerment or Warfare?"

51. As Marion Fourcade and Keyran Healy observe, the capture of data often starts as a speculative project. This was the case for Kamande's start-up. Fourcade and Healy, "Seeing Like a Market."

52. For a nuanced critique of this framing, see Gagliardone, *China, Africa.*

53. Gravett, "Digital Neo-Colonialism." But see Gagliardone, *China, Africa.*

54. Chen et al., "China as a 'Black Box.'"

55. Bratton, *The Revenge of the Real*, 54. See also Kwet, "Digital Colonialism."

56. Couldry and Mejias, "Data Colonialism."

57. Mouton and Burns, "(Digital) Neo-Colonialism."

58. See Bernards, "Colonial Financial Infrastructures"; Bhagat and Roderick, "Banking on Refugees"; Birhane, "Algorithmic Colonization"; Langley and Leyshon, "Neo-Colonial Credit"; Rodima-Taylor, "Platformizing Ubuntu."

59. Smith, *The Eyes.*

60. See Downey and Fisher, "Introduction."

61. On the polysemy of frontier/edge as a space of continuity, as a relation, and as a form of uncertainty, see Saguin, *Urban Ecologies.* I thank Morgan Mouton for the suggestion.

3. PLATFORMS OF ALGORITHMIC SUTURING

1. Saxenian, *The New Argonauts.*

2. See Chan, *Networking Peripheries.* See also Datta, "The informational Periphery."

3. On the haigui phenomenon in China, see Dal Maso, *Risky Expertise.*

4. Hong, *Networking China.*

5. Achola, "Colonial Policy."

6. Nangulu-Ayuku, "Politics, Urban Planning." See also Kimari, "The Story of a Pump."

7. See Ng'weno, "Growing Old."

8. Ogot and Ogot, *History of Nairobi*; Ese and Ese, *The City Makers.*

9. See Akallah and Hård, "Under the Historian's Radar."

10. Mutongi, *Matatu.*

11. See Guma, "Incompleteness." For a critical perspective on the politics of the infrastructure "gap," see Goodfellow, "Finance, Infrastructure and Urban Capital." See also Cirolia and Pollio, "Spectrums of Infrastructural Hybridity."

12. De Boeck, "Divining the City."

13. De Boeck, "Divining the City," 56.

14. Simone, "Ritornello." A recurring thread in the scholarly contributions that have been inspired by Simone's formulation of "people as infrastructure" is that in contexts of infrastructural breakages and absences, urban dwellers and state actors find ways of "suturing" and "completing" these systemic fragments in order to make-do against dysfunction and ruination. See, e.g., Baptista, "Electricity Services"; Cirolia et al., "Infrastructure Governance"; Kasper and Schramm, "Storage City"; Silver, "Incremental Infrastructures."

15. The idea of "splintering urbanism" was introduced by Steve Graham and Simon Marvin in their field-defining book of the same title. See Graham and Marvin, *Splintering Urbanism*. Since then, several scholars have also pointed out the limitations of this framing. See, e.g., Jaglin, "Differentiating Networked Services."

16. See also Friederici et al., *Digital Entrepreneurship*, 109–10.

17. Fejerskov, "The New Technopolitics." A similar argument is made more specifically about Nairobi's tech scene in the last chapter of Wahome, *Fabricating Silicon Savannah.*

18. Fejerskov, *The Global Lab.*

19. Pollio, "Acceleration."

20. Here my argument slightly differs from Nemer's description (Nemer, *Technology of the Oppressed*) of technological bricolage (*gambiarra*) as a practice of technical make-do through which marginal citizens in Brazilian favelas survive infrastructural neglect while creating spaces of disobedience. While these practices do exist in Nairobi, my focus is on start-ups that imagine technological bricolage as a site of value through algorithmic optimization.

21. Among others, see Al Dahdah, "Digital Markets"; Cirolia et al., "Silicon Savannahs"; Cirolia et al., "Fintech 'Frontiers'"; Mann and Iazzolino, "From Development State."

22. Qiu, *Working-Class Network Society*. Another interesting corporate history is that of the household electronics manufacturer Haier. See Yi, *The Haier Way.*

23. With all its contradictions and violences. See Zhang, *The Labour of Reinvention.* Also in Nairobi, scholars have written about the forms of predatory inclusion enabled by digital platforms. See, e.g., Donovan and Park, "Knowledge/Seizure"; Donovan and Park, "Algorithmic Intimacy."

24. Pollio et al., "Algorithmic Suturing."

25. Simone, "Ritornello," 1343.

26. Seaver, *Computing Taste.*

27. For a spatial genealogy of algorithms, see Pasquinelli, "Three Thousand Years." See also Daston, *Rules*. As my colleague Liam Magee pointed out in private correspondence, the spatial nature of algorithmic thinking in software development also owes a debt to the curiously enormous influence of Christopher Alexander's 1970s work on architectural and urban design patterns, so that the "algorithm" began to be thought as less a long expanding recipe of instruments and more a set of interlinked and recursive functions straddling the real world and its modeling.

28. Lee, *The Specter of Global China*.

29. See Cupers and Meier, "Infrastructure Between Statehood."

30. About the speculative nature of this densification along Nairobi's bypasses, see Maina and Cirolia, "Ring Roads." See also Huchzermeyer, "Tenement City." And for a broader discussion of these multifarious processes of plotted expansion in urban Africa, see Karaman et al., "Plot by Plot"; Choplin, *Concrete City*.

31. Gillespie, "The Real Estate Frontier"; Choplin, *Concrete City*.

32. Writing more broadly about East Africa, Tom Goodfellow shows how the unique pace of urbanization in the region depends on distinctive political circumstances that marry the power of local elites, domestic capital, and urban political movements. See Goodfellow, *Politics and the Urban Frontier*. In Nairobi, the northeastern suburbs along Thika Road are the political bedrock of Mount Kenya politics and an important voting pool along one of the branches of the colonial railway that connects Nairobi to Mount Kenya (Nanyuki).

33. Kasper and Schramm, "Storage City."

34. On the contradictory nature of Safaricom as the custodian of a public infrastructure and a corporation beholden to its shareholders, see Park, "Intimacy." On the developmental mandate to reach universal access in China, see Hong, *Networking China*.

35. Ogone, "Mobile phones in Africa."

36. Prahalad, *The Fortune*.

37. Donovan and Park. "Knowledge/Seizure."

38. However, the kadogo economy also extends to the poorest sections of the population, and in settlements like Kibera many economic activities are organized around the principle of kadogo parceling. See Mukeku, "Urban Slum Morphology."

39. Anwar and Graham, *The Digital Continent*; Muldoon et al., "The Poverty of Ethical AI."

40. Charting a history of the urban dashboard, Shannon Mattern argues that such a mode of visualizing data renders complex, technical matters into legible and actionable problems. Tzkak also makes a related point, ultimately analyzing dashboards as formats, layouts that at once constrain and translate data in determinate ways. See Mattern, "Mission Control;" Beverungen, "Executive Dashboard"; Tkacz, *Being with Data*.

41. In a more critical view, Altenried describes this as "digital Taylorism." See Altenried, *The Digital Factory*, 6.

42. Fourcade and Healy, "Seeing Like a Market."

43. Donovan and Park, "Knowledge/Seizure."

44. Even though they may rely on the same underlying infrastructure, such as Taobao villages that serve more than one e-commerce platform. See Chu et al., "Placing the Platform Economy."

45. Kimari, "We Will Be Back"; Guma, "Smart Urbanism."

46. See Steinberg et al., "Media Power."

47. According to some accounts, boda bodas owe their name to the word *border*, as the first riders working on such pillion services were ferrying passengers from Busia, in Uganda, to the Kenyan border in the 1960s. See Courtwright, "Uganda's Boda Bodas."

48. See Rizzo, *Taken for a Ride*; Goodfellow, "Taming the Rogue Sector."

49. As Courtwright writes, in the context of nearby Uganda, "It also didn't take long for politicians to see . . . that boda bodas were highly visible and mobile, and that they could move constituents both physically and metaphorically to vote for them." Courtwright, "Uganda's Boda Bodas."

50. At the time of this writing, the most recent attempt at regulation was the bill introduced to the Kenyan Senate in late 2023.

51. Nyairo, "The Boda Boda," 109.

52. Cirolia et al., "Fintech 'Frontiers.'"

53. Cirolia et al., "Silicon Savannahs."

54. See Darbon, "The Political Role."

55. On the centrality of addressability in computational architectures, see Dhaliwal, "On Addressability."

56. See Fei, "Transnationalizing Intrapreneurship."

57. In many respects, Dasher's business model was not unique. Research on platforms has shown time and again that on-demand work can make labor less rather than more precarious but not necessarily better. See Schor, "Dependence and Precarity."

58. This confirms and extends C. K. Lee's argument that corporate China in Africa is often involved in practices of profit optimization rather than immediate profit maximization. While Lee's point is specifically about state capital as opposed to other varieties of capital, Chinese tech start-ups in Kenya also operate across diverse temporalities of profitability. I return to this point in chapter 5. See Lee, *The Specter*.

59. See, e.g., Seaver, *Computing Taste*.

60. On the theme of convenience, see Cirolia and Pollio, "Beyond Inclusion"; and the broader reflections in the same collection, Neves and Steinberg, "In Convenience."

61. Chen, "The Mirage."

62. Chen, "The Mirage."

63. Shen, *Alibaba*. More broadly, see Hong and Harwit, *China's Globalizing Internet*.

64. See Fejerskov, *The Global Lab*.

65. On the precariousness of labor enrolled in China's platform giants, see Chen and Qiu, "Digital Utility"; Sun, "Your Order"; Zhang, "Platformizing Family Production"; Zhou, "Trapped in the Platform"; De Kloet et al., "The Platformization of Chinese Society." Of course, the notion of platform labor more generally has underscored the fungibility and surplus nature of workers in the platform economy; see Van Doorn "Platform Labor"; Van Doorn and Chen, "Odd Stacked." It is digital China at large, as Elaine Zhao explains, that lives between formal and informal, precarious and stable economic arrangements. See Zhao, *Digital China's Informal Circuits*.

66. See Meagher, "Cannibalizing the Informal Economy." For a different view of repair practices through mundane technologies, see Nemer, *Technology of the Oppressed*.

67. Thieme, "Turning Hustlers."

68. Donovan and Park, "Knowledge/Seizure."

69. Donovan and Park, "Algorithmic Intimacy." See also Neves and Steinberg, "In Convenience."

70. See Halpern et al., "Test-Bed Urbanism."

71. Tadiar, "Remaindered Life."

72. Stengers, "Comparison as a Matter of Concern."

4. MICROGEOPOLITICS OF STANDARDS

1. Sottek, "Google Pulls Huawei."

2. Chen and Haldane, "Explainer."

3. For an equivalent story in Xiaomi, see Zhao, *Digital China's Informal Circuits*, chap. 2.

4. Osamuyi, "Transsion's Trojan Horses."

5. Miller, *Chip War*.

6. Palmer, "An Act of War."

7. Fei, "Internationalizing China Standards."

8. Pohlmann and Buggenhagen, "Who Is Leading."

9. For a critique of this framing, see Gagliardone, *China, Africa*; Nanni, "Digital Sovereignty."

10. Drawing on research on China's contributions to ITU and ICANN, Gianluigi Negro suggests that, contrary to expectations that China is contributing to the fragmentation of the internet, Chinese delegates are pushing for a multistakeholder model in which states are the only players that can voluntarily agree to suspend their sovereign rights to cede more power to private actors. This model is designed to contrast with the overwhelming power of large tech companies, as well as the dominance of US institutions in the assignment of network space. See Negro, "A History."

11. Qiu et al., "A New Approach." One may even notice an oddly contradictory stance in the 2021 "National Standardization Development Outline," whereby Chinese industries need to better follow international standards while making new ones. The strategy is framed against the overarching principles of Xi's Thought on Socialism with Chinese Characteristics for a New Era and against the more recent "five-in-one" goals, which articulate China's path to development in five inseparable trajectories.

12. Palmer, "An Act of War."

13. Ecofin agency, "Kenya Pledges."

14. Munda and Njau, "Kenya Backs Safaricom."

15. See Leigh Star and Lampland, "Reckoning with Standards."

16. Easterling, *Extrastatecraft*, 171. For a less standard-centric analysis, see Wiig and Silver, "Turbulent Presents."

17. International Standards Organization, https://www.iso.org/standards.html [09/08/2023].

18. Bowker and Star, *Sorting Things Out*.

19. Note, however, that Bowker and Star also highlight the limitations of standardization (both as an analytical entry point and as a strategy for ensuring consistency) and offer a wider vocabulary of analysis through their work on "boundary objects." See Bowker and Star, *Sorting Things Out*.

20. Timmermans and Epstein, "A World of Standards."

21. Thévenot, "Rules and Implements." The making of standards can also be seen as a key process of rent-seeking in what Kean Birch and Fabian Muniesa call the "asset" form. See Birch and Muniesa, "Introduction."

22. In Paula Bialski's words, these were "good-enough" solutions, even though the companies building them were not "middle tech" but rather small start-ups. See Bialski, *Middle Tech*.

23. Note that protocols, like standards, have a similar definitional fuzziness. See Galloway, *Protocol*.

24. For a discussion of the *chi ku*—eating bitterness—ethos, see Driessen, "Pushed to Africa."

25. For more about the evolving contractual nature of Chinese-funded infrastructure in Africa, see Huang and Pollio, "Between Highways."

26. The first wave of privatization of Kenya's public enterprises took place in the decade from the early 1990s to the early 2000s, during which the entirety of nonstrategic parastatals established in the wake of the country's independence (1963) was partially or fully liquidated. A much more complex set of public sector reforms ensued in the early 2000s. Both these programs were championed and sometimes enforced by Western development finance institutions, which at the time owned the majority of Kenya's foreign debt.

27. On the diversity of finance, see, e.g., Maurer, *Mutual Life*; Miyazaki, *Arbitraging Japan*.

28. Only a week earlier, an unsettling scandal had reverberated across the continent. Flutterwave, the Nigerian fintech company that so many tech reporters had heralded as the first, truly African unicorn—a start-up valued more than US$1 billion—had revealed itself to be built on shaky financial grounds and on unsavory practices of corporate harassment. Shockwaves had been felt in Nairobi too. I first saw this piece of investigative journalism in David Hundeyin's *West Africa Weekly* (Hundeyn, "Flutterwave"). The story was picked up by *Rest of the World* on April 28, 2022 (Idris, "Inside the Scandal at Flutterwave").

29. See Morozov, *To Save Everything*. While these forms of promethean optimism undoubtedly permeate the African development-technology nexus, I have argued that other rationalities are also at play in the making of African cultures of digital innovation. See Pollio, "Acceleration."

30. Gowa, *Closing the Gold Window*.

31. Scott and Zachariadis, *The Society*, 7–26.

32. De Goede, "Finance/Security Infrastructure," 352.

33. De Goede, "Finance/Security Infrastructure," 353.

34. Scott and Zachariadis, *The Society*.

35. Wise does not actually need accounts in each country for a number of reasons: there are integrated payment spaces, such as the European Union's SEPA, which allow all payments made in euros to be handled in a single jurisdiction; similarly, there are pan-African aggregators such as the already mentioned Flutterwave that handle many African currencies through a single switch, on behalf of companies like Wise. Also note that Wise does use SWIFT for clearing transactions.

36. "Float" is a financial term for money that is briefly counted twice. Float strategies are behind many fintech innovations, not just cross-border payment platforms. See Roitman, "Platform Economies."

37. Price, "London's $1 Billion Finance Startup." Not incidentally, Western Union, a US corporation that started more than 170 years ago as a telegraph company, was also behind the telex system, which, as we have seen, primed the development of the SWIFT standard. See Scott and Zachariadis, *The Society*.

38. Joy, *Chinese Underground Banking*.

39. See De Goede, "Hawala Discourses."

40. A great account of the making of "good" and "bad" destinations for capital invest-ment in Africa is in Ralph's *Forensic of Capital*.

41. During our conversation, June also made an interesting remark concerning this tightening of the legal leeways of informal value transfer practices. She argued that this phenomenon had happened everywhere, not just in China. In a more academic form, the essentialism of this view of China's intervention in the fintech sector has been made in Zhang and Chen, "A Regional and Historical Approach."

42. Daston, *Rules*.

43. See Rosenberg and Brent, "Infrastructure Disruption."

44. See Cirolia et al., "Silicon Savannahs."

45. Chen, *Influence Empire*. See chap. 2.

46. Hong, *Networking China*, 17.

47. Tan, *Chinnovation*.

48. Pollio, "Acceleration."

49. See Latour, "Visualization and Cognition"; Beckert, *Imagined Futures*.

50. See Thrift, *Knowing Capitalism*.

51. In sociological terms, these would be both terminological standards and procedural standards. See Timmermans and Epstein, "A World of Standards."

52. Qiu, *Working Class*.

53. Ries, *The Lean Startup*.

54. Holweg, "The Genealogy of Lean Production." For a "lean" genealogy of contempo-rary platform economies, see also Steinberg, *The Platform Economy*.

55. Zhang, *The Labor of Reinvention*.

56. A point that I cannot explore in full here is that this labor of reinvention is also the reinvention of the laborer, as argued by Zhang in *The Labor of Reinvention*.

57. Ries, *The Lean Startup*.

58. See Huang and Pollio, "Between Highways."

59. Lee, *The Specter*.

60. These were June's actual words: "It will be different from all other remittance [pro-viders] in Kenya . . . in Africa. Because we have modeled it using the Chinese control sys-tem, which is actually better for controlling risk. Because you gather more information. And it's not like I need to get information others don't. It's: others don't have that informa-tion, then they don't think about it."

61. See Fei, "The Compound Labor"; Fei, "Networked Internationalization"; Huang and Chen, "Is China Building Africa."

62. Maurer, "Payment." See also O'Dwyer, "Cache Society."

63. Zhu, "Sinophobia." In *Racism for Sale*, BBC journalists tracked a Chinese hustler and his questionable business of filming videos of African children dancing while being instructed to chant self-demeaning insults in Mandarin. These clips belonged to a bigger, somewhat more benign, though perhaps not less problematic, online business of video greeting cards: birthday and other well wishes pronounced by Black kids in heavily accent-ed Mandarin. In China, these videos could be ordered on online platforms like Taobao and gifted as unique, personalized tokens. Unsurprisingly, the release of the BBC documentary

generated shock and outrage but also reflections on the politics of representation implied in it. Some of my Kenyan friends, for example, praised the investigative efforts but expressed frustrations about the theatrical tone of the piece, which in their view portrayed Africans as hapless victims of racist scammers. My Chinese research interlocutors, on the other hand, raised questions about the sinophobic metonymy they recognized in the video. "Why was the BBC chasing a single Chinese rascal and making it into a story of China in Africa?" I was asked by Bobby, a Chongqingnese entrepreneur introduced in the final chapter.

64. See Kimari, "Under Construction"; Maweu, "Journalists."

65. And its hitherto hegemony in the dollarized infrastructures of remittance, even alternative ones. See Cirolia et al., "Remittance Micro-Worlds."

66. Mizes and Donovan, "Capitalizing Africa." See also Mizes, "Investing in Independence"; Roitman, "Platform Economies." For a longer lineage of this, see Sylla, "Fighting Monetary Colonialism."

67. See Thévenot, "Rules and Implements."

68. Mathews et al., *The World in Guangzhou.*

69. This resonates with an important point made by Alex Galloway about protocols: they may operate in a contradictory manner, by fostering horizontality while creating vertical institutions that define the access and the modes of access. See Galloway, *Protocol.*

70. Fourcade and Healy, "Seeing Like a Market."

5. LABORS OF INVESTABILITY

1. Mkalama and Ouma, "To Whom Does the Money Go"; Wahome, *Fabricating Silicon.*

2. I use the idea of investability drawing on the work of the anthropologist Tania Li, who writes more specifically about the making of land into an investable asset. See Li, "What Is Land," 589.

3. Rosenberg and Brent, "Infrastructure Disruption."

4. Antenucci, "The Making"; Pollio and Cirolia, "Fintech Urbanism."

5. For a reflection on the contradictions of Nairobi's nightlife from a queer perspective, see the beautiful essay by Eddie Ombagi, "Nairobi Is a Shot of Whiskey."

6. Ogot and Ogot, *History of Nairobi.*

7. Nyairo, *Kenya@50*, 49.

8. They are also zones of exception and expulsion for the many refugees and other stateless people who reside in Nairobi. On "gated" Nairobi, see Owuor, *Security.*

9. On these erasures, see Kimari, "Resisting Imperial Erasures."

10. Saxenian, *The New Argonauts.*

11. Pollio, "Making the Silicon Cape."

12. Tsing, "Inside the Economy," 117–18.

13. Coban, *Performing Technocapitalism.*

14. See Franceschini and Loubere, *Global China as Method.*

15. Ogot and Ogot, *History of Nairobi.*

16. Lee, *The Specter*, 10.

17. Elyachar, *Markets of Dispossession*; Roy, *Poverty Capital.*

18. Dolan and Rajak, "Remaking Africa's Informal Economies," 53. See also Dolan and Gordon, "Worker, Businessman, Entrepreneur?"

19. Zhang, *The Labor of Reinvention.*

20. A similar intervention about the collective nature of what Gina Neff calls "venture labor" is in her book of the same name. See Neff, *Venture Labor.*

21. Hong, *Passionate Work.*

22. See Saxenian, *Regional Advantage.* On these modes of sociality, see also Cockayne, "Entrepreneurial Affects."

23. A sympathetic yet gripping portrayal of Beijing's innovation scene is Ning, *Zhong Guan Village.*

24. Data from Refinitiv shows that by 2021 almost half of global VC was coming from China, a peak followed by a downfall.

25. Hannah Appel makes a fundamental point that is useful to these reflections. *Risks* are at once taken and offloaded (those that *should not* be taken) to more precarious and less privileged people. Some of the activities described in this chapter, in my reading, were about reconciling these two kinds of risks. See Appel, *The Licit Life,* 71.

26. I return to these reflections in the next chapter.

27. On the parable of New York city's tech scene, two books are crucial beyond Neff's *Venture Labor.* See Indergaard, *Silicon Alley*; Zukin, *The Innovation Complex.*

28. I borrow the term "entrepreneurial solidarity" from Cheryll Soriano and Jason Cabañes, who describe the solidarities forged by Filipino digital workers. Soriano and Cabañes, "Entrepreneurial Solidarities," 2. See also Rosenberg and Brent, "Infrastructure Disruption"; Wahome, *Fabricating Silicon Savannah.*

29. Coleman, "The Hacker Conference."

30. For a similar argument see Chan, *Networking Peripheries,* 121.

31. In a different context, see Elyachar, "Phatic Labor."

32. This argument resonates with Neff's description of venture labor, although the latter captures "workers" in a more traditional sense rather than self-employed entrepreneurs. See Neff, *Venture Labor.*

33. Cooiman, "Veni Vidi VC," 230.

34. Of course, risky equity investments have a longer history. Tom Nicholas, for example, describes whaling investments as an early form of US venture capitalism. See Nicholas, *VC.*

35. Block and Keller, "Where Do Innovations Come From."

36. These are matters inscribed in the investment negotiation.

37. VC funds can also be state owned or participated in by state capital, as is the case with some VC funds in Asia. See Klingler-Vidra, *The Venture Capital State.*

38. Cooiman, "Imprinting the Economy."

39. Pollio, "Acceleration, Development and Technocapitalism."

40. At the heart of these derisking processes is, of course, financial valuation, a subject that I do not address in this book. See Doganova, *Discounting.*

41. See Benjamin, "Assessing Risk"; Coleman, "Race as Technology"; Chun, *Discriminating Data*; Eubanks, *Automating Inequality*; Migozzi, "Selecting Spaces"; Roy, "Subjects of Risk."

42. See Birch, "Reflexive Expectations."

43. On VC patience, see Klingler-Vidra, "When Venture Capital Is Patient."

44. See Friederici et al., *Digital Entrepreneurship.*

45. In fact, only a handful of cities in the continent, Nairobi, Cairo, Lagos, Cape Town, and Johannesburg, claim the lion's share of these capital circulations. Pollio and Cirolia, *Financing ICT*.

46. Ross, *No Collar*.

47. Mkalama and Ouma, "To Whom Does the Money Go."

48. See Steinberg et al., "Media Power."

49. I borrow this notion from the seminal work of Jane Guyer. See Guyer, *Marginal Gains*.

50. Shestakofsky, *Behind the Startup*.

51. Shestakofsky, *Behind the Startup*, x.

52. Shestakofsky, *Behind the Startup*, xi; Geiger, "Silicon Valley" (on eschatology); Shiller, *Irrational Exuberance*. For a similar argument about "caution," see Chen, *Networking Peripheries*.

53. Berlant, *Cruel Optimism*.

54. Coban, *Performing Technocapitalism*, 17.

55. Lee, *The Specter*.

6. ETHNOGRAPHIES OF TECHNO-OPTIMISM

1. Huang and Pollio, "Between Highways"; Guma et al., "Plug-In Urbanism"; Kimari, "Under Construction."

2. Wasuna, "Chinese Billionaire."

3. Adeyemi, "A Closer Look."

4. For a discussion of democratic ideals in this technological optimism, see Nyambola, *Digital Democracy*.

5. Pollio, "Incubators"; Pollio, "Reading Development Failure."

6. Pollio, "Acceleration."

7. Saxenian, "Regional Networks"; Barbrook and Cameron, "The Californian Ideology."

8. Barbrook and Cameron, "The Californian Ideology," 45.

9. Barbrook and Cameron, "The Californian Ideology," 47; Gilmore, *Golden Gulag*; Heppler, *Silicon Valley*.

10. Geiger, "Silicon Valley"; Morozov, *To Save Everything*.

11. Mac and Schleifer, "How a Network"; Pollio, "Acceleration."

12. Fejerskov, *The Global Lab*.

13. Mitchell, *Rule of Experts*.

14. See the collection Cooper and Packard, *International Development*. See also the reflections in Táíwò, *Africa Must Be Modern*.

15. Ferguson, *The Anti-Politics Machine*.

16. A good example of this is Léopold Sédar Senghor's writings about the relationship between technical expertise and the socialist state.

17. Rostow, *The Stages*.

18. Barbrook and Cameron, "The Californian Ideology," 48.

19. Toffler, *Future Shock*.

20. Toffler, *The Third Wave*.

21. Toffler, *The Third Wave*, chap. 23.

22. Adeyemi, "Sorry Kenya."

23. Feigenbaum, *China's Techno-Warriors*

24. Gewirtz, "The Futurists," 115.

25. Lindtner, *Prototype nation*; Liu, *The Shenzhen Model*; Zhang, *The Labor of Reinvention*.

26. Franceschini et al., "Prometheus in China."

27. See Issaka, "Techno-Optimism"; and Mazzarella, "Beautiful Balloon."

28. Dolan and Gordon, "Worker, Businessman, Entrepreneur?"; Pollio, "Acceleration."

29. Liu, *The Shenzhen Model*; Liu, *Start-Up Wolf*; Zhang, *The Labor of Reinvention*. Cedric Durand specifically argues that China is an example of a state-capitalist Silicon Valley consensus; Durand, *How Silicon Valley*.

30. On the centrality of scaling up, see Avle et al., "Scaling."

31. Cockayne, "Entrepreneurial Affect."

32. See Latour, *Aramis*.

33. Danaher, "Techno-Optimism"; Königs, "What Is Techno-Optimism?"

34. Said, *Orientalism*.

35. Wang, *The Politics*.

36. I borrowed this from Ang, *On Not Speaking Chinese*.

37. Of course, this is a perspective that has been variously challenged. See An, "Renarrating China-Africa Relations."

38. Li, *The Will to Improve*.

39. Lepore, "The Disruption Machine."

40. See, e.g., Ralph, *Thin Description*.

41. Nader, "Ethnography," 217. See also Zaloom, *Out of the Pits*.

42. Gerwitz, "The Futurists of Beijing," 117.

43. Pandian, *A Possible Anthropology*, 107.

44. Malinowski, *Argonauts*, 20.

45. Cirolia and Pollio, "Queer Infrastructures."

46. Berlant, "The Commons," 393.

47. Boellstorff, "Queer Techne," 230. On the field site as a network, see Burrell, "The Field Site."

48. Ahmed, "Orientations."

49. Cirolia and Pollio, "Queer Infrastructures."

50. Ahmed, "Orientations,"545.

51. Cirolia and Pollio, "Queer Infrastructures," 242.

52. Günel and Watanabe, "Patchwork Ethnography."

53. Gill and Pratt, "In the Social Factory."

54. See Cockayne, "What Is a Startup."

55. Coleman, "The Hacker Conference"; Liu, "To Be 'Entrepreneured'"; Pollio, "Incubators."

56. Malinowski, *Argonauts of the Western Pacific*.

57. Geertz, "Thick Description."

58. Günel and Watanabe, "Patchwork Ethnography."

59. E.g., Cenere, "Making Translation"; Coban, *Performing Technocapitalism*; Irani, *Chasing Innovation*; Shestakofsky, *Behind the Startup*.

60. Rist, "Blitzkrieg Ethnography."

61. Geertz, "Thick Description," 20–21.

62. Jackson, *Thin Description*.

63. Pollio, "Reading Development Failure."

CODA: THINKING TECHNOLOGY ELSEWHERE, AND OTHERWISE

1. One of Ruto's signature policies had been a "hustler fund," a set of flat-rate, digitally enabled personal and start-up loans targeted to entrepreneurial citizens. The fund, controversial from the beginning, ended up having a higher default rate than the portfolios of commercial banks. Abiodun, "Default." For a discussion on hustling in Nairobi, see Thieme, "Turning Hustlers."

2. Chan, *Networking Peripheries*.

3. Neumark, "Hypeful Worlds," 537.

4. See, e.g., the work of Oscar Otele at Afrobarometer. Otele, "What Explains African Perceptions."

5. Ouma, "The Difference."

6. McElroy, *Silicon Valley Imperialism*, 209. For a discussion of the relationship between digital technology (specifically, AI) and capital through the lens of labor, see Pasquinelli, *The Eye*.

7. Harvey, *Spaces of Hope*.

8. Chari, "African Extraction," 84.

9. Hui, "Cosmotechnics," 9.

BIBLIOGRAPHY

Abiodun, Bolu. "Default on the Government-Backed Hustler Fund in Kenya Has Reached $20m." *Techpoint Africa*, August 22, 2023. https://techpoint.africa/2023/08/22/20m-default -on-hustlers-fund/ [8/7/2024].

Achola, Milcah Amolo. "Colonial Policy and Urban Health: The Case of Colonial Nairobi." *AZANIA: Journal of the British Institute in Eastern Africa* 36, no. 1 (2001): 119–37.

Adeyemi, Daniel. "A Closer Look at Opera's 'Africa First Approach.'" *Techcabal*, January 7, 2021. https://techcabal.com/2021/01/07/a-closer-look-at-operas-africa-first-approach/ [6/21/2023].

Adeyemi, Daniel. "Sorry Kenya! Google Drops Balloon Internet Project." *Techcabal*, January 22, 2021. https://techcabal.com/2021/01/22/googles-moonshot-project-that-promised -kenyans-affordable-internet-shuts-down/ [7/1/2024].

Ahmed, Sara. "Orientations: Toward a Queer Phenomenology." *GLQ: A Journal of Lesbian and Gay Studies* 12, no. 4 (2006): 543–74.

Aitken, Rob. *Performing Capital: Toward a Cultural Economy of Popular and Global Finance.* New York: Palgrave Macmillan, 2007.

Akallah, Jethron Ayumbah, Nelson Arellano-Escudero, Animesh Chatterjee, Sławomir Łotysz, Saara Matala, Min Fanxiang, Stefan Poser, Hugh R. Slotten, and Magdalena Zdrodowska. "History of Technology in Global Perspectives." *ICON: Journal of the International Committee for the History of Technology* 29, no. 1 (2024): 9–45.

Akallah, Jethron Ayumbah, and Mikael Hård. "Under the Historian's Radar: Local Water Supply Practices in Nairobi, 1940–1980." *Water Alternatives* 13, no. 3 (2020): 886–901.

Al-Bulushi, Yousuf. "Dar es Salaam on the Frontline: Red and Black Internationalisms." *Third World Thematics: A TWQ Journal* 8, no. 1–3 (2023): 21–37.

Al-Bulushi, Yousuf. *Ruptures in the Afterlife of the Apartheid City.* Cham: Springer Nature, 2024.

Al Dahdah, Marine. "Digital Markets and the Commercialization of Healthcare in Africa: The Case of Kenya." *Globalizations* (2022): 1–13.

Alami, Ilias, and Adam D. Dixon. "The Strange Geographies of the 'New' State Capitalism." *Political Geography* 82 (2020): 102237.

Alden, Chris. "China in Africa." *Survival* 47, no. 3 (2005): 147–64.

Alden, Christopher, Daniel Large, and Ricardo Soares de Oliveira. "Introduction: China Returns to Africa." In *China Returns to Africa: A Rising Power and a Continent Embrace*, ed. Christopher Alden, Daniel Large, and Ricardo Soares de Oliveira, 1–26. New York: Columbia University Press, 2008.

Altenried, Moritz. *The Digital Factory: The Human Labor of Automation.* Chicago: University of Chicago Press, 2022.

Alves, Ana Cristina. "China's 'Win-Win' Cooperation: Unpacking the Impact of Infrastructure-for-Resources Deals in Africa." *South African Journal of International Affairs* 20, no. 2 (2013): 207–26.

An, Ning. "Renarrating China-Africa Relations: Perspectives from New Chinese Immigrants in Zimbabwe." *South African Geographical Journal* 106, no. 3 (2024): 249–67.

Andreas, Joel. *Rise of the Red Engineers: The Cultural Revolution and the Origins of China's New Class.* Stanford: Stanford University Press, 2009.

Ang, Ien. *On not Speaking Chinese: Living Between Asia and the West.* London: Routledge, 2001.

Antenucci, Ilia. "The Making of Urban Computing Environments." *Synoptique* 8, no. 1 (2019): 54–64.

Anwar, Mohammad Amir, and Mark Graham. *The Digital Continent: Placing Africa in Planetary Networks of Work.* Oxford: Oxford University Press, 2022.

APA News. "Africa Should Take Advantage of China's BRI—Kenyatta." Agence de Press Africaine News, April 26, 2019. https://www.apanews.net/en/news/africa-should-take -advantage-of-chinas-bri-kenyatta [12/31/2022].

Appel, Hannah. *The Licit Life of Capitalism: US Oil in Equatorial Guinea.* Durham, NC: Duke University Press, 2019.

Asante, Lewis Abedi, and Ilse Helbrecht. "Hybrid Entrepreneurial Urban Governance in Post-Colonial Ghana: An Analysis of Chinese Funding of the Kotokuraba Market Project in Cape Coast." *Urban Geography* 43, no. 10 (2022): 1519–43.

Attoh, Kafui, Katie Wells, and Declan Cullen. "'We're Building Their Data': Labor, Alienation, and Idiocy in the Smart City." *Environment and Planning D: Society and Space* 37, no. 6 (2019): 1007–24.

Avle, Seyram. "Hardware and Data in the Platform Era: Chinese Smartphones in Africa." *Media, Culture & Society* 44, no. 8 (2022): 1473–89.

Avle, Seyram, Cindy Lin, Jean Hardy, and Silvia Lindtner. "Scaling Techno-Optimistic Visions." *Engaging Science, Technology, and Society* 6 (2020): 237–54.

Baptista, Idalina. "Electricity Services Always in the Making: Informality and the Work of Infrastructure Maintenance and Repair in an African city." *Urban Studies* 56, no. 3 (2019): 510–25.

Baraka, Carey. "The Failed Promise of Kenya's Smart City." *Rest of the World*, June 1, 2021. https://restofworld.org/2021/the-failed-promise-of-kenyas-smart-city/ [5/24/2023].

Barbrook, Richard, and Andy Cameron. "The Californian Ideology." *Science as Culture* 6, no. 1 (1996): 44–72.

Basil, Ibrahim, and Kevin P. Donovan. "Costly Propositions." *Sidecar*, August 18, 2023. https://newleftreview.org/sidecar/posts/costly-propositions?s=08 [8/29/2023].

Beckert, Jens. *Imagined Futures: Fictional Expectations and Capitalist Dynamics*. Cambridge, MA: Harvard University Press, 2016.

Benjamin, Ruha. "Assessing Risk, Automating Racism." *Science* 366, no. 6464 (2019): 421–22.

Benjamin, Ruha. *Race After Technology: Abolitionist Tools for the New Jim Code*. Cambridge: Polity, 2019.

Benyera, Everisto. *The Fourth Industrial Revolution and the Recolonisation of Africa: The Coloniality of Data*. London: Taylor & Francis, 2021.

Berlant, Lauren. "The Commons: Infrastructures for Troubling Times." *Environment and Planning D: Society and Space* 34, no. 3 (2016): 393–419.

Berlant, Lauren. *Cruel Optimism*. Durham, NC: Duke University Press, 2020.

Bernards, Nick. "Colonial Financial Infrastructures and Kenya's Uneven Fintech Boom." *Antipode* 54, no. 3 (2022): 708–28.

Beverungen, Armin. "Executive Dashboard." In *The Oxford Handbook of Media, Technology, and Organization Studies*, ed. Timon Beyes, Robin Holt, and Claus Pias, 225–37. Oxford: Oxford University Press, 2019.

Bhagat, Ali, and Leanne Roderick. "Banking on Refugees: Racialized Expropriation in the Fintech Era." *Environment and Planning A: Economy and Space* 52, no. 8 (2020): 1498–1515.

Bialski, Paula. *Middle Tech: Software Work and the Culture of Good Enough*. Princeton: Princeton University Press, 2024.

Birch, Kean. "Reflexive Expectations in Innovation Financing: An Analysis of Venture Capital as a Mode of Valuation." *Social Studies of Science* 53, no. 1 (2023): 29–48.

Birch, Kean, and Fabian Muniesa. "Introduction: Assetization and Technoscientific Capitalism." In *Assetization: Turning Things into Assets in Technoscientific Capitalism*, ed. Kean Birch and Fabian Muniesa, 1–41. Cambridge, MA: MIT Press, 2020.

Birhane, Abeba. "Algorithmic Colonization of Africa." *SCRIPTed* 17 (2020): 389.

Block, Fred, and Matthew R. Keller. "Where Do Innovations Come From? Transformations in the US Economy, 1970–2006." *Socio-Economic Review* 7, no. 3 (2009): 459–83.

Boellstorff, Tom. "Queer Techne: Two Theses on Methodology and Queer Studies." In *Queer Methods and Methodologies: Intersecting Queer Theories and Social Science Research*, ed. Kath Browne, and Catherine J. Nash, 215–30. London: Routledge, 2016.

Bowker, Geoffrey C., and Susan Leigh Star. *Sorting Things Out: Classification and Its Consequences*. Cambridge, MA: MIT Press, 2000.

Braman, Sandra. *Change of State: Information, Policy, and Power*. Cambridge, MA: MIT Press, 2009.

Branch, Daniel. *Kenya: Between Hope and Despair, 1963–2011*. New Haven, CT: Yale University Press, 2011.

Bratton, Benjamin H. *The Revenge of the Real: Politics for a Post-Pandemic World*. London: Verso Books, 2022.

Bratton, Benjamin H. *The Stack: On Software and Sovereignty*. Cambridge, MA: MIT Press, 2016.

Brautigam, Deborah. *The Dragon's Gift: The Real Story of China in Africa*. Oxford: Oxford University Press, 2011.

Brautigam, Deborah. "'Flying Geese' or 'Hidden Dragon' Chinese Business and African Industrial Development." In *China Returns to Africa: A Rising Power and a Continent*

Embrace, ed. Christopher Alden, Daniel Large, and Ricardo Soares de Oliveira, 51–68. New York: Columbia University Press, 2008.

Brautigam, Deborah A., and Tang Xiaoyang. "China's Engagement in African Agriculture: 'Down to the Countryside.'" *China Quarterly* 199 (2009): 686–706.

Brautigam, Deborah, Tang Xiaoyang, and Ying Xia. "What Kinds of Chinese 'Geese' Are Flying to Africa? Evidence from Chinese Manufacturing Firms." *Journal of African Economies* 27, no. 1 (2018): 29–51.

Breckenridge, Keith. *Biometric State: The Global Politics of Identification and Surveillance in South Africa, 1850 to the Present*. Cambridge: Cambridge University Press, 2014.

Breznitz, Dan, and Michael Murphree. *Run of the Red Queen: Government, Innovation, Globalization, and Economic Growth in China*. New Haven, CT: Yale University Press, 2011.

Buire, Chloé. "The Dream and the Ordinary: An Ethnographic Investigation of Suburbanisation in Luanda." *African Studies* 73, no. 2 (2014): 290–312.

Bunnell, Tim. *Malaysia, Modernity and the Multimedia Super Corridor: A Critical Geography of Intelligent Landscapes*. London: Routledge, 2004.

Bunnell, Tim. "Where Is the Future? Geography, Expectation and Experience Across Three Decades of Malaysia's Vision 2020." *International Journal of Urban and Regional Research* 46, no. 5 (2022): 885–95.

Burrell, Jenna. "The Field Site as a Network: A Strategy for Locating Ethnographic Research." *Field Methods* 21, no. 2 (2009): 181–99.

Burrell, Jenna. *Invisible Users: Youth in the Internet Cafés of Urban Ghana*. Cambridge, MA: MIT Press, 2012.

Business Daily. "Shift Kenya's Economic Model to Fasten Growth Urges NESC Advisor." *Business Daily*, June 22, 2013.

Camba, Alvin. "The Sino-Centric Capital Export Regime: State-Backed and Flexible Capital in the Philippines." *Development and Change* 51, no. 4 (2020): 970–97.

Camner, Gunnar, Caroline Pulver, and Emil Sjöblom. *What Makes a Successful Mobile Money Implementation? Learnings from M-PESA in Kenya and Tanzania*. London: GMSA, 2011.

Carmody, Pádraig. *The New Scramble for Africa*. New York: John Wiley & Sons, 2017.

Carmody, Pádraig, and Francis Owusu. "Neoliberalism, Urbanization and Change in Africa: The Political Economy of Heterotopias." *Journal of African Development* 18, no. 1 (2016): 61–73.

Cenere, Samantha. "Making Translations, Translating Making: Actor-Networks, Spatialities, and Forms of Makers' Work in Turin." *City* 25, no. 3–4 (2021): 355–75.

Chan, Anita Say. *Networking Peripheries: Technological Futures and the Myth of Digital Universalism*. Cambridge, MA: MIT Press, 2014.

Chari, Sharad. "African Extraction, Indian Ocean Critique." *South Atlantic Quarterly* 114, no. 1 (2015): 83–100.

Cheeseman, Nic. "'No Bourgeoisie, No Democracy?' The Political Attitudes of the Kenyan Middle Class." *Journal of International Development* 27, no. 5 (2015): 647–64.

Chen, Celia, and Matt Haldane. "Explainer: Will Huawei's Harmony Operating System End the Global Duopoly of Google's Android and Apple's iOS?" *South China Morning Post*, June 4, 2021. https://www.scmp.com/tech/big-tech/article/3136017/will-huaweis-harmony-operating-system-end-global-duopoly-googles [7/25/2023].

Chen, Hao, and Meg Rithmire. "The Rise of the Investor State: State Capital in the Chinese Economy." *Studies in Comparative International Development* 55, no. 3 (2020): 257–77.

Chen, Julie Yujie. "The Mirage and Politics of Participation in China's Platform Economy." *Javnost—The Public* 27, no. 2 (2020): 154–70.

Chen, Julie Yujie, and Jack Linchuan Qiu. "Digital Utility: Datafication, Regulation, Labor, and DiDi's Platformization of Urban Transport in China." *Chinese Journal of Communication* 12, no. 3 (2019): 274–89.

Chen, Ling. *Manipulating Globalization: The Influence of Bureaucrats on Business in China.* Stanford: Stanford University Press, 2020.

Chen, Lulu. *Influence Empire: the Story of Tencent and China's Tech Ambition.* London: Hodder & Stoughton, 2022.

Chen, Yuchen, Alex Jiahong Lu, and Angela Xiao Wu. "'China' as a 'Black Box'? Rethinking Methods Through a Sociotechnical Perspective." *Information, Communication & Society* 26, no. 2 (2023): 253–69.

Cheng, Han, Emma Mawdsley, and Weidong Liu. "Reading the Forum on China–Africa Cooperation (2000–2021): Geoeconomics, Governance, and Embedding 'Creative Involvement.'" *Area Development and Policy 8*, no. 1 (2023): 60–83.

Choplin, Armelle. *Concrete City: Material Flows and Urbanization in West Africa.* Hoboken, NJ: John Wiley & Sons, 2023.

Chu, Han, Robert Hassink, Dixiang Xie, and Xiaohui Hu. "Placing the Platform Economy: The Emerging, Developing and Upgrading of Taobao Villages as a Platform-Based Place Making Phenomenon in China." *Cambridge Journal of Regions, Economy and Society* 16, no. 2 (2023): 319–34.

Chun, Lin. *China and Global Capitalism: Reflections on Marxism, History, and Contemporary Politics.* New York: Palgrave Macmillan, 2013.

Chun, Lin. *Revolution and Counterrevolution in China.* London: Verso Books, 2021.

Chun, Wendy Hui Kyong. *Discriminating Data: Correlation, Neighborhoods, and the New Politics of Recognition.* Cambridge, MA: MIT Press, 2021.

Cirolia, Liza Rose. "Contested Fiscal Geographies: Urban Authority, Everyday Practice, and Emerging State-Finance Relations." *Geoforum* 117 (2020): 33–41.

Cirolia, Liza Rose. "(W)Escaping the Challenges of the City: A Critique of Cape Town's Proposed Satellite Town." *Urban Forum* 25, no. 3 (2014): 295–312.

Cirolia, Liza Rose, Tesfaye Hailu, Julia King, Nuno F. da Cruz, and Jo Beall. "Infrastructure Governance in the Post-Networked City: State-Led, High-Tech Sanitation in Addis Ababa's Condominium Housing." *Environment and Planning C: Politics and Space* 39, no. 7 (2021): 1606–24.

Cirolia, Liza Rose, Suzanne Hall, and Henrietta Nyamnjoh. "Remittance Micro-Worlds and Migrant Infrastructure: Circulations, Disruptions, and the Movement of Money." *Transactions of the Institute of British Geographers* 47, no. 1 (2022): 63–76.

Cirolia, Liza Rose, and Andrea Pollio. "Queer Infrastructures: Objects of and Orientations Towards Urban Research Practice." *Urban Forum* 34, no. 2 (2023): 235–44.

Cirolia, Liza Rose, and Andrea Pollio. "Spectrums of Infrastructural Hybridity: Insights from Urban Africa for a Propositional Research Agenda." In *Handbook of Infrastructures and Cities*, ed. Olivier Coutard and Daniel Florentin, 179–95. Cheltenham: Edward Elgar, 2024.

Cirolia, Liza Rose, Andrea Pollio, Rike Sitas, Alicia Fortuin, Jack Ong'iro Odeo, and Alexis Sebarenzi. "Fintech 'Frontiers' and the Platformed Motorcycle: Emergent Infrastructures of Value Creation in African Cities." *Environment and Planning D: Society and Space* (2024). https://journals.sagepub.com/doi/full/10.1177/02637758241276324.

Cirolia, Liza Rose, Rike Sitas, Andrea Pollio, Alexis Gatoni Sebarenzi, and Prince K. Guma. "Silicon Savannahs and Motorcycle Taxis: A Southern Perspective on the Frontiers of Platform Urbanism." *Environment and Planning A: Economy and Space* 55, no. 8 (2023): 1989–2008.

CITIC Securities. *Transsion Holdings: Prospectus for Initial Public Offering and Listing on the Science and Technology Innovation Board.* Shanghai: CITIC Securities, 2019. [My translation of 中信证券．传音控股：首次公开发行股票并在科创板上市招股说明书．]

Coban, Alev. *Performing Technocapitalism: The Politics and Affects of Postcolonial Technology Entrepreneurship in Kenya.* Bielefeld: Transcript, 2024.

Coban, Alev. "Same, Same but Different: Storytelling of Innovative Places and Practices in Nairobi." In *Schafft Wissen: Gemeinsames und geteiltes Wissen in Wissenschaft und Technik: Proceedings of the 2 Tagung des Nachwuchsnetzwerks INSIST, October 7–8, 2016, Munich,* 139–52. Munich: INSIST, 2016.

Cockayne, Daniel. "Entrepreneurial Affect: Attachment to Work Practice in San Francisco's Digital Media Sector." *Environment and planning D: Society and Space* 34, no. 3 (2016): 456–73.

Cockayne, Daniel. "What Is a Startup Firm? A Methodological and Epistemological Investigation into Research Objects in Economic Geography." *Geoforum* 107 (2019): 77–87.

Coleman, Beth. "Race as Technology." *Camera Obscura: Feminism, Culture, and Media Studies* 24, no. 1 (2009): 177–207.

Coleman, Gabriella. "The Hacker Conference: A Ritual Condensation and Celebration of a Lifeworld." *Anthropological Quarterly* 83, no. 1 (2010): 47–72.

Cooiman, Franziska. "Imprinting the Economy: The Structural Power of Venture Capital." *Environment and Planning A: Economy and Space* 56, no. 2 (2024): 586–602.

Cooiman, Franziska. "Veni Vidi VC: The Backend of the Digital Economy and Its Political Making." *Review of International Political Economy* 30, no. 1 (2023): 229–51.

Cooper, Frederick, and Randall M. Packard, eds. *International Development and the Social Sciences: Essays on the History and Politics of Knowledge.* Berkeley: University of California Press, 1997.

Côté-Roy, Laurence, and Sarah Moser. "'Does Africa Not Deserve Shiny New Cities?' The Power of Seductive Rhetoric Around New Cities in Africa." *Urban Studies* 56, no. 12 (2019): 2392.

Couldry, Nick, and Ulises A. Mejias. *The Costs of Connection: How Data Is Colonizing Human Life and Appropriating It for Capitalism*: Stanford: Stanford University Press, 2019.

Couldry, Nick, and Ulises A. Mejias. "Data Colonialism: Rethinking Big Data's Relation to the Contemporary Subject." *Television & New Media* 20, no. 4 (2019): 336–49.

Courtwright, Tom. "Uganda's Boda Bodas: Half a Century of Getting to Places, Madly." *African Arguments*, August 20, 2023.

Croese, Sylvia. "State-Led Housing Delivery as an Instrument of Developmental Patrimonialism: The Case of Post-War Angola." *African Affairs* 116, no. 462 (2017): 80–100.

Cupers, Kenny, and Prita Meier. "Infrastructure Between Statehood and Selfhood: The Trans-African Highway." *Journal of the Society of Architectural Historians* 79, no. 1 (2020): 61–81.

Dal Maso, Giulia. "China as a Laboratory to Renegotiate Globalization: Statecraft Through the Selective Exclusion of Foreign Capital." *Dialogues in Human Geography* (2025): 20438206251316016.

Dal Maso, Giulia. *Risky Expertise in Chinese Financialisation: Returned Labour and the State-Finance Nexus.* Singapore: Springer, 2020.

Danaher, John. "Techno-Optimism: An Analysis, an Evaluation and a Modest Defence." *Philosophy & Technology* 35, no. 2 (2022): 54.

Darbon, Dominique. "The Political Role of the African Middle Class: The Over-Politicization of an Elusive Category." In *Oxford Research Encyclopedia of Politics.* Oxford: Oxford University Press, 2019.

Daston, Lorraine. *Rules: A Short History of What We Live By.* Princeton: Princeton University Press, 2022.

Datta, Ayona. "The Informational Periphery: Territory, Logistics and People in the Margins of a Digital Age." *Asian Geographer* (2023): 1–18.

Datta, Ayona, and Dennis M. Muthama. "Sorting Paper: The Archival Labour of Digitising Land Records in Kenya." *Geographical Journal* 190, no. 4 (2024): 1–12.

De Boeck, Filip. "'Divining' the City: Rhythm, Amalgamation and Knotting as Forms of 'Urbanity.'" *Social Dynamics* 41, no. 1 (2015): 47–58.

De Goede, Marieke. "Finance/Security Infrastructures." *Review of International Political Economy* 28, no. 2 (2020): 351–68.

De Goede, Marieke. "Hawala Discourses and the War on Terrorist Finance." *Environment and Planning D: Society and Space* 21, no. 5 (2003): 513–32.

De Kloet, Jeroen, Yiu Fai Chow, and Lena Scheen. *Boredom, Shanzhai, and Digitisation in the Time of Creative China.* Amsterdam: Amsterdam University Press, 2019.

De Kloet, Jeroen, Thomas Poell, Zeng Guohua, and C. H. O. W. Yiu Fai. "The Platformization of Chinese Society: Infrastructure, Governance, and Practice." *Chinese Journal of Communication* 12, no. 3 (2019): 249–56.

Dhaliwal, Ranjodh S. "On Addressability, or What Even Is Computation?" *Critical Inquiry* 49, no. 1 (2022): 1–27.

Dittgen, Romain, and Gerald Chungu. "(Un)writing 'Chinese Space' in Urban Africa: Of City-Making, Lived Experiences, and Entangled Processes." *China Perspectives* 119, no. 4 (2019): 3–8.

Doganova, Liliana. *Discounting the Future: The Ascendancy of a Political Technology.* Princeton: Princeton University Press, 2024.

Dolan, Catherine, and Claire Gordon. "Worker, Businessman, Entrepreneur? Kenya's Shifting Labouring Subject." *Critical African Studies* 11, no. 3 (2019): 301–21.

Dolan, Catherine, and Dinah Rajak. "Remaking Africa's Informal Economies: Youth, Entrepreneurship and the Promise of Inclusion at the Bottom of the Pyramid." In *Globalization, Economic Inclusion and African Workers*, ed. Kate Meagher, Laura Mann, and Maxim Bolt, 52–67. London: Routledge, 2018.

Donovan, Kevin P., and Emma Park. "Algorithmic Intimacy: The Data Economy of Predatory Inclusion in Kenya." *Social Anthropology/Anthropologie Sociale* 30, no. 2 (2022): 120–39.

Donovan, Kevin P., and Emma Park. "Knowledge/Seizure: Debt and Data in Kenya's Zero Balance Economy." *Antipode* 54, no. 4 (2022): 1063–85.

Downey, Greg, and Melissa S. Fisher. "Introduction: The Anthropology of Capital and the Frontiers of Ethnography." In *Frontiers of Capital: Ethnographic Reflections on the New Economy*, ed. Melissa S. Fisher and Greg Downey, 1–30. Durham, NC: Duke University Press, 2020.

Dreher, Axel, Andreas Fuchs, Bradley Parks, Austin Strange, and Michael J. Tierney. *Banking on Beijing: The Aims and Impacts of China's Overseas Development Program*. Cambridge: Cambridge University Press, 2022.

Driessen, Miriam. "Pushed to Africa: Emigration and Social Change in China." *Journal of Ethnic and Migration Studies* 42, no. 15 (2016): 2491–2507.

Driessen, Miriam. *Tales of Hope, Tastes of Bitterness: Chinese Road Builders in Ethiopia*. Hong Kong: Hong Kong University Press, 2019.

Durand, Cédric. *How Silicon Valley Unleashed Techno-Feudalism: The Making of the Digital Economy*. London: Verso Books, 2024.

Easterling, Keller. *Extrastatecraft: The Power of Infrastructure Space*. London: Verso Books, 2014.

Ecofin Agency. "Kenya Pledges Support for Huawei, as Does South Africa." July 26, 2019. https://www.ecofinagency.com/telecom/2607–40362-kenya-pledges-support-for-huawei-as-does-south-africa [9/6/2021].

Eldridge, Claire. "Algiers, Mecca of Revolutions." *History Workshop Journal* 91, no. 1 (2021): 240–47.

Elyachar, Julia. "Empowerment Money: The World Bank, Non-Governmental Organizations, and the Value of Culture in Egypt." *Public Culture* 14, no. 3 (2002): 493–513.

Elyachar, Julia. *Markets of Dispossession: NGOs, Economic Development, and the State in Cairo*. Durham, NC: Duke University Press, 2005.

Elyachar, Julia. "Phatic Labor, Infrastructure, and the Question of Empowerment in Cairo." *American Ethnologist* 37, no. 3 (2010): 452–64.

Ese, Anders, and Kristin Ese. *The City Makers of Nairobi: An African Urban History*. London: Routledge, 2020.

Etta, Florence. "Policy Making: The New Development Eldorado." In *At the Crossroads: ICT Policy Making in East Africa*, ed. Florence Etta and Laurent Elder, 3–15. Ottawa and Nairobi: IDRC and East African Educational Publisher, 2005.

Eubanks, Virginia. *Automating Inequality: How High-Tech Tools Profile, Police, and Punish the Poor*. New York: St. Martin's Press, 2018.

Fei, Ding. "The Compound Labor Regime of Chinese Construction Projects in Ethiopia." *Geoforum* 117 (2020): 13–23.

Fei, Ding. "Internationalizing China Standards Through Corporate Social Responsibility: An Exploratory Study of Chinese State-Owned Enterprises in Africa." *Journal of Contemporary China* (2023): 1–21.

Fei, Ding. "Networked Internationalization: Chinese Companies in Ethiopia's Infrastructure Construction Sector." *Professional Geographer* 73, no. 2 (2021): 322–32.

Fei, Ding. "Transnationalizing Intrapreneurship of Chinese Private Investment in Africa." *Environment and Planning A: Economy and Space* 56, no. 6 (2024): 1595–1613.

Feigenbaum, Evan A. *China's Techno-Warriors: National Security and Strategic Competition from the Nuclear to the Information Age*. Stanford: Stanford University Press, 2003.

Fejerskov, Adam Moe. *The Global Lab: Inequality, Technology, and the Experimental Movement*. Oxford: Oxford University Press, 2022.

Fejerskov, Adam Moe. "The New Technopolitics of Development and the Global South as a Laboratory of Technological Experimentation." *Science, Technology, & Human Values* 42, no. 5 (2017): 947–68.

Ferguson, James. *The Anti-Politics Machine: Development, Depoliticization, and Bureaucratic Power in Lesotho*. Minneapolis: University of Minnesota Press, 1994.

Ferguson, James. *Global Shadows: Africa in the Neoliberal World Order*. Durham, NC: Duke University Press, 2006.

Fourcade, Marion, and Kieran Healy. "Seeing Like a Market." *Socio-Economic Review* 15, no. 1 (2017): 9–29.

Fourie, Elsje. "Model Students: Policy Emulation, Modernization, and Kenya's Vision 2030." *African Affairs* 113, no. 453 (2014): 540–62.

Franceschini, Ivan, and Nicholas Loubere. *Global China as Method*. Cambridge: Cambridge University Press, 2022.

Franceschini, Ivan, Nicholas Loubere, and Andrea E. Pia. "Prometheus in China: Techno-Optimism and Its Discontents." *Made in China Journal* 7, no. 2 (2022): 8–9.

Frank, Andre Gunder. *ReOrient: Global Economy in the Asian Age*. Berkeley: University of California Press, 1998.

Friederici, Nicolas, Michel Wahome, and Mark Graham. *Digital Entrepreneurship in Africa: How a Continent Is Escaping Silicon Valley's Long Shadow*. Cambridge, MA: MIT Press, 2020.

Fuchs, Christian. "Industry 4.0: The Digital German Ideology." *TripleC: Communication, Capitalism & Critique* 16, no. 1 (2018): 280–89.

Gagliardone, Iginio. *China, Africa, and the Future of the Internet*. London: Zed Books, 2019.

Gainer, Maya. "Planning Transformation in a Divided Nation: Creating Kenya Vision 2030, 2005–2009." In *Innovations for Successful Societies, Case Study*, 1–22. Princeton: Princeton University, 2015.

Galloway, Alexander R. *Protocol: How Control Exists After Decentralization*. Cambridge, MA: MIT Press, 2004.

Geertz, Clifford. "Thick Description: Toward an Interpretive Theory of Culture." In *The Interpretation of Cultures: Selected Essays*, 3–30. New York: Basic Books, 1975.

Geiger, Susi. "Silicon Valley, Disruption, and the End of Uncertainty." *Journal of Cultural Economy* 13, no. 2 (2020): 169–84.

Gewirtz, Julian. "The Futurists of Beijing: Alvin Toffler, Zhao Ziyang, and China's 'New Technological Revolution,' 1979–1991." *Journal of Asian Studies* 78, no. 1 (2019): 115–40.

Gill, Rosalind, and Andy Pratt. "In the Social Factory? Immaterial Labour, Precariousness and Cultural Work." *Theory, Culture & Society* 25, no. 7–8 (2008): 1–30.

Gillespie, Tom. "The Real Estate Frontier." *International Journal of Urban and Regional Research* 44, no. 4 (2020): 599–616.

Gilmore, Ruth Wilson. *Golden Gulag: Prisons, Surplus, Crisis, and Opposition in Globalizing California*. Berkeley: University of California Press, 2007.

Githiora, Chege J. *Sheng: Rise of a Kenyan Swahili Vernacular*. Rochester: Boydell & Brewer, 2018.

Githongo, John. "Kenya: Riding the Tiger." *Journal of Eastern African Studies* 2, no. 2 (2008): 359–67.

Gitonga, Jimmy. "Conversation #1: The Past, Present, and Future of 'Digital Nyika': How to Fix an Aircraft in Flight." In *Digital Kenya: An Entrepreneurial Revolution in the Making*, ed. Bitange Ndemo and Tim Weiss, 13–24. London: Palgrave Macmillan, 2017.

Goldman, Michael. "Speculative Urbanism and the Making of the Next World City." *International Journal of Urban and Regional Research* 35, no. 3 (2011): 555–81.

Goodfellow, Tom. "Finance, Infrastructure and Urban Capital: The Political Economy of African 'Gap-Filling.'" *Review of African Political Economy* 47, no. 164 (2020): 256–74.

Goodfellow, Tom. *Politics and the Urban Frontier: Transformation and Divergence in Late Urbanizing East Africa*. Oxford: Oxford University Press, 2022.

Goodfellow, Tom. "Taming the 'Rogue' Sector: Studying State Effectiveness in Africa Through Informal Transport Politics." *Comparative Politics* 47, no. 2 (2015): 127–47.

Goodfellow, Tom, and Zhengli Huang. "Contingent Infrastructure and the Dilution of 'Chineseness': Reframing Roads and Rail in Kampala and Addis Ababa." *Environment and Planning A: Economy and Space* 53, no. 4 (2021): 655–674.

Government of Kenya. *Digital Economy Blueprint: Powering Kenya's Transformation*. Nairobi: Ministry of Information, Communication and the Digital Economy. 2019.

Government of Kenya. *Economic Recovery Strategy for Wealth and Employment Creation 2003–2007*. Nairobi: Ministry of Planning and National Development, 2003.

Government of Kenya. *The Kenya National Digital Master Plan 2022–2032*. Nairobi: Ministry of ICT, Innovation and Youth Affairs, 2021.

Government of Kenya. *Kenya National ICT Masterplan: Towards a Digital Kenya*. Nairobi: Ministry of Information Communications and Technology, 2013.

Government of Kenya. *Kenya Vision 2030: A Globally Competitive and Prosperous Kenya*. Nairobi: Government of Kenya, 2007.

Government of Kenya. *National Spatial Plan 2015–2045: An Integrated Spatial Plan for Balanced and Sustainable National Development*. Nairobi: Ministry of Lands and Physical Planning, 2014.

Government of Kenya. *Status Report on Preparatory Activities and Way Forward for the Economic Recovery Strategy Paper (ERS) for Kenya*. Nairobi: Government of Kenya and IMF, 2003.

Gowa, Joanne. *Closing the Gold Window: Domestic Politics and the End of Bretton Woods*. Ithaca, NY: Cornell University Press, 2019.

Graham, Mark, and Laura Mann. "Imagining a Silicon Savannah? Technological and Conceptual Connectivity in Kenya's BPO and Software Development Sectors." *Electronic Journal of Information Systems in Developing Countries* 56, no. 1 (2013): 1–19.

Graham, Stephen, and Simon Marvin. *Splintering Urbanism: Networked Infrastructures, Technological Mobilities and the Urban Condition*. London: Routledge, 2001.

Gravett, Willem. "Digital Neo-Colonialism: The Chinese Model of Internet Sovereignty in Africa." *African Human Rights Law Journal* 20, no. 1 (2020): 125–46.

Gu, Tianshi, Peng Zhang, and Xujia Zhang. "Spatio-Temporal Evolution Characteristics and Driving Mechanism of the New Infrastructure Construction Development Potential in China." *Chinese Geographical Science* 31 (2021): 646–58.

Guma, Prince K. "Incompleteness of Urban Infrastructures in Transition: Scenarios from the Mobile Age in Nairobi." *Social Studies of Science* 50, no. 5 (2020): 728–50.

Guma, Prince K. "Nairobi's Rise as a Digital Platform Hub." *Current History* 121, no. 835 (2022): 184–89.

Guma, Prince K. "Recasting Provisional Urban Worlds in the Global South: Shacks, Shanties and Micro-Stalls." *Planning Theory & Practice* 22, no. 2 (2021): 211–26.

Guma, Prince K. "Smart Urbanism? ICTs for Water and Electricity Supply in Nairobi." *Urban studies* 56, no. 11 (2019): 2333–52.

Guma, Prince K., Jethron Ayumbah Akallah, and Jack Ong'iro Odeo. "Plug-In Urbanism: City Building and the Parodic Guise of New Infrastructure in Africa." *Urban Studies* 60, no. 13 (2023): 2550–63.

Guma, Prince K., and Mwangi Mwaura. "Infrastructural Configurations of Mobile Telephony in Urban Africa: Vignettes from Buru Buru, Nairobi." *Journal of Eastern African Studies* 15, no. 4 (2021): 527–45.

Günel, Gökçe, and Chika Watanabe. "Patchwork Ethnography." *American Ethnologist* 51, no. 1 (2024): 131–39.

Guyer, Jane I. *Marginal Gains: Monetary Transactions in Atlantic Africa*. Chicago: University of Chicago Press, 2004.

Halpern, Orit, Jesse LeCavalier, Nerea Calvillo, and Wolfgang Pietsch. "Test-Bed Urbanism." *Public Culture* 25, no. 2 (2013): 272–306.

Han, Byung-Chul. *Shanzhai: Deconstruction in Chinese*. Cambridge, MA: MIT Press, 2017.

Harrison, Philip, and Sylvia Croese. "The Persistence and Rise of Master Planning in Urban Africa: Transnational Circuits and Local Ambitions." *Planning Perspectives* 38, no. 1 (2023): 25–47.

Harwit, Eric. *China's Telecommunications Revolution*. Oxford: Oxford University Press, 2008.

He, Yujia. "Chinese Digital Platform Companies' Expansion in the Belt and Road Countries." *Information Society* (2024): 1–24.

Hecht, Gabrielle. *Being Nuclear: Africans and the Global Uranium Trade*. Cambridge, MA: MIT Press, 2012.

Heeks, Richard. "ICT4D 3.0? Part 1: The Components of an Emerging 'Digital-for-Development' Paradigm." *Electronic Journal of Information Systems in Developing Countries* 86, no. 3 (2020): e12124.

Heeks, Richard, and Yujia He. "Analysing the US-China 'AI Cold War' Narrative." *Manchester Centre for Digital Development Working Paper* 110 (2024). https://papers.ssrn.com/sol3/papers.cfm?abstract_id=5026574.

Heppler, Jason A. *Silicon Valley and the Environmental Inequalities of High-Tech Urbanism*. Norman: University of Oklahoma Press, 2024.

Holweg, Matthias. "The Genealogy of Lean Production." *Journal of Operations Management* 25, no. 2 (2007): 420–37.

Hong, Caylee. "'Safe Cities' in Pakistan: Knowledge Infrastructures, Urban Planning, and the Security State." *Antipode* 54, no. 5 (2022): 1476–96.

Hong, Renyi. *Passionate Work: Endurance After the Good Life*. Durham, NC: Duke University Press, 2022.

Hong, Yu. *Networking China: The Digital Transformation of the Chinese Economy*. Chicago: University of Chicago Press, 2017.

Hong, Yu, and Eric Harwit, eds. *China's Globalizing Internet: History, Power, and Governance*. London: Routledge, 2022.

Horst, Heather, and Daniel Miller. *The Cell Phone: An Anthropology of Communication*. Abingdon: Routledge, 2006.

Huang, Zhengli, and Xiangming Chen. "Is China Building Africa?" *European Financial Review* (2016): 7.

Huang, Zhengli, and Andrea Pollio. "Between Highways and Fintech Platforms: Global China and Africa's Infrastructure State." *Geoforum* 147 (2023): 103876.

Huchzermeyer, Marie. "Tenement City: The Emergence of Multi-Storey Districts Through Large-Scale Private Landlordism in Nairobi." *International Journal of Urban and Regional Research* 31, no. 4 (2007): 714–32.

Hundeyin, David. "Flutterwave: The African Unicorn Built on Quicksand." *West Africa Weekly*, April 12, 2022. https://westafricaweekly.substack.com/p/flutterwave-the-african -unicorn-built [1/4/23].

Hui, Yuk. *Art and Cosmotechnics*. Minneapolis: University of Minnesota Press, 2021.

Hui, Yuk. "Cosmotechnics as Cosmopolitics." *E-Flux Journal* 87 (2017): 1–10.

Hui, Yuk. *Post-Europe*. Falmouth: Urbanomic, 2024.

Hui, Yuk. *The Question Concerning Technology in China: An Essay in Cosmotechnics*. Cambridge, MA: MIT Press, 2019.

Idris, Abubakar. "Inside the Scandal at Flutterwave, Nigeria's Fintech Champion." *Rest of the World*, April 28, 2022. https://restofworld.org/2022/inside-the-scandal-at-flutterwave -nigerias-fintech-champion/ [1/4/2023].

Indergaard, Michael. *Silicon Alley: The Rise and Fall of a New Media District*. New York: Routledge, 2004.

Irani, Lilly. *Chasing Innovation: Making Entrepreneurial Citizens in Modern India*. Princeton: Princeton University Press, 2019.

Issaka, Adams. "Techno-Optimism: Framing Data and Digital Infrastructure for Public Acceptance in Ghana." *Big Data & Society* 10, no. 2 (2023): 20539517231215359.

Jackson, John L. *Thin Description: Ethnography and the African Hebrew Israelites of Jerusalem*. Cambridge, MA: Harvard University Press, 2013.

Jaglin, Sylvy. "Differentiating Networked Services in Cape Town: Echoes of Splintering Urbanism?" *Geoforum* 39, no. 6 (2008): 1897–1906.

Joy, Meghana. *Chinese Underground Banking*. Pune: Indiaforensic, 2021. https://regtech times.com/exclusive-guide-to-chinese-underground-banking/ [1/12/2023].

Kadiri, Par Ghadi, and Joan Tilouine. "À Addis-Abeba, le siège de l'Union africaine espionné par Pékin." *Le Monde Afrique*, January 26, 2018.

Kagwanja, Peter, and Roger Southall, eds. *Kenya's Uncertain Democracy: The Electoral Crisis of 2008*. London: Routledge, 2013.

Kanyinga, Karuti. "Devolution and the New Politics of Development in Kenya." *African Studies Review* 59, no. 3 (2016): 155–67.

Kasper, Moritz, and Sophie Schramm. "Storage City: Water Tanks, Jerry Cans, and Batteries as Infrastructure in Nairobi." *Urban Studies* 60, no. 12 (2023): 2400–2417.

Karaman, Ozan, Lindsay Sawyer, Christian Schmid, and Kit Ping Wong. "Plot by Plot: Plotting Urbanism as an Ordinary Process of Urbanisation." *Antipode* 52, no. 4 (2020): 1122–51.

Keane, Michael, Haiqing Yu, Elaine J. Zhao, and Susan Leong. *China's Digital Presence in the Asia-Pacific: Culture, Technology and Platforms*. London: Anthem Press, 2021.

Keane, Michael, and Elaine J. Zhao. "Renegades on the Frontier of Innovation: The Shanzhai Grassroots Communities of Shenzhen in China's Creative Economy." *Eurasian Geography and Economics* 53, no. 2 (2012): 216–30.

Kenya Gazette Supplement. *The Kenya Communications Act, 1998, and the Postal Corporation Act, 1998*. Nairobi, November 1998.

Kimari, Wangui. "Resisting Imperial Erasures: Matigari Ruins and Relics in Nairobi." *Journal of Eastern African Studies* 17, no. 1–2 (2023): 207–21.

Kimari, Wangui. "The Story of a Pump: Life, Death and Afterlives Within an Urban Planning of 'Divide and Rule' in Nairobi, Kenya." *Urban Geography* 42, no. 2 (2021): 141–60.

Kimari, Wangui. "'Under Construction': Everyday Anxieties and the Proliferating Social Meanings of China in Kenya." *Africa* 91, no. 1 (2021): 135–52.

Kimari, Wangui. "'We Will Be Back to the Street!': Protest and the 'Empires' of Water in Nairobi." In *Refractions of the National, the Popular and the Global in African Cities*, ed. Simon Bekker, Edgar Pieterse, and Sylvia Croese, 99–109. Cape Town: African Minds, 2021.

Kimari, Wangui, and Henrik Ernstson. "Imperial Remains and imperial Invitations: Centering Race Within the Contemporary Large-Scale Infrastructures of East Africa." *Antipode* 52, no. 3 (2020): 825–46.

King, Kenneth. *Jua Kali Kenya: Change and Development in an Informal Economy, 1970–95*. Columbus: Ohio State University Press, 1996.

Kirui, Sammy, and Godfrey Muhatia. "Universal Access: The Kenyan Experience." In *At the Crossroads: ICT Policy Making in East Africa*, ed. Florence Etta and Laurent Elder, 84–99. Ottawa and Nairobi: IDRC and East African Educational Publisher, 2005.

Klingler-Vidra, Robyn. *The Venture Capital State: The Silicon Valley Model in East Asia*. Ithaca, NY: Cornell University Press, 2018.

Klingler-Vidra, Robyn. "When Venture Capital Is Patient Capital: Seed Funding as a Source of Patient Capital for High-Growth Companies." *Socio-Economic Review* 14, no. 4 (2016): 691–708.

Königs, Peter. "What Is Techno-Optimism?" *Philosophy & Technology* 35, no. 3 (2022): 63.

Kuo, Lily. "Mark Zuckerberg Has Made a Surprise Visit to Nairobi to Learn About Mobile Money." *Quartz*, September 1, 2016. https://qz.com/africa/771809/mark-zuckerberg-has-made-a-surprise-visit-to-nairobi-to-learn-about-mobile-money [7/26/2024].

Kusimba, Sibel. *Reimagining Money: Kenya in the Digital Finance Revolution*. Stanford: Stanford University Press, 2021.

Kwet, Michael. "Digital Colonialism: US Empire and the New Imperialism in the Global South." *Race & Class* 60, no. 4 (2019): 3–26.

Langley, Paul, and Andrew Leyshon. "Neo-Colonial Credit: FinTech Platforms in Africa." *Journal of Cultural Economy* 15, no. 4 (2022): 401–15.

Latour, Bruno. *Aramis, or the Love of Technology*. Cambridge, MA: Harvard University Press, 1996.

Latour, Bruno. "Visualization and Cognition." *Knowledge and Society* 6, no. 6 (1986): 1–40.

Lee, Ching Kwan. "Introduction: Global China at 20: Why, How and So What?" *China Quarterly* 250 (2022): 313–31.

Lee, Ching Kwan. *The Specter of Global China: Politics, Labor, and Foreign Investment in Africa*. Chicago: University of Chicago Press, 2018.

Lepore, Jill. "The Disruption Machine." *New Yorker* 23 (2014): 30–36.

Lesutis, Gediminas. "Infrastructural Territorialisations: Mega-Infrastructures and the (Re)making of Kenya." *Political Geography* 90 (2021): 102459.

Li, Hongwen. *Ren Zhengfei and Huawei: A Business and Life Biography*. Madrid: LID Publishing, 2017.

Li, Tania Murray. "What Is Land? Assembling a Resource for Global Investment." *Transactions of the Institute of British Geographers* 39, no. 4 (2014): 589–602.

Li, Tania Murray. *The Will to Improve: Governmentality, Development, and the Practice of Politics.* Durham, NC: Duke University Press, 2007.

Lindtner, Silvia M. *Prototype Nation: China and the Contested Promise of Innovation.* Princeton: Princeton University Press, 2020.

Liu, Olivia Yijian. *Start-Up Wolf: The Shenzhen Model of High-Tech Entrepreneurship.* London: Routledge, 2024.

Liu, Olivia Yijian. "To Be 'Entrepreneured': An Ethnographic Study of Tech Entrepreneurship Competitions in China." *Journal of Business Anthropology* 13, no. 1 (2024): 33–53.

Liu, Xiao. *Information Fantasies: Precarious Mediation in Postsocialist China.* Minneapolis: University of Minnesota Press, 2019.

Lu, Miao. "Designed for the Bottom of the Pyramid: A Case Study of a Chinese Phone Brand in Africa." *Chinese Journal of Communication* 14, no. 1 (2020): 24–39.

Lu, Miao, and Jack Linchuan Qiu. "Empowerment or Warfare? Dark Skin, AI Camera, and Transsion's Patent Narratives." *Information, Communication & Society* 25, no. 6 (2022): 768–84.

Lu, Miao, and Jack Linchuan Qiu. "Transfer or Translation? Rethinking Traveling Technologies from the Global South." *Science, Technology, & Human Values* 48, no. 2 (2023): 272–94.

Lumumba-Kasongo, Tukumbi. "China-Africa Relations: A Neo-Imperialism or a Neo-Colonialism? A Reflection." *African and Asian Studies* 10, no. 2–3 (2011): 234–66.

Mac, Ryan, and Theodore Schleifer. "How a Network of Tech Billionaires Helped J. D. Vance Leap into Power." *The New York Times*, July 17, 2024. https://www.nytimes.com/2024/07/17/technology/jd-vance-tech-silicon-valley.html [7/23/2024].

Mahoney, Josef Gregory. "China's Rise as an Advanced Technological Society and the Rise of Digital Orientalism." *Journal of Chinese Political Science* 28, no. 1 (2023): 1–24.

Maina, Miriam, and Liza Cirolia. "Ring Roads, Revived Plans, and Plotted Practice: The Multiple Makings of Nairobi's Urban Periphery." *Habitat International* 142 (2023): 102932.

Malinowski, Bronisław. *Argonauts of the Western Pacific: An Account of Native Enterprise and Adventure in the Archipelagoes of Melanesian New Guinea.* Vol. 2 of *Collected Works.* London: Routledge, 2013.

Manji, Ambreena. "Bulldozers, Homes and Highways: Nairobi and the Right to the City." *Review of African Political Economy* 42, no. 144 (2015): 206–24.

Mann, Laura, and Gianluca Iazzolino. "From Development State to Corporate Leviathan: Historicizing the Infrastructural Performativity of Digital Platforms Within Kenyan Agriculture." *Development and Change* 52, no. 4 (2021): 829–54.

Marcinkoski, Christopher. *The City That Never Was.* Princeton: Princeton Architectural Press, 2015.

Mathews, Gordon, Linessa Dan Lin, and Yang Yang. *The World in Guangzhou: Africans and Other Foreigners in South China's Global Marketplace.* Chicago: University of Chicago Press, 2017.

Mattern, Shannon. "Mission Control: A History of the Urban Dashboard." *Places Journal* (2015). https://doi.org/10.22269/150309 [07/15/2025].

Maurer, Bill. "Mobile Money: Communication, Consumption and Change in the Payments Space." *Journal of Development Studies* 48, no. 5 (2012): 589–604.

Maurer, Bill. *Mutual Life, Limited: Islamic Banking, Alternative Currencies, Lateral Reason.* Princeton: Princeton University Press, 2011.

Maurer, Bill. "Payment: Forms and Functions of Value Transfer in Contemporary Society." *Cambridge Journal of Anthropology* 30, no. 2 (2012): 15–35.

Mavhunga, Clapperton Chakanetsa. "Introduction: What Do Science, Technology, and Innovation Mean from Africa?" In *What Do Science, Technology, and Innovation Mean from Africa?*, ed. Clapperton Mavhunga, 1–27. Cambridge, MA: MIT Press, 2017.

Mavhunga, Clapperton Chakanetsa. *Transient Workspaces: Technologies of Everyday Innovation in Zimbabwe.* Cambridge, MA: MIT Press, 2014.

Maweu, Jacinta Mwende. "Journalists' and Public Perceptions of the Politics of China's Soft Power in Kenya Under the 'Look East' Foreign Policy." In *China's Media and Soft Power in Africa: Promotion and Perceptions*, ed. Xiaoling Zhang, Herman Wasserman, and Winston Mano, 123–34. London: Palgrave Macmillan, 2016.

Mazzarella, William. "Beautiful Balloon: The Digital Divide and the Charisma of New Media in India." *American Ethnologist* 37, no. 4 (2010): 783–804.

Mazzucato, Mariana. *The Entrepreneurial State: Debunking Public vs. Private Sector Myths.* London: Anthem Press, 2013.

Mbembe, Achille, and Sarah Nuttall. "Writing the World from an African Metropolis." *Public Culture* 16, no. 3 (2004): 347–72.

McElroy, Erin. *Silicon Valley Imperialism: Techno Fantasies and Frictions in Postsocialist Times.* Durham, NC: Duke University Press, 2024.

Meagher, Kate. "Cannibalizing the Informal Economy: Frugal Innovation and Economic Inclusion in Africa." *European Journal of Development Research* 30 (2018): 17–33.

Medina, Eden. *Cybernetic Revolutionaries: Technology and Politics in Allende's Chile.* Cambridge, MA: MIT Press, 2011.

Meiu, George Paul. "Panics over Plastics: A Matter of Belonging in Kenya." *American Anthropologist* 122, no. 2 (2020): 222–35.

Menon, Dilip M. "Changing Theory: Thinking Concepts from the Global South." In *Changing Theory: Concepts from the Global South*, ed. Dilip M. Menon, 1–30. London: Routledge, 2022.

Merab, Elizabeth. "How Melinda Gates Plans to Promote Growth in Africa." *The Nation*, January 28, 2018.

Mercer, Claire. "Boundary Work: Becoming Middle Class in Suburban Dar es Salaam." *International Journal of Urban and Regional Research* 44, no. 3 (2020): 521–36.

Miao, Julie T., Nicholas A. Phelps, and Hyungmin Kim. "Urban Entrepreneurialism 3.0 and the Export of Urban Expertise: The Case of South Korea's International Information and Telecommunication Technology Program." *Competition & Change* 27, no. 5 (2023): 790–808.

Migozzi, Julien. "Selecting Spaces, Classifying People: The Financialization of Housing in the South African city." *Housing Policy Debate* 30, no. 4 (2020): 640–60.

Miller, Chris. *Chip War: The Fight for the World's Most Critical Technology.* New York: Simon and Schuster, 2022.

Mitchell, Timothy. *Rule of Experts: Egypt, Techno-Politics, Modernity.* Berkeley: University of California Press, 2002.

Miyazaki, Hirokazu. *Arbitraging Japan: Dreams of Capitalism at the End of Finance.* Berkeley: University of California Press, 2013.

Mizes, James Christopher. "Investing in Independence: Popular Shareholding on the West African Stock Exchange." *Africa* 92, no. 4 (2022): 644–62.

Mizes, James Christopher, and Kevin P. Donovan. "Capitalizing Africa: High Finance from Below." *Africa* 92, no. 4 (2022): 540–60.

Mkalama, Ben, and Stefan Ouma. "To Whom Does the Money Go? Mapping the Uneven Financial Geographies of Venture Capital in 'Silicon Savannah,' Kenya." *Finance and Space* 1, no. 1 (2024): 517–41.

Mkandawire, P. Thandika. "Neopatrimonialism and the Political Economy of Economic Performance in Africa: Critical Reflections." *World Politics* 67, no. 3 (2015): 563–612.

Mkandawire, P. Thandika. "Thinking About Developmental States in Africa." *Cambridge Journal of Economics* 25, no. 3 (2001): 289–314.

Mkandawire, P. Thandika, and Charles Chukwuma Soludo. *Our Continent, Our Future: African Perspectives on Structural Adjustment.* Dakar: CODESRIA, 1998.

Moisio, Sami, and Ugo Rossi. "The Start-Up State: Governing Urbanised Capitalism." *Environment and Planning A: Economy and Space* 52, no. 3 (2020): 532–52.

Monson, Jamie. *Africa's Freedom Railway: How a Chinese Development Project Changed Lives and Livelihoods in Tanzania.* Bloomington: Indiana University Press, 2009.

Morawczynski, Olga. "Exploring the Usage and Impact of 'Transformational' Mobile Financial Services: The Case of M-PESA in Kenya." *Journal of Eastern African Studies* 3, no. 3 (2009): 509–25.

Morozov, E. *To Save Everything, Click Here: The Folly of Technological Solutionism.* New York: Public Affairs Books, 2013.

Moser, Sarah. "New Cities: Old Wine in New Bottles?" *Dialogues in Human Geography* 5, no. 1 (2015): 31–35.

Mouton, Morgan, and Ryan Burns. "(Digital) Neo-Colonialism in the Smart City." *Regional Studies* 55, no. 12 (2021): 1890–1901.

Mu, Junnan. "How Not to Define the 'Smart City.'" In *The Smartification of Everything, Technoscience and Society*, ed. Mascha Gugganin, Kelly Bronson, and Vincent Mirza. Toronto: University of Toronto Press, 2025.

Mukeku, Joseph. "Urban Slum Morphology and Socio-Economic Analogies: A Case Study of Kibera Slum, Nairobi, Kenya." *Urbanisation* 3, no. 1 (2018): 17–32.

Muldoon, James, Callum Cant, Mark Graham, and Funda Ustek Spilda. "The Poverty of Ethical AI: Impact Sourcing and AI Supply Chains." *AI & Society* (2023): 1–15.

Mullaney, Thomas S. *The Chinese Computer: A Global History of the Information Age.* Cambridge, MA: MIT Press, 2024.

Mullaney, Thomas S. *The Chinese Typewriter: A History.* Cambridge, MA: MIT Press, 2017.

Munda, Constant, and Salaton Njau. "Kenya Backs Safaricom in US, Huawei 5G fight." *Business Daily*, August 3, 2020. https://www.businessdailyafrica.com/bd/economy/kenya-backs-safaricom-in-us-huawei-5g-fight-2297586 [8/8/2023].

Muniesa, Fabian. "On the Political Vernaculars of Value Creation." *Science as Culture* 26, no. 4 (2017): 445–54.

Muniesa, Fabian. *The Provoked Economy: Economic Reality and the Performative Turn.* London: Routledge, 2014.

Munyua, Alice W., and Muriuki Mureithi. "Kenya: Kenya ICT Action Network (KICTANet)." In *Global Information Society Watch 2007*, 164–66. Stockholm: Association for Progressive Communications and the Third World Institute, 2007.

Murray, Martin J. "'City Doubles': Re-Urbanism in Africa." In *Cities and Inequalities in a Global and Neoliberal World*, ed. Faranak Miraftab, David Wilson, and Kenneth Salo, 92–109. London: Routledge, 2015.

Murunga, Godwin R. "Governance and the Politics of Structural Adjustment in Kenya." In *Kenya: The Struggle for Democracy*, ed. Godwin R. Murunga and Shadrack W. Nasong'o, 263–300. Dakar: CODESRIA Books, 2007.

Mwangi, Oscar Gakuo. "Political Corruption, Party Financing and Democracy in Kenya." *Journal of Modern African Studies* 46, no. 2 (2008): 267–85.

Nader, Laura. "Ethnography as Theory." *HAU: Journal of Ethnographic Theory* 1, no. 1 (2011): 211–19.

Nangulu-Ayuku, Anne. "Politics, Urban Planning and Population Settlement: Nairobi, 1912–1916." *Journal of Third World Studies* 17, no. 2 (2000): 171–204.

Nanni, Riccardo. "Digital Sovereignty and Internet Standards: Normative Implications of Public-Private Relations Among Chinese Stakeholders in the Internet Engineering Task Force." *Information, Communication & Society* 25, no. 16 (2022): 2342–62.

Narins, Thomas P., and John Agnew. "Missing from the Map: Chinese Exceptionalism, Sovereignty Regimes and the Belt Road Initiative." *Geopolitics* 25, no. 4 (2020): 809–37.

Ndemo, E. Bitange. "Inside a Policymaker's Mind: An Entrepreneurial Approach to Policy Development and Implementation." In *Digital Kenya: An Entrepreneurial Revolution in the Making*, ed. Bitange Ndemo and Tim Weiss, 349–51. London: Palgrave Macmillan, 2017.

Ndemo, E. Bitange. "Political Entrepreneurialism: Reflections of a Civil Servant on the Role of Political Institutions in Technology Innovation and Diffusion in Kenya." *Stability: International Journal of Security and Development* 4, no. 1 (2015): 1–14.

Ndemo, E. Bitange, and Tim Weiss, eds. *Digital Kenya: An Entrepreneurial Revolution in the Making*. London: Palgrave Macmillan, 2017.

Ndlovu-Gatsheni, Sabelo J. "Provincializing Europe and Deprovincialising Africa: Prospects for Decolonizing the Humanities." *Présence Africaine* 1 (2018): 337–62.

Nduati, Charles, and Warigia Bowman. "Working from the Sidelines: The Kenya Private Sector Foundation ICT Board Story." In *At the Crossroads: ICT Policy Making in East Africa*, ed. Florence Etta and Laurent Elder, 56–67. Ottawa and Nairobi: IDRC and East African Educational Publisher, 2005.

Needham, Joseph. *The Grand Titration: Science and Society in East and West*. London: George Allen & Unwin, 1969.

Neff, Gina. *Venture Labor: Work and the Burden of Risk in Innovative Industries*. Cambridge, MA: MIT Press, 2012.

Negro, Gianluigi. "A History of Chinese Global Internet Governance and Its Relations with ITU and ICANN." *Chinese Journal of Communication* 13, no. 1 (2020): 104–21.

Neilson, Brett. "Working the Digital Silk Road: Alibaba's Digital Free Trade Zone in Malaysia." In *Digital Work in the Planetary Market*, ed. Mark Graham and Fabian Ferrari, 117–36. Cambridge, MA: MIT Press, 2022.

Nellor, David C. L. "The Rise of Africa's 'Frontier' Markets." *Finance and Development* 45, no. 3 (2008): 30–33.

Nemer, David. *Technology of the Oppressed: Inequity and the Digital Mundane in Favelas of Brazil*. Cambridge, MA: MIT Press, 2022.

Neves, Joshua, and Marc Steinberg. "In Convenience." In *In/Convenience: Inhabiting the Logistical Surround*, ed. Joshua Neves and Marc Steinberg, 11–33. Theory on Demand 54. Amsterdam: Institute of Network Cultures, 2024.

Ng'weno, Bettina. "Growing Old in a New City: Time, the Post-Colony and Making Nairobi Home." *City* 22, no. 1 (2018): 26–42.

Nicholas, Tom. *VC: An American History*. Cambridge, MA: Harvard University Press.

Ning, Ken. *Zhong Guan Village: Tales from the Heart of China's Silicon Valley*. London: Alan Charles Publishing (ACA), 2022.

Nyabola, Nanjala. *Digital Democracy, Analogue Politics: How the Internet Era Is Transforming Politics in Kenya*. London: Zed Books, 2018.

Nyairo, Joyce. "The Boda Boda (R)age: Economies of Affection in the Motorbike Taxis of Kenya." *English Studies in Africa* 66, no. 1 (2023): 109–23.

Nyairo, Joyce. *Kenya@50: Trends, Identities and the Politics of Belonging*. Nairobi: Contact Zones NRB, 2015.

Nyairo, Joyce, and James Ogude. "Popular Music, Popular Politics: Unbwogable and the Idioms of Freedom in Kenyan Popular Music." *African Affairs* 104, no. 415 (2005): 225–49.

Nyong'o, Peter Anyang'. "Planning for Policy Making and Implementation in Kenya: Problems and Prospects." In *At the Crossroads: ICT Policy Making in East Africa*, ed. Florence Etta and Laurent Elder, 16–24. Ottawa and Nairobi: IDRC and East African Educational Publisher, 2005.

O'Dwyer, Rachel. "Cache Society: Transactional Records, Electronic Money, and Cultural Resistance." *Journal of Cultural Economy* 12, no. 2 (2019): 133–53.

Ogone, James Odhiambo. "Mobile Phones in Africa: The Politics of Cultural and Material Integration into Local Economies." *International Journal of Cultural Studies* 23, no. 4 (2020): 531–46.

Ogot, Bethwell A. *Who, if Anyone Owns the Past? Reflections on the Meaning of "Public History."* Kisumu: Anyange Press, 2010.

Ogot, Bethwell A., and Madara Ogot. *History of Nairobi 1899–2012: From a Railway Camp and Supply Depot to a World-Class African Metropolis*. Kisumu: Anyange Press, 2020.

Okolloh, Ory. "Ushahidi, or 'Testimony': Web 2.0 Tools for Crowdsourcing Crisis Information." *Participatory Learning and Action* 59, no. 1 (2009): 65–70.

Omanga, Duncan, and Pamela Mainye. "Digital Media Politics in Kenya: Of Nerds, Missionaries and Mercenaries." In *Digital Technologies, Elections and Campaigns in Africa*, ed. Duncan Omanga, Admire Mare, and Pamela Mainye, 46–63. London: Routledge, 2023.

Ombagi, Eddie. "Nairobi Is a Shot of Whisky: Queer (Ob)scenes in the City." *Journal of African Cultural Studies* 31, no. 1 (2019): 106–19.

Omondi, Dominic. "Darling of Private Investors, Mwai Kibaki Did Not Leave Any Money to Lie Idle." *The Standard*, April 23, 2022.

Omondi, Dominic. "How Huawei Charmed Its Way into the Heart of Kenya's Data." *The Standard*, April 20, 2021.

Omwansa, Tonny K., and Nicholas P. Sullivan. *Money, Real Quick: Kenya's Disruptive Mobile Money Innovation*. New Romney: Balloon View, 2012.

Osamuyi, Osarumen. "Transsion's Trojan Horses." *The Subtext*, July 20, 2018. https://www.thesubtext.io/transsions-trojan-horses [5/3/2021].

Otele, Oscar Meywa. *What Explains African Perceptions of China as a Model of Development?* Berlin: Megatrends Afrika, 2023.

Ouma, Stefan. "The Difference That 'Capitalism' Makes: On the Merits and Limits of Critical Political Economy in African Studies." *Review of African Political Economy* 44, no. 153 (2017): 499–509.

Owino, Vincent. "Kenya Is Africa's Start-Up Funding Top Destination." *East African*, March 24, 2024. https://www.theeastafrican.co.ke/tea/business/kenya-is-africa-s-start-up -funding-top-destination-4566202 [7/26/2024].

Owuor, Samuel. "Security, Community Organization and Privatization of Public Space: An Analysis of Gated Neighbourhoods in Nairobi, Kenya." Paper presented at the International Workshop on Privatization of Security in Sub-Saharan African Cities: Urban Dynamics and New Forms of Governance, Ibadan, Nigeria, November 21–25, 2005.

Palmer, Alex W. "'An Act of War': Inside America's Silicon Blockade Against China." *The New York Times Magazine*, July 12, 2023. https://www.nytimes.com/2023/07/12/magazine /semiconductor-chips-us-china.html [8/7/2023].

Pandian, A. *A Possible Anthropology: Methods for Uneasy Times*. Durham, NC: Duke University Press, 2019.

Park, Emma. "'Human ATMs': M-Pesa and the Expropriation of Affective Work in Safaricom's Kenya." *Africa* 90, no. 5 (2020): 914–33.

Park, Emma. "Intimacy and Estrangement: Safaricom, Divisibility, and the Making of the Corporate Nation-State." *Comparative Studies of South Asia, Africa and the Middle East* 41, no. 3 (2021): 423–40.

Pasquinelli, Matteo. *The Eye of the Master: A Social History of Artificial Intelligence*. London: Verso Books, 2023.

Pasquinelli, Matteo. "Three Thousand Years of Algorithmic Rituals: The Emergence of AI from the Computation of Space." *E-Flux Journal* 101 (2019): 1–10.

Pasquinelli, Matteo, and Vladan Joler. "The Nooscope Manifested: AI as Instrument of Knowledge Extractivism." *AI & Society* 36 (2021): 1263–80.

Perrigo, Billy. "OpenAI Used Kenyan Workers on Less Than $2 per Hour to Make ChatGPT Less Toxic." *Time*, January 23, 2023.

Plantin, Jean-Christophe. "The Data Archive as Factory: Alienation and Resistance of Data Processors." *Big Data & Society* 8, no. 1 (2021): 20539517211007510.

Poggiali, Lisa. "Seeing (from) Digital Peripheries: Technology and Transparency in Kenya's Silicon Savannah." *Cultural Anthropology* 31, no. 3 (2016): 387–411.

Pohlmann, Tim, and Magnus Buggenhagen. "Who Is Leading the 5G Patent Race?" *IPlytics Platform* (Berlin), June 2022.

Pollio, Andrea. "Acceleration, Development and Technocapitalism at the Silicon Cape of Africa." *Economy and Society* 51, no. 1 (2022): 46–70.

Pollio, Andrea. "The Digital Silk Road as Planetary Intelligence: A Story of China in Africa." In *Parables of AI in/from the Majority World*, ed. Ranjit Singh, Rigoberto Lara Guzmán, and Patrick Davison, 88–99. New York: Data & Society Research Institute, 2022.

Pollio, Andrea. "Incubators at the Frontiers of Capital: An Ethnographic Encounter with Startup Weekend in Khayelitsha, Cape Town." *Annals of the American Association of Geographers* 110, no. 4 (2020): 1244–59.

Pollio, Andrea. "Making the Silicon Cape of Africa: Tales, Theories and the Narration of Startup Urbanism." *Urban Studies* 57, no. 13 (2020): 2715–32.

Pollio, Andrea. "Of Bloatware and Spreadsheets: Nairobi, Chinese Phones, and the Limits of Data Coloniality." *Journal of Urban Technology* (2024): 1–22.

Pollio, Andrea. "Reading Development Failure: Experts and Experiments at the Bottom of the Pyramid in Cape Town." *Third World Quarterly* 42, no. 12 (2021): 2974–92.

Pollio, Andrea, and Liza Rose Cirolia. "Beyond Inclusion: Glitchy Economies and the Promise of Platformization in African Cities." In *In/Convenience: Inhabiting the Logistical Surround*, ed. Joshua Neves and Marc Steinberg, 148–61. Theory on Demand #54. Amsterdam: Institute of Network Cultures, 2024.

Pollio, Andrea, and Liza Rose Cirolia. *Financing ICT and Digitalisation in Africa: Current Trends and Key Sustainability Issues*. Cape Town: African Centre for Cities, 2022.

Pollio, Andrea, and Liza Rose Cirolia. "Fintech Urbanism in the Startup Capital of Africa." *Journal of Cultural Economy* 15, no. 4 (2022): 508–23.

Pollio, Andrea, Liza Rose Cirolia, and Jack Ong'iro Odeo. "Algorithmic Suturing: Platforms, Motorcycles and the 'Last Mile' in Urban Africa." *International Journal of Urban and Regional Research* 47, no. 6 (2023): 957–74.

Posadam, Julian. "Embedded Reproduction in Platform Data Work." *Information, Communication & Society* 25, no. 6 (2022): 816–34.

Power, Marcus, and Ana Alves Cristina. "Introduction: China and Angola's Partnership." In *China and Angola: a Marriage of Convenience?*, ed. Marcus Power and Ana Alves Cristina, 1–9. Cape Town: Pambazuka Press, 2012.

Prahalad, C. K. *The Fortune at the Bottom of the Pyramid: Eradicating Poverty Through Profits*. Upper Saddle River, NJ: Wharton School Publishing, 2005.

Pratt, Mary Louise. "Arts of the Contact Zone." *Profession* (1991): 33–40.

Price, Rob. "London's $1 Billion Finance Startup TransferWise Is Just Like an Ancient Islamic Money Transfer System." *Business Insider*, January 27, 2015. https://www.businessinsider.com/transferwises-similarities-to-hawala-2015-1 [10/1/2023].

Qiu, Jack Linchuan. *Working-Class Network Society: Communication Technology and the Information Have-Less in Urban China*. Cambridge, MA: MIT Press, 2009.

Qiu, Jack Linchuan, Peter K. Yu, and Elisa Oreglia. "A New Approach to the Geopolitics of Chinese Internets." *Information, Communication & Society* 25, no. 16 (2022): 2335–41.

Ralph, Michael. *Forensics of Capital*. Chicago: University of Chicago Press, 2020.

Repnikova, Maria, and Keyu Alexander Chen. "Asymmetrical Discursive Competition: China–United States Digital Diplomacy in Africa." *International Communication Gazette* 85, no. 1 (2023): 15–31.

Republic of Kenya. *African Socialism and Its Application to Planning in Kenya*. 1965. https://www.treasury.gov.za/coopbank/publications/Kenya%20document.pdf [7/13/2025].

Reyes-Carranza, Mariana, and Dennis M. Muthama. "Urban Sprawl and the Automation of Building Control in the Peripheries of Nairobi." *Urban Geography* (2025): 1–17.

Ricaurte, Paola. "Data Epistemologies, the Coloniality of Power, and Resistance." *Television & New Media* 20, no. 4 (2019): 350–65.

Ries, Eric. *The Lean Startup: How Today's Entrepreneurs Use Continuous Innovation to Create Radically Successful Businesses*. New York: Crown Business, 2011.

Rist, Ray C. "Blitzkrieg Ethnography: On the Transformation of a Method into a Movement." *Educational Researcher* 9, no. 2 (1980): 8–10.

Rizzo, Matteo. *Taken for a Ride: Grounding Neoliberalism, Precarious Labour, and Public Transport in an African Metropolis*. Oxford: Oxford University Press, 2017.

Roberts, George. *Revolutionary State-Making in Dar es Salaam: African Liberation and the Global Cold War, 1961–1974*. Cambridge: Cambridge University Press, 2022.

Robinson, Jennifer. *Comparative Urbanism: Tactics for Global Urban Studies.* New York: John Wiley & Sons, 2022.

Rodima-Taylor, Daivi. "Platformizing Ubuntu? FinTech, Inclusion, and Mutual Help in Africa." *Journal of Cultural Economy* 15, no. 4 (2022): 416–35.

Roh, David S., Betsy Huang, and Greta A. Niu. *Techno-Orientalism: Imagining Asia in Speculative Fiction, History, and Media.* New Brunswick, NJ: Rutgers University Press, 2015.

Roitman, Janet. "Platform Economies: Beyond the North–South Divide." *Finance and Society* 9, no. 1 (2023): 1–13.

Rosenberg, Lauren, and Alan Brent. "Infrastructure Disruption in 'Silicon Savannah': Exploring the Idea of the Creative Class and Their Relation to Quality of Place in Nairobi, Kenya." *International Journal of Urban and Regional Research* 44, no. 5 (2020): 809–20.

Ross, Andrew. *No-Collar: The Humane Workplace and Its Hidden Costs.* Philadelphia: Temple University Press, 2004.

Rostow, Walter W. *The Stages of Economic Growth: A Non-Communist Manifesto.* Cambridge: Cambridge University Press, 1960.

Rouse, Marybeth, Bernardo Bátiz-Lazo, and Santiago Carbó-Valverde. "M-Pesa and the Role of the Entrepreneurial State in a Cashless Technology to Deliver an Inclusive Financial Sector." *Essays in Economic & Business History* 41, no. 1 (2023): 109–33.

Roy, Ananya. "Ethnographic Circulations: Space-Time Relations in the Worlds of Poverty Management." *Environment and Planning A* 44, no. 1 (2012): 31–41.

Roy, Ananya. *Poverty Capital: Microfinance and the Making of Development.* New York: Routledge, 2010.

Roy, Ananya. "Subjects of Risk: Technologies of Gender in the Making of Millennial Modernity." *Public Culture* 24, no. 1 (2012): 131–55.

Saguin, Kristian Karlo. *Urban Ecologies on the Edge: Making Manila's Resource Frontier.* Berkeley: University of California Press, 2022.

Said, Edward. *Orientalism.* New York: Pantheon Books, 1978.

Saxenian, AnnaLee. *The New Argonauts: Regional Advantage in a Global Economy.* Cambridge, MA: Harvard University Press, 2006.

Saxenian, AnnaLee. *Regional Advantage: Culture and Competition in Silicon Valley and Route 128.* Cambridge, MA: Harvard University Press, 1996.

Saxenian, AnnaLee. "Regional Networks and the Resurgence of Silicon Valley." *California Management Review* 33, no. 1 (1990): 89–112.

Scarfe, Jade, and Jing Cai. "Agency, Bargaining Power, and African Leadership Visits to China." *The Diplomat,* May 24, 2021.

Schindler, Seth, Ilias Alami, Jessica DiCarlo, Nicholas Jepson, Steve Rolf, Mustafa Kemal Bayırbağ, Louis Cyuzuzo, et al. "The Second Cold War: US-China Competition for Centrality in Infrastructure, Digital, Production, and Finance Networks." *Geopolitics* 29, no. 4 (2024): 1083–1120.

Schindler, Seth, and Jessica DiCarlo, eds. *The Rise of the Infrastructure State: How US-China Rivalry Shapes Politics and Place Worldwide.* Bristol: Bristol University Press, 2022.

Schindler, Seth, Jessica DiCarlo, and Dinesh Paudel. "The New Cold War and the Rise of the 21st-Century Infrastructure State." *Transactions of the Institute of British Geographers* 47, no. 2 (2022): 331–46.

Schor, Juliet B., William Attwood-Charles, Mehmet Cansoy, Isak Ladegaard, and Robert Wengronowitz. "Dependence and Precarity in the Platform Economy." *Theory and Society* 49 (2020): 833–61.

Scott, James C. "Intellectual Diary of an Iconoclast." *Annual Review of Political Science* 27 (2024): 1–7.

Scott, Susan V., and Markos Zachariadis. *The Society for Worldwide Interbank Financial Telecommunication (SWIFT): Cooperative Governance for Network Innovation, Standards, and Community*. London: Routledge, 2014.

Seaver, Nick. *Computing Taste: Algorithms and the Makers of Music Recommendation*. Chicago: University of Chicago Press, 2022.

Shen, Hong. *Alibaba: Infrastructuring Global China*. New York: Routledge, 2021.

Shen, Hong. "Building a Digital Silk Road? Situating the Internet in China's Belt and Road Initiative." *International Journal of Communication* 12 (2018): 2683–2701.

Shen, Hong, and Yujia He. "The Geopolitics of Infrastructuralized Platforms: The Case of Alibaba." *Information, Communication & Society* 25, no. 16 (2022): 2363–80.

Shestakofsky, Benjamin. *Behind the Startup: How Venture Capital Shapes Work, Innovation, and Inequality*. Oakland: University of California Press, 2024.

Shiller, Robert J. *Irrational Exuberance*. Princeton: Princeton University Press, 2016.

Shinn, David H. "The Environmental Impact of China's Investment in Africa." *Cornell International Law Journal* 49, (2016): 25–67.

Silver, Jonathan. "Incremental Infrastructures: Material Improvisation and Social Collaboration Across Post-Colonial Accra." *Urban Geography* 35, no. 6 (2014): 788–804.

Simone, AbdouMaliq. "Ritornello: 'People as Infrastructure.'" *Urban Geography* 42, no. 9 (2021): 1341–48.

Smith, James H. *The Eyes of the World: Mining the Digital Age in the Eastern DR Congo*. Chicago: University of Chicago Press, 2021.

Soriano, Cheryll Ruth R., and Jason Vincent A. Cabañes. "Entrepreneurial Solidarities: Social Media Collectives and Filipino Digital Platform Workers." *Social Media + Society* 6, no. 2 (2020): 2056305120926484.

Sottek, T. C. "Google Pulls Huawei's Android License, Forcing It to Use Open Source Version: A Dramatic Escalation in the US War on Chinese Tech Firms." *The Verge*, May 19, 2019. https://www.theverge.com/2019/5/19/18631558/google-huawei-android-suspension [7/23/2023].

Soulé, Folashadé. *Negotiating Africa's Digital Partnerships amid Geopolitical Competition*. Oxford: Centre for International Governance Innovation, 2024.

Star, Susan Leigh, and Martha Lampland. "Reckoning with Standards." In *Standards and Their Stories: How Quantifying, Classifying, and Formalizing Practices Shape Everyday Life*, ed. Martha Lampland and Susan Leigh Star, 3–34. Ithaca, NY: Cornell University Press, 2009.

Steinberg, Marc. *The Platform Economy: How Japan Transformed the Consumer Internet*. Minneapolis: University of Minnesota Press, 2019.

Steinberg, Marc, Rahul Mukherjee, and Aswin Punathambekar. "Media Power in Digital Asia: Super Apps and Megacorps." *Media, Culture & Society* 44, no. 8 (2022): 1405–19.

Steinberg, Marc, Lin Zhang, and Rahul Mukherjee. "Platform Capitalisms and Platform Cultures." *International Journal of Cultural Studies* (2024): 13678779231223544.

Stengers, Isabelle. "Comparison as a Matter of Concern." *Common Knowledge* 17, no. 1 (2011): 48–63.

Stengers, Isabelle. *Cosmopolitics*. Minneapolis: University of Minnesota Press, 2010.

Stevens, Hallam. "Teleview and the Aspirations of the Infrastructural State in Singapore." In *Infrastructure and the Remaking of Asia*, ed. Max Hirsh and Till Mostowlansky, 134–54. Honolulu: University of Hawai'i Press, 2023.

Sun, Ping. "Your Order, Their Labor: An Exploration of Algorithms and Laboring on Food Delivery Platforms in China." *Chinese Journal of Communication* 12, no. 3 (2019): 308–23.

Sun, Yutao, and Cong Cao. "Planning for Science: China's 'Grand Experiment' and Global Implications." *Humanities and Social Sciences Communications* 8, no. 1 (2021): 1–9.

Sylla, Ndongo Samba. "Fighting Monetary Colonialism in Francophone Africa: Samir Amin's Contribution." *Review of African Political Economy* 48, no. 167 (2021): 32–49.

Sylla, Ndongo Samba. "From a Marginalised to an Emerging Africa? A Critical Analysis." *Review of African Political Economy* 41, no. 1 (2014): 7–25.

Tadiar, Neferti X. M. "Remaindered Life of Citizen-Man, Medium of Democracy." *Japanese Journal of Southeast Asian Studies* 49, no. 3 (2011): 464–95.

Táíwò, Olúfẹ́mi O. *Africa Must Be Modern: A Manifesto*. Bloomington: Indiana University Press, 2014.

Takhteyev, Yuri. *Coding Places: Software Practice in a South American City*. Cambridge, MA: MIT Press, 2012.

Tan, Yinglan. *Chinnovation: How Chinese Innovators Are Changing the World*. Singapore: John Wiley & Sons, 2011.

Tang, Min. *Tencent: The Political Economy of China's Surging Internet Giant*. London: Routledge, 2019.

Taylor, Ian. "China's Foreign Policy Towards Africa in the 1990s." *Journal of Modern African Studies* 36, no. 3 (1998): 443–60.

Taylor, Ian. *The Forum on China-Africa Cooperation (FOCAC)*. London: Routledge, 2010.

Taylor, Ian. "Kenya's New Lunatic Express: The Standard Gauge Railway." *African Studies Quarterly* 19, no. 3–4 (2020): 29–52.

Taylor, Ian, and Tim Zajontz. "In a Fix: Africa's Place in the Belt and Road Initiative and the Reproduction of Dependency." *South African Journal of International Affairs* 27, no. 3 (2020): 277–95.

Terrefe, Biruk. "Infrastructures of Renaissance: Tangible Discourses in the EPRDF's Ethiopia (Infrastructures de Renaissance; Discours tangible dans l'Ethiopie de le FDRPE)." *Critical African Studies* 14, no. 3 (2022): 250–73.

Thévenot, Laurent. "Rules and Implements: Investment in Forms." *Social Science Information* 23, no. 1 (1984): 1–45.

Thieme, Tatiana A. "Turning Hustlers into Entrepreneurs, and Social Needs into Market Demands: Corporate–Community Encounters in Nairobi, Kenya." *Geoforum* 59 (2015): 228–39.

Thrift, Nigel. *Knowing Capitalism*. London: Sage, 2004.

Timmermans, Stefan, and Steven Epstein. "A World of Standards but Not a Standard World: Toward a Sociology of Standards and Standardization." *Annual Review of Sociology* 36 (2010): 69–89.

Tkacz, Nathaniel. *Being with Data: The Dashboarding of Everyday Life*. Cambridge: Polity, 2022.

Toffler, Alvin. *Future Shock*. New York: Random House, 1970.

Toffler, Alvin. *The Third Wave*. New York: William Morrow, 1980.

Tsing, Anna. *Friction: An Ethnography of Global Connection*. Princeton: Princeton University Press, 2004.

Tsing, Anna. "Inside the Economy of Appearances." *Public Culture* 12, no. 1 (2000): 115–44.

Tugendhat, Henry, and Julia Voo. "China's Digital Silk Road in Africa and the Future of Internet Governance. No. 2021/50." Washington, DC: China Africa Research Initiative (CARI), School of Advanced International Studies (SAIS), Johns Hopkins University.

Tuwei, David, and Melissa Tully. "Producing Communities and Commodities: Safaricom and Commercial Nationalism in Kenya." *Global Media and Communication* 13, no. 1 (2017): 21–39.

Van Doorn, Niels. "Platform Labor: On the Gendered and Racialized Exploitation of Low-Income Service Work in the 'On-Demand' Economy." *Information, Communication & Society* 20, no. 6 (2017): 898–914.

Van Doorn, Niels, and Julie Yujie Chen. "Odds Stacked Against Workers: Datafied Gamification on Chinese and American Food Delivery Platforms." *Socio-Economic Review* 19, no. 4 (2021): 1345–67.

Van Noorloos, Femke, and Marjan Kloosterboer. "Africa's New Cities: The Contested Future of Urbanisation." *Urban Studies* 55, no. 6 (2018): 1223–41.

Von Schnitzler, Antina. *Democracy's Infrastructure: Techno-Politics and Protest After Apartheid*. Princeton: Princeton University Press.

Wahome, Michel Njeri. *Fabricating Silicon Savannah: The Making of a Digital Entrepreneurship Arena of Development*. Cham: Springer, 2023.

Wai, Zubairu. "Neo-Patrimonialism and the Discourse of State Failure in Africa." *Review of African Political Economy* 39, no. 131 (2012): 27–43.

Wainaina, Binyavanga. "Generation Kenya." *Vanity Fair*, June 25, 2007.

Wang, Gungwu. *China Reconnects: Joining a Deep-Rooted Past to a New World Order*. Singapore: World Scientific, 2019.

Wang, Hui. *The Politics of Imagining Asia*. Cambridge, MA: Harvard University Press, 2011.

Wasserman, Herman. "The Incompleteness of Knowledge Production: An Interview with Francis Nyamnjoh." *African Journalism Studies* 43, no. 3 (2022): 1–9.

Wasuna, Brian. "Chinese Billionaire Behind Kenya's Popular Mobile Money Lending Apps." *The Nation*, April 9, 2021. https://nation.africa/kenya/news/chinese-billionaire-behind-kenya-s-popular-mobile-money-lending-apps—3355020 [8/12/2022].

Watson, Vanessa. "African Urban Fantasies: Dreams or Nightmares?" *Environment and Urbanization* 26, no. 1 (2014): 215–31.

Weber, Isabella M. *How China Escaped Shock Therapy: The Market Reform Debate*. London: Routledge, 2021.

Weber, Isabella M. "State Capitalism, Imperialism and China: Bringing History Back In." *Environment and Planning A: Economy and Space* 55, no. 3 (2023): 774–81.

Wen, Yun. *The Huawei Model: The Rise of China's Technology Giant*. Urbana: University of Illinois Press, 2020.

Wiig, Alan, and Jonathan Silver. "Turbulent Presents, Precarious Futures: Urbanization and the Deployment of Global Infrastructure." *Regional Studies* 53, no. 6 (2019): 912–23.

Winter, Tim. *Geocultural Power: China's Quest to Revive the Silk Roads for the Twenty-First Century*. Chicago: University of Chicago Press, 2019.

World Bank. *Accelerated Development in Sub-Saharan Africa: An Agenda for Action* [Berg Report]. Washington, DC: World Bank Group, 1981.

Xi, Jingping. "Open a New Era of China-Africa Win-Win Cooperation and Common Development." Address at the opening ceremony of the Johannesburg Summit of the Forum on China–Africa Cooperation, December 4, 2015.

Yang, Fan. "From Bandit Cell Phones to Branding the Nation: Three Moments of Shanzhai in WTO-Era China." *Positions: East Asia Cultures Critique* 24, no. 3 (2016): 589–619.

Yang, Guobin. *The power of the Internet in China: Citizen activism online*. New York: Columbia University Press, 2009.

Yi, Jeannie Jinsheng, and Shawn Xian Ye. *The Haier Way: The Making of a Chinese Business Leader and a Global Brand*. Paramus, NJ: Homa & Sekey Books, 2003.

Zajontz, Tim. "Debt, Distress, Dispossession: Towards a Critical Political Economy of Africa's Financial Dependency." *Review of African Political Economy* 49, no. 171 (2022): 173–83.

Zaloom, Caitlin. *Out of the Pits: Traders and Technology from Chicago to London*. Chicago: University of Chicago Press, 2006.

Zhang, Lin. *The Labor of Reinvention: Entrepreneurship in the New Chinese Digital Economy*. New York: Columbia University Press, 2023.

Zhang, Lin. "Platformizing Family Production: The Contradictions of Rural Digital Labor in China." *Economic and Labour Relations Review* 32, no. 3 (2021): 341–59.

Zhang, Lin, and Julie Yujie Chen. "A Regional and Historical Approach to Platform Capitalism: The Cases of Alibaba and Tencent." *Media, Culture & Society* 44, no. 8 (2022): 1454–72.

Zhang, Lin, and Anthony Fung. "The Myth of 'Shanzhai' Culture and the Paradox of Digital Democracy in China." *Inter-Asia Cultural Studies* 14, no. 3 (2013): 401–16.

Zhao, Elaine Jing. *Digital China's Informal Circuits: Platforms, Labour and Governance*. London: Routledge, 2019.

Zheng, Chen. "China Debates the Non-Interference Principle." *Chinese Journal of International Politics* 9, no. 3 (2016): 349–74.

Zheng, Yongnian, and Yanjie Huang. *Market in State: The Political Economy of Domination in China*. Cambridge: Cambridge University Press, 2018.

Zhi, Qiang, and Margaret M. Pearson. "China's Hybrid Adaptive Bureaucracy: The Case of the 863 Program for Science and Technology." *Governance* 30, no. 3 (2017): 407–24.

Zhou, Yang. "Trapped in the Platform: Migration and Precarity in China's Platform-Based Gig Economy." *Environment and Planning A: Economy and Space* (2022): 0308518X221119196.

Zhu, April. "Can a Chinese Import Ever Be Authentically African?" *African Arguments*, August 21, 2019. https://africanarguments.org/2019/08/can-chinese-import-authentically-african-kitenge/ [8/14/2024].

Zhu, April. "Sinophobia Spreads Faster Than the Coronavirus." *The Elephant*, February 28, 2020. https://www.theelephant.info/culture/2020/02/28/sinophobia-spreads-faster-than-the-coronavirus/ [9/8/2023].

Zukin, Sharon. *The Innovation Complex: Cities, Tech, and the New Economy*. Oxford: Oxford University Press, 2020.

INDEX

Ahmed, Sarah, 152–53
algorithmic optimization, 14, 70, 82, 89–91, 165
algorithmic suturing, 18, 68–70, 87, 89–91, 165
Alibaba, 21–22, 24, 38, 87, 88–89, 118, 139, 160–61; Alipay, 108, 113; as model, 18, 69, 78, 85
Amazon, 84, 86, 88
ambivalence of technology, 12, 151, 163–64
Apple, 53, 93
arbitraging China, 15, 18, 122, 138–39
ATM: ethanol, 63; human, 2; water, 81
Avle, Seyram, 58, 61

Beijing connection, 4, 14–16, 128–30, 139–41, 165, 168n17
Belt and Road Initiative (BRI), 7–8, 26, 37–38, 122, 128, 159
Berlant, Lauren, 152
Birhane, Abeba, 48
bloatware, 61, 93, 95
boda boda, 79, 82–89, 104, 179n47,49
bottom of the pyramid (BOP), 54–55, 61, 69–70, 72–73, 97, 134
Bowker, Geoffrey, 96
Branch, Daniel, 26
Bratton, Benjamin, 64
Brautigam, Deborah, 22
business process offshoring (BPO), 3, 29, 39–40, 43, 73

Californian ideology, 69, 144–47
capital: ethnography of techno-capital, 15, 151; frontiers of techno-capital, 48; techno-capital, 3–5, 9–14, 31, 44, 116–17, 164–65; varieties of capital, 9–11, 64, 107, 133, 173n80, 179n58; varieties of techno-capital, 9–11, 140. *See also* venture capital
central location tests (CLTs), 56
Chan, Anita, 12
Chari, Sharad, 165
Chen, Julie, 89
Chen, Lulu, 104
Chen, Yuchen, 12, 64
China: China-Africa relations, 5–9, 22; China Global Television Network (CGTN), 2, 47; China Telecom, 38, 74; digital champions, 4, 8, 17, 32, 37–39; Export-Import Bank of the Republic of China (Chexim), 8, 42; going out (or going global) policy, 9, 34–35, 78, 123, 175n30; Internet Plus, 37; Made in China 2025, 37, 94, 106; Mass Entrepreneurship and Innovation (MEI), 37–38, 106. *See also* Global China
chinku, 17, 47, 174n2; phones, 17, 47, 48–51, 55, 58, 61, 64–65
Chun, Lin, 7
Cirolia, Liza R., 70
Coban, Alev, 10, 140
Cold War, 4; second cold war, 4; tech cold war, 18, 92–95, 96, 164

Founded in 1893,
UNIVERSITY OF CALIFORNIA PRESS
publishes bold, progressive books and journals
on topics in the arts, humanities, social sciences,
and natural sciences—with a focus on social
justice issues—that inspire thought and action
among readers worldwide.

The UC PRESS FOUNDATION
raises funds to uphold the press's vital role
as an independent, nonprofit publisher, and
receives philanthropic support from a wide
range of individuals and institutions—and from
committed readers like you. To learn more, visit
ucpress.edu/supportus.